TWELVE ESSAYS ON TERRORISM

A VIF Analysis

TWELVE ESSAYS ON TERRORISM

A VIF Analysis

Edited by

Lt Gen Gautam Banerjee

Foreword by

Gen NC Vij, PVSM, UYSM, AVSM

Director, Vivekananda International Foundation, New Delhi

Vivekananda International Foundation
New Delhi

PENTAGON PRESS

Twelve Essays on Terrorism

Editor: Lt Gen Gautam Banerjee

Vivekananda International Foundation, New Delhi

ISBN 978-81-8274-942-9

First Published in 2017

Published by

PENTAGON PRESS

206, Peacock Lane, Shahpur Jat,

New Delhi-110049

Phones: 011-64706243, 26491568

Telefax: 011-26490600

email: rajan@pentagonpress.in

website: www.pentagonpress.in

Printed at Aegean Offset Printers, Greater Noida, U.P.

CONTENTS

FOREWORD

Upon Independence, India had been afflicted with many shades of insurgencies, as indeed it usually happens with new nation-states. It was the remarkable resilience of our nationhood and exemplary commitments of our military formations which prevented this anti-national phenomena from debilitating the nation's integrity. It was thus that by the late 1970s the estranged and misguided elements had been finally controlled to manageable levels. However, the 1980s saw a new turn of anti-nationalism manifesting in the form of rise of terrorism. It appeared fist in Punjab and then in Kashmir, just as Maoist terrorism raised its head in Central India. Meanwhile, unable to retain relevance, remnant insurgencies in certain pockets of our North Eastern States have taken to terrorist activities. Thus for more than three decades past, India has been afflicted with various shades of terrorism.

Terrorism in India has its roots in Pakistan's existential pinning on anti-Indian ideology that has found radical religious moorings during the past decade. It is so that Pakistan's policy of terror export has found powerful underwriters in the form of 'all-weather' and fundamentalist endorsers. Agreeably, distractive inclinations of our polity has permitted these India-inimical forces to perpetrate their trade. Though the situations in other areas are well under control, the situation in Kashmir continues to remain somewhat disturbed, due to complicity of our Western neighbours. Added to this matter of strategic concern is the spread of indigenous anti-nationals who fall victim to various forms of poisonous incitements from external propagators and their internal collaborators.

Today terrorism, *per se* is counted as one of the three major danger issues in the world. Even the new President of US has mentioned it in his recent remark. For India, it has been a problem born with the partition of the country.

We, the strategic fraternity of the Vivekananda International Foundation, are seized of this growing menace. Accordingly, it has been our endeavour to analyse the phenomenon of terrorism and propagate appropriate considerations in defeating this poisonous hydra. To that end, I found it appropriate to disseminate some of the salient works carried out by the scholars of this Foundation. This book is a result of that idea. It is a compilation of twelve analytical papers on various aspects of terrorism, the purpose being to share facts and thoughts that might provide for the courses and options in tackling the menace.

Jai Hind.

February 2017

Gen NC Vij, PVSM, UYSM, AVSM
(Former Chief of the Army Staff & Founder Vice Chairman,
National Disaster Management Authority)
Director
Vivekananda International Foundation, New Delhi

PREAMBLE

As the mankind takes giant strides towards a dispensation of technological and economic empowerment, one of the darker fallouts of that progress is the scourge of terrorism. Individuals today are exposed to propagations of iniquitous political and religious beliefs, and facilitated by instant networking, find it easy to coalesce into groupings of like-minded catalysts for their version of societal 'corrections'. Opportunities of fund 'collection' and virtually unbridled access to 'technology of violence' completes the diabolic circle of mindless mayhem upon the innocent and defenceless people that terrorism has come to represent.

Beside a lunatic attraction for the role of 'angels' who are ordained to impose such bestial 'objectives' which the society finds abhorrent, terrorism is also seen by its propagators, controllers and executioners as a profitable commerce, a trade to live on and a ladder to political power. These lunatics – jihadists, Maoists or various factions of militants – propose to find those objectives through indiscriminate killings, funded by ruthless extortion and all manners of illegal transactions, that would purportedly force the societies and its ideologues to 'convert' to specified ways of radicalism. The truth, that notwithstanding the sufferings, terrorism has never triumphed against societal resilience, does not seem to penetrate the cocoon of ignorance in which the terrorists prefer to ensconce themselves.

Terrorism has come to stay - till its failings mount to a level that even its most corrupt- brained adherer learns the futility of it all. Tackling terrorism is therefore no more a secondary responsibility for the governing establishments and its various institutions, it has notched up the State's liability towards its citizen's safety and societal stability. Study and analysis of this barbarous phenomenon is therefore a prime responsibility for the thinking and scholastic community. The purpose must be to dig into its causes, roots, ramifications, sustenance – and of course, remedy.

The Vivekananda International Foundation, India's premier think tank on strategic affairs has been engaged in consistent dissection of the phenomenon of terrorism that has injected a sense of despondency in India. This book is a compilation of twelve essays penned by its scholars over the past couple of years to bring out the various facets of understanding and control of the phenomenon of terrorism.

Jai Hind.

Lt Gen Gautam Banerjee, PVSM, AVSM, YSM (Retd)

(Former Chief of Staff Central Command &
Commandant Officers' Training Academy, Chennai)

Member Executive Council, Distinguished Fellow & Editor,
Vivekananda International Foundation, New Delhi

List of Contributors

Alvite Singh Ningthoujam, is a Research Associate at the VIF. Earlier, he has served as a Fellow at the Begin-Sadat (BESA) Centre for Strategic Studies, Bar-Ilan University, Israel. He has published articles in the *Middle East Review of International Affairs* (*MERIA*), *The Diplomat*, *Asia Times*, *The Jerusalem Post*, International Strategic and Security Studies Programme (ISSSP), Bangalore. He was also a contributing writer for the magazine *Unmanned Flying Machines*. He is the author of the chapter titled "Iran" in P.R. Kumaraswamy (ed.) *Persian Gulf 2014: India's Relations with the Region*, published by Sage, New Delhi. Currently, he is also a final year Doctoral Candidate at the Centre for West Asian Studies, School of International Studies, Jawaharlal Nehru University, New Delhi.

Rohit Singh graduated in History (Honours) from Hansraj College, Delhi University.He holds a post-graduate diploma in Electronic Media from Guru Gobind Singh Indraprastha University, Delhi, and a Masters in Mass Communication from Guru Jambeshwar University, Hisar. He had been a Research Assistant and later Associate Fellow at the Centre for Land Warfare Studies (CLAWS), and a Senior Research Associate and Special Assistant to the Director at the Vivekananda International Foundation (VIF), New Delhi.

Lt Gen Gautam Banerjee, PVSM, AVSM, YSM (Retd), a former Chief of Staff, Central Command and Commandant, Officers' Training Academy, Chennai, is a prolific writer on strategic issues, authoring so far over fifty papers and five books. He is a Member of the Executive Council and a Distinguished Fellow at the Vivekananda International Foundation, New Delhi.

C.D. Sahay is the Dean, the Centre for Neighbourhood Studies and Internal Security Studies, at the Vivekananda International Foundation, New Delhi. He is a Former Secretary (Research and Analysis Wing), Cabinet Secretariat.

Dr Abhinav Pandya is a public relations, economics and policy consultant. He is also a free-lance journalist.

Brigadier Sushil Kumar Sharma has been the Deputy General Officer Commanding of a Mountain Division in Assam. He is a PhD from IGNOU; the topic of his study being North-East India. He is presently posted as DIGP, CRPF in the North-East Region.

Ambassador Tariq Karim is the former High Commissioner of Bangladesh to India. He has had ambassadorial assignments also in the United States, South Africa, Iran and Beijing. As Additional Foreign Secretary at the Ministry of Foreign Affairs of Bangladesh, he was instrumental in normalising troubled relations with India and resolving long outstanding problems relating to water sharing, cross-border insurgency and boundary demarcation. He was entrusted with the role of finalising the landmark Ganges Water Sharing Treaty between Bangladesh and India. State fragility, civil society, democratic transition, human rights and rule of law, governance issues, political Islam and globalisation issues are among his primary areas of academic interest. Opting for early retirement from the Foreign Service, Ambassador Karim joined as a senior faculty at the University of Maryland in 1999 and was associated with the George Washington and the Virginia International Universities. Currently a Distinguished Fellow at the Vivekananda International Foundation in New Delhi, Ambassador Tariq Karim is concurrently an Advisor to the World Bank on their South Asian Regional Economic Integration Programme.

Dr Madhumita Srivastava Balaji, a student of political science, is an alumna of the Benaras Hindu University, Varanasi. She is a PhD in Political Science and the subject of her dissertation has been 'International Dimensions of Ethnic Conflicts: A Case Study of Kashmir and Northern Ireland', reviewed by the Indian Council of Social Sciences Research, New Delhi, and published under the ICSSR in 1999-2000. Having taught in colleges of Delhi University, she is presently a Senior Research Associate with the Vivekananda International Foundation, New Delhi.

Ms Navroz Singh is a Research Intern with the Vivekananda International Foundation, focusing on the Central Asian Republics. She is a graduate with honours in Political Science from Miranda House, University of Delhi, and a post-graduate diploma holder in Conflict Transformation and Peace Building from the Aung San Suu Kyi Centre for Peace, Lady Sri Ram College, University of Delhi.

Col Ashish Sirsikar is a Senior Research Fellow with the Vivekananda International Foundation, working in the field of National Security and Strategy with a focus on China. His areas of study encompass Chinese security perspectives and vision for the 21st Century, with particular emphasis on the ongoing PLA modernisation.

Gen N C Vij, PVSM, UYSM, AVSM is a former Army Chief and founder Vice Chairman of the National Disaster Management Authority. He is the Director of the Vivekananda International Foundation, New Delhi.

1

Islamic State of Iraq and Syria (ISIS) and its South Asian Connection: An Indian Perspective

Alvite Singh Ningthoujam

A Brief Background to the Evolution of ISIS

Today, one of the most serious threats that have engulfed a large portion of the Middle East is the emergence of the Sunni Muslim extremist group, infamously known as the Islamic State of Iraq and Syria (ISIS), or Islamic State of Iraq and Levant (ISIL). After capturing sizeable territory in Iraq and Syria, the group changed its name to Islamic State (IS). The main objective behind the inception of this dreaded armed group was to establish a caliphate, or an Islamic statebased on Sharia law, across the world. On June 29, 2014, IS declared its leader Abu Bakr al-Baghdadi as the new caliph, or the "leader of the faithful". His real name is Ibrahim Awwad Ibrahim Ali al-Badri al-Samarrai, but to his followers, he is Caliph Ibrahim. The word Caliph or Khilafa in Arabic means "successor" and this signifies the ultimate ambition of the leader to establish the above-mentioned state (the last Caliphate had been destroyed with the fall of the Ottoman Empire in the World War I).[1]

A rather quick unfolding of such a situation in this already war-torn region has shaken up security establishments in the region. Most importantly, the alarming pace at which the militant group is gaining control over large swathes of territory in Iraq and Syria is something that the affected countries' political and security establishments need to grapple with. The IS's resonance is being felt in Europe, Central Asia and South Asia, including India.

Before getting into the emerging trends of the IS and how it is impacting India, it is imperative to understand the origins of the group, its main motives, source of funding, global outreach and the kinds of military it has come to deploy in the fight against the state forces of Iraq and Syria.

The roots of the IS can be traced back to the early 2000s—particularly, the US invasion of Saddam Hussein's Iraq in 2003. While the US-led coalition forces were trying to establish control in Iraq, a group by the name al-Qaeda in Iraq (AQI) was formed in 2004, primarily to wage a guerrilla war against the coalition forces and their domestic allies within Iraq.[2] In other words, IS had started as an al-Qaeda franchise. The first leader of AQI was an Arab of Jordanian descent named Abu Musab al-Zarqawi. The US State Department declared AQI as a terrorist organisation. Al-Zarqawi's AQI started an extremely brutal campaign to "ignite a sectarian war against the majority Shia community".[3] However, al-Zarqawi's leadership was cut short as he was killed in a US airstrike, and was replaced by Abu Ayyub al-Masri in October 2006. Abu Ayyub al-Masri changed the name of the group from AQI to Islamic State in Iraq (ISI), and named Abu Omar al-Baghdadi as its leader.

The name ISI was given with an aim to garner support from the people of Iraq. In 2010, Abu Ayyub al-Masri and Abu Omar al Baghdadi met the same fate as al-Zarqawi (killed in a joint US–Iraq operation). From April 2010 onwards, the onus of running ISI fell on Abu Bakr al-Baghdadi, who again changed the name of the outfit to Islamic State in Iraq and the Levant (ISIL) or ISIS. ISIL was named thus when Abu Bakr al-Baghdadi, in early 2013, declared the absorption of the al-Qaeda backed militant group in Syria, known as Jabhat al-Nusra or Al-Nusra Front.[4] By this time, Al-Nusra's popularity in Syria had already gained prominence and this came in conflict with the proclamation of Abu al-Baghdadi for the merger of AQI and Al-Nusra to form the ISIS or ISIL. The ISI's declaration of adding Al-Nusra to its group clearly expressed the vision of its leader for a broadened objective of controlling a larger territory of Syria by fighting the regime of President Bashar al-Assad and the various opposition groups in the country. It should also be noted that Al-Nusra is considered to be one of the best armed and most successful groups fighting against Bashar al-Assad, and it is also known for carrying out some of the deadliest attacks in the ongoing Syrian crisis, including several suicide bombings.

The rift between Al-Nusra and Abu Bakr al-Baghdadi's ISIS was first exposed in April 2013 when the former's leader Abu Mohammed al-Jawlani publicly denied the announcement of their merger. This was a clear indication that things had turned sour between the two militant groups, which was attributed to their quest for dominance in the region, particularly, inside Syria. The merger announcement did not go down well with the parent organisation of the al-Qaeda. After failed attempts to ease out differences between the ISIS and the Jabhat al-Nusra, on February 3, 2014, the al-Qaeda formally dissociated itself from its onetime affiliate in Iraq and Syria, and announced that ISIS "is not a branch of the al-Qaeda group...does not have an organizational relationship with it and [al-Qaeda] is not the group responsible for their actions".[5] This brought to an end the love–hate relationship between the two militant groups. The ISIS's targeting of civilians alienated local populations and ran contrary to the al-Qaeda's mission to unite all Muslims across the region and became one of the most important factors for the break between the two outfits.

The ISIS, right from its establishment, has followed stringent behavioural norms and strategies, which makes it starkly different from the other militant organisations operating in the region. It is known for its brutal tactics and also for its harsh implementation of the Islamic laws. Actually, it first came into notice when it started massacring its rivals. But it attracted global attention after it executed thousands of Iraqi soldiers and 100-odd Syrian troops, during mid-2014. The ISIS's extreme intolerance to external intervention in the Middle Eastern crisis, particularly in Iraq and Syria, has been signified by the killings of foreign nationals, including aid workers and journalists. The ISIS's administering of Islamic punishments like flogging, imposing ban on smoking and music and other social restrictions, which are deemed as un-Islamic, do not go well with the Syrians as well. As a result, considering the extreme brutalities of the ISIS, terror outfits such as the al-Qaeda appears to be more lenient.

Another dimension that is of global concern is the ISIS's source of funding. One of the most important sources is the kidnap-for-ransom tactics, and often European citizens (mostly corporation employees) have been their prime targets. In one such case, a Scandinavian corporation reportedly paid a ransom of US$ 70,000 to release a kidnapped employee.[6] But this was not the case with James Foley, the American journalist beheaded by the ISIS. The failure of the US to pay a ransom of approximately US$ 132 million[7] as demanded by his ISIS captors became one of the reasons for his murder. But the ISIS also used Foley's death to send a message of defiance to the US which had started intervening to stall its march in Iraq.

There are also reports of funds being transferred to the ISIS by the Persian Gulf countries such as Kuwait, Qatar, Turkey and Saudi Arabia. This was believed to have been done through Kuwait, with the tacit approval of the regimes in the above-mentioned countries.[8] Iraq's former Prime Minister Nouri al-Maliki even accused Saudi Arabia and Qatar of financial assistance to the ISIS. But along the journey, ISIS exploited various means to garner financial support.

During its initial days, the ISIS had could gather a large sum of money out of petty crimes and bank robberies. After capturing Mosul's central bank, ISIS was believed to have looted 500 billion Iraqi dinars (approximately US$ 425 million) and, with a total fund worth about US$ 2 billion, it has become the "world's richest terrorist group".[9] With such an enormous amount, the ISIS has acquired the capability of paying about 60,000 people, who are associated with the group, a salary of US$ 600 a month a year.[10] According to a recent estimate by the Central Intelligence Agency (CIA), there are about 20,000 to 31,500 fighters across Iraq and Syria.[11] This dramatic rise is due to the strong recruitment tactics used by the group. Another breakthrough happened when they captured large oil fields in Syria and Iraq.[12] The oil seized from these fields is sold at a discounted price, which is estimated at US$ 25 to US$ 60 for a barrel, as against the market price of US$ 100, and the total profits from such sales are over US$ 3 million a day.[13] The suspected recipient of such oils is Turkey. Beyond this, using the latest technology and social media, the ISIS is believed to have appealed for funds from individual donors.

The ISIS's military capabilities are another important feature of the group. This terror organisation has been successful in acquiring a few sophisticated weapons systems of different origins. The large sum of funds that it has accumulated is used in buying military items, apart from those captured from the Syrian and Iraqi troops. While the exact figures and types of the weapons are hard to identify, there are a few estimations. For instance, the ISIS has

Russian-made T55 and T72 tanks which it captured from the Syrian troops and the Iraqi Army, respectively.[14] Other items include rifles, grenades, machine guns, truck-mounted machine guns and munitions. The ISIS fighters are believed to possess towed and mounted anti-aircraft guns, including the powerful 12.7mm DShK machine guns and a Chinese-made Type 65 or Type 74 37mm twin-barrelled anti-aircraft gun.[15] During mid-July, the ISIS captured from the Iraqi military around 52 155mm M198 howitzers, 1,500 US-made Humvees and 4,000 PKC machine guns.[16]

A report which documented a few weapons captured from the ISIS by Kurdish forces in Iraq and Syria included the following items: US M16A4 rifles, two Chinese Type 80 machine guns, a Croatian sniper rifle, a 9mm Glock pistol, various Soviet-era small arms and anti-tank weapons (manufactured in former Yugoslavia).[17] Adding to its military prowess, the ISIS also captured a major military air base in north-eastern Syria during late August. However, it is still unknown as to how much of what it captured from the airbase, or from the troops, could actually be utilised. That said, the continuous stockpiling of arms and ammunitions is a rather worrisome factor in the long run.

ISIS and its Impact on India

The rapidly unfolding events in Iraq have become a matter of great concern for the Indians (approximately 16,000 before the crisis erupted), living there as well for the newly-installed Bharatiya Janata Party (BJP) government, under the leadership of Narendra Modi, in New Delhi. Apart from the safety of the Indians in Iraq, and the economic impact this crisis would have on India, the most serious concerns is the likely impact on the internal security of India. The following section discusses the abduction episode of the Indian workers and nurses and how the present government is planning to tackle the possible resonance of ISIS within the country, particularly among the radicalised Muslim youth.

When the wave of this dreaded phenomenon began in the Middle Eastern countries of Iraq and Syria, India was watching the developments very cautiously. However, the wait-and-watch policy did not last for long after 40 Indian workers were kidnapped by suspected ISIS militants from Mosul during mid-June 2014, the city wracked by heavy clashes between the Shia-dominated[18] Iraqi government and the Sunni militant groups. In quick succession, 46 Indian nurses where taken captive by ISIS militants from the city of Tikrit. These events sent a shock across India. New Delhi responded by dispatching a career-diplomat, and the former Indian ambassador to Iraq, Suresh Reddy. The said Indian diplomat is well-known for his contacts in Iraq, and he was instrumental in establishing contacts, not only with the Iraqi officials but with the larger regional powers and several American security and intelligence officials. There was also speculation that India had approached Middle Eastern countries such as Iran, Turkey and Israel for assistance while rescuing the abducted Indians. Besides reaching out to Saudi Arabia, a country which has a significant influence in the region, India also sought assistance from Russia to secure the safe release of the Indians.

The abduction crisis posed the first big challenge to Modi after he became the Prime Minister of India. The Indian Minister of External Affairs (MEA) Sushma Swaraj and the National Security Advisor (NSA) Ajit Doval, also played important roles in the rescue efforts of the kidnapped citizens.

During the initial days into the kidnapping, it was a huge challenge for the Indian authorities, particularly the security establishment, as no one knew exactly where they had been kept, and who had abducted them, although hints were pointed towards the ISIS. Moreover, as the ISIS was being considered even more brutal than the al-Qaeda and other militant organisations, the room for negotiations was limited. The absence of any ransom calls added to the sense of disquiet. It was at such a juncture that the Indian officials came up with the probabilities of the kidnapped workers being used as "human shields", or a "first line of defence"[19] in the possible advent of any combined airstrikes by the US and Iraqi forces. However, the successful rescue operations during early-July which resulted in the release of the kidnapped Indian nurses from the clutches of the ISIS militants were lauded back home. But what has remained as a major challenge is how to rescue those Indian workers who are still in the captivity of the IS militants.

After the rescue operations of the nurses, a few questions that cropped up were how the Indian officials negotiated with the militants; what were their terms and conditions for the release of the Indians and was there any cooperation between India and the Middle Eastern intelligence agencies during the rescue efforts? These questions were left unanswered as the nature of the entire operation was considered to be an "extremely difficult" one, and this continues to be a mystery, till today. Even while briefing the media, the Indian MEA spokesperson Syed Akbaruddin said,

> "At the diplomatic level these negotiations were involving the External Affairs Minister herself. At the ground level, obviously we will not be able to share, and I had repeated it previously, because diplomacy works through the front door. I had said we are using other doors. How those doors were used and knocked on, how they were opened up, is a story for another day. The story for today is that one of those doors opened and we were able to extricate our nationals."[20]

Serious concerns have been expressed over the possible spill-over of this latest Middle Eastern crisis to India. While the problem is actually taking place in a distant region, it is being considered as a "danger far closer home than it appears".[21] In the first place, the main objective behind the establishment of an outfit like ISIS is to create an Islamic state of which India would also be a part. A map released by the outfit shows a large part of India as part of the Islamic province of Khorasan.[22] To some, this might appear to be rhetoric because of the party's ambition to carve its own unique niche, but it is a matter of grave concern for India, for various reasons.

Prior to the abduction crisis, one of the earliest impacts of the ISIS that hit India was the news of the 30,000-odd Indian Muslims who had reportedly signed up to defend Iraq's holy Shia shrines and fight the Sunni Islamist militants in the country.[23] Although this did not lead to any immediate impact on India, the willingness of the volunteers, who are mainly engineers, students and police officers, raised warning bells for the security agencies in India. It is the presence of such educated and middle-class Indian Muslims that is posing to be a major challenge while trying to douse the fire that is spreading due to the Middle Eastern crisis. For India, which is home to about a 175 million Muslim population, such acts could trigger an untoward sectarian crisis. The Intelligence Bureau officials have warned concerned authorities to plan sensitisation measures as there were reports of a clear division among the Shia and Sunni religious leaders on supporting either the Sunni outfit ISIS, or the Shia-dominated al-Maliki government. Moreover, the demographic nature of the Indian subcontinent where many Muslim youth appear to be dissatisfied and the instant communication that is facilitated by the cyber technology, have become key factors for ISIS's successful penetration in India.

The above-mentioned development, in a subtle manner, has indicated the gradual and growing connection between the ISIS and India. Moreover, as most Jihadist groups have their eyes set on India, the ISIS's influence in the country is not a surprising outcome. An Indian strategist was of the view that,

> "Strategy is a function of capability. We are not focusing on events in the Middle East because we have no capability to influence them. Earlier too, people have been kidnapped in the region and we have had to depend on third party negotiators. All global jihad will have India in its crosshairs. We can ignore them only at our own peril."[24]

There is a growing concern that is developing within India with regard to the ISIS's gaining influence, and the above-mentioned statement reflects one of those voices. Moreover, the short duration within which the ISIS has gained prominence can be considered as the most important feature of this group. India's worst nightmare came into a reality when Abu Bakr al-Baghdadi, during his Ramzan speech, vowed war against several countries, including India.[25] The reiteration of India a few times in his speech strongly signalled the possibilities of India being one of the prime targets of the ISIS, and he connected this with the plight of the Muslims in Myanmar, Pakistan and Jammu and Kashmir. The call of the self-proclaimed Caliph to the Indian Muslims did not go well with most Indian Muslim leaders. Despite their opposition, the radicalised Muslims are getting attracted to the IS, something that was illustrated by the radical Kashmiri youth—believed to be deeply indoctrinated by the Deobandi school of thought—seen waving ISIS flags during a demonstration against the Israeli invasion of the Gaza Strip during July and August.[26] This is a serious issue which the Indian government needs to grapple with in the days to come.

Radicalisation of the Indian Muslim Youth: The Impact on Internal Security

The rapid radicalisation of a few Indian Muslim youth, in consonance with the rising influence of the ISIS, has turned out to be one of the most critical challenges for the Indian security agencies. The Sunni militant outfit, which is very techno-savvy unlike other militant groups, has been able to lure young Muslims not only from India, but also from Central Asia and the European countries. The group is known for its heavy usage of internet and social media tools. Moreover, the ability of the group to convey its messages using a few Indian regional languages—namely, Hindi, Tamil and Urdu—for subtitles, makes the recruitment process easier. In this regard, Facebook and Twitter have become hotspots for the various "ads" posted by the ISIS.[27] Most of the youth who are believed to be highly radicalised hail from the states of Kerala, Maharashtra, Tamil Nadu and Jammu and Kashmir.

Interestingly, unemployment or poverty is not the only factor attributed for joining the ISIS; youth with proper educational backgrounds and from middle-income families are being increasingly enticed towards this dreaded phenomenon. This was the exact case with four youth from Kalyan (in Maharashtra) who reportedly joined the ISIS to fight in Syria and Iraq, as early as July.[28] A similar participation of the Indian youth was also reported for fighting in Syria. In a strange case, 26-year-old Adil Fayaz, an Indian student (from Srinagar) in Australia, reportedly joined the ISIS in Syria to fight against the al-Assad regime. Similarly, a Kerala youth who was studying in Dubai and another one of Hyderabad-origin from Texas, have reportedly joined the Islamist fighters in Syria.[29] However, there are no concrete reports on how many Indians from the expatriate communities in the Middle East have joined the ISIS.

Most of the youth have been so brainwashed that they have left their jobs in India and decided to take up the terrorist path. What needs to be investigated thoroughly is the root cause of the problem that has driven the youth to travel to Iraq and Syria. While the angle of ideological commitment as a main motive behind joining the ISIS cannot be ignored, some of the recruits could be joining the ISIS for purely mercenary motives. According to a report, there are about "1.2 to 1.3 lakh mercenaries fighting in Syria alone, and only 15-20 per cent of ISIS members are ideologically driven".[30] The Indians, according to this report, could also be a part of the mercenary group.

With the passage of time, the severity of the ISIS's influence on India is also on the rise. Amid investigations of the movements of the Indian youth to Iraq, a photograph of 26 Muslim youth sporting black T-shirts with the emblem of the ISIS in front of a mosque at the coastal town of Thondi in Ramanathapuram district (in Tamil Nadu) in early August rang further warning bells.[31] As a quick follow-up to this, an Imam responsible for procuring the T-shirts with the pro-ISIS slogans on them was arrested, and he revealed, during the investigation, "that the main accused were active supporters of the ISIS and allegedly trying to brainwash Muslim youths for the cause that the ISIS was fighting for".[32] This incident is a serious issue as religious leaders have been involved in promoting the extremist ideologies propagated by the ISIS, which is deeply anti-India. The India-based Islamic organisation, Jamaat-e-Islami Hind, has reportedly said that the "ISIS caliphate is binding on all Muslims"[33] and a similar support was also endorsed by a cleric from the Darul Uloom Nadwatul Ulama. In a letter allegedly written by the cleric, he expressed "confidence that Iraqi Sunnis were with ISIS and that Bagdhadi's clean and pious character is worth praise", and he also allegedly asked the "Saudi government to prepare an army of five lakh Indian Sunni Muslim youth to fight against the Shia militias in Iraq and elsewhere.[34] Another man from Bhatkal in Karnataka, who is also a cleric reportedly trained at the Darul Uloom Nadwatul Ulama seminary in Lucknow, called on the Indian Muslims "to join the global jihad".[35] He is highly believed to be impressed by the advancements made by the Islamic State's success. Such acts could also have far-reaching implications at this juncture when discontent among the Muslim youth is wide, owing to real and imagined social and economic deprivations. An Indian Mujahideen (IM) man was believed to be instrumental in recruiting for the ISIS poor Muslims in the aforementioned states. If this nexus between the ISIS and India's home-grown terror groups manages to establish a robust link, then the headache of combating such amalgamated force will be a hard task for the Indian security agencies.

The involvement of a few Indian Muslim youth with the crisis going on in Syria and Iraq is worrying for a few reasons. The first reason is that it could set a trend for other like-minded youth who are easily susceptible to the radicalisation process. Although a large section of the Indian Muslim society is well-integrated with the rest of the society, there seems to be a growing unrest in many areas where the youth and influential leaders have taken up a staunch anti-India stance. Even if the number of the youth that adheres to the ideology of the ISIS is minuscule, the act of siding with such an organisation itself is very dangerous. A second reason, and a more dangerous one, is as to how the returnees (from Syria and Iraq), with their first-hand experience of the entire turmoil could easily brainwash their peers at home. That said, this would depend on how far they have been indoctrinated during their stay either in Iraq or Syria. Investigations upon their arrival back in India could only give a picture as to why they joined the militant outfit, and how they travelled to the conflict-ridden countries. Another critical issue is the use of the social networking sites and the internet-related activities that are fuelling this problem. There is already a paramount concern within the Indian security establishment about the use of information technology and other cyber-related activities while fanning the ISIS propaganda.

Furthermore, the news of the death of one of the four youth from Maharashtra while fighting in Iraq was quite a disturbing one. Although this is one isolated incident, the act of giving up one's life could be considered as the depth of commitment of such youth towards the cause of the ISIS, and the influence the organisation has gained in India in the span of few months. The al-Qaeda, despite operating widely in Pakistan and Afghanistan, has not been able to leave such imprints wherein it could recruit Indians and make them fight to death. Likewise, the unconfirmed report of a young suicide bomber of the ISIS, who was from Tamil Nadu, blowing himself up in the Syria–Iraq theatre became a matter of grave concern.[36] If this report is found to be true, it is going to be the first suicide attack by an Indian in the world and it will have a serious repercussion on matters related to India's internal security. Such incidents should be viewed especially by the security establishment with utmost importance as there is a fear that those youth with similar intentions, upon their return to India, could introduce this form of extreme terrorism. Reports of Indian jihadists having received training on the extreme form of terrorism abroad[37] raise fears that the home-grown terrorists could be leaning towards suicide attacks, although no such incidents have occurred so far. Attempts have already been made, i.e., during the attack against an election campaign rally of the current Prime Minister in December 2013 in Patna. The recently-released report by the National Investigation Agency (NIA) mentioned that "the terrorists planned everything from using firearms to employing a suicide bomber and ultimately using a series of bomb blasts to assassinate the BJP leader and then Gujarat chief minister".[38] NIA's report also mentioned the usage of videos and lectures by the Students Islamic Movement of India (SIMI) cadres to recruit young boys from Ranchi.[39] As a result, the burgeoning enticement of the Indian youth towards such extreme terror organisations is posing a major challenge to the Indian internal security.

The above developments have come at a time when the leader of the al-Qaeda Ayman al-Zawahri released a video-tape wherein he mentioned the establishment of the al-Qaida in Indian Subcontinent (AQIS). Given the low-profile activities of the al-Qaeda in India since the last few years, the Indian security apparatus does not see an immediate threat emerging out of this announcement, but it has not taken it lightly either. In fact, this is a worrisome factor as both the militant groups, that is, the al-Qaeda and the ISIS, have a similar objective to target India and to turn this South Asian country as one of the recruiting grounds for extremists. With such motives, the rapid radicalisation of the youth could go in their favour.

The Way Ahead for India

As the influence of the ISIS has already been felt in India, New Delhi will be compelled to take certain steps to prevent it from making further inroads into the country. The establishment of robust intelligence sharing networks with the Persian Gulf countries, where there is a huge Indian expatriate population, should be a priority for the new government in New Delhi. Although such efforts were initiated by the previous Congress-led United Progressive Alliance (UPA) government, cooperation in this particular aspect lacks substance. The time has come to look at the Middle East not only from the prism of oil, energy and commercial angle, but from that military-security arena, too. The already-existing military cooperation between countries such as Oman, Qatar, Kuwait, Saudi Arabia and the UAE should be promoted further, where counter-terrorism, intelligence and information-sharing cooperation should be high on the agenda. The least-explored opportunities of the India–Iraq military cooperation should also be revived.

At this moment, the possibility of India joining hands with the US-led military attack on ISIS does not seem to be a feasible option. The US President Barack Obama had expressed his desire to rope in India in his efforts to tackle the menace militarily. Although India has major concerns with the pace at which the ISIS and al-Qaeda are gaining visible influence in the country, New Delhi will ponder upon the participation in any military strike in a distant country where it has major interests. Alongside this, the safety of the Indians in Iraq as well as in the other Persian Gulf countries remains a major concern for India. India would like to avoid similar circumstances as faced by those three foreigners, including journalists and an aid worker (of American and British origin) for their respective country's military operations in Iraq.

At this stage, when India is exploring mechanisms to curb the influence of the ISIS, New Delhi has shown some signs of advancement. The present government which is known for its no-tolerance attitude to any form of terrorism has started to keep strict vigilance over the movement of youth from India to Iraq and Syria, other Middle Eastern and the neighbouring countries as well. Moreover, the NSA and IB, with a robust cooperation with the Ministry of Home Affairs (MHA) and security establishments, are expected to play a greater role in affairs related to internal security, including home-grown radicalisation. The Indian MHA is particularly interested in the de-radicalisation process of the youth and this itself is an enormous challenge.

As a part of the ongoing efforts to prevent the rise of the ISIS-related activities in India, the Anti-Terrorism Squad (ATS) in Mumbai reportedly interrogated a few people who were suspected to have indoctrinated and motivated the Kalyan boys for their ISIS-related activities. Similarly, a special branch detained four college dropouts in Kolkata, who were originally from Hyderabad. They were believed to be on their way to Iraq via Bangladesh for allegedly joining the ISIS, a claim refuted by a few Muslim leaders. But it is clear from vigilance that the authorities have started taking steps before the matter spirals out of control.

Owing to the burgeoning ISIS-connected activities within India, it is highly probable that the government is likely to ask the NIA to file an FIR against unknown persons affiliated to the organisation, with an aim to prevent more Muslim youth from going to Iraq and this would also be applicable to those who return after a brief stint. According to a report, the NIA can register an FIR on the basis of the UN Security Council Resolution 2170 that has placed the ISIS under terror sanctions and asked the member countries not to allow fighters from joining the extremist Wahabi group headed by Abu Bakr al-Baghdadi.[40] The Indian security agencies are also believed to be exploring the possibility of banning of ISIS as a terrorist organisation by listing it under the Unlawful Activities Prevention Act (UAPA).[41] But a section in the government is of the view that this move could be detrimental to those Indian workers who are still under the captivity of the ISIS in Mosul.

Conclusion

It is evident from the above developments that India faces a major challenge of tackling the rising influence of the ISIS in the country. For this, New Delhi, under the leadership of Prime Minister Narendra Modi, should build up a strong network of intelligence-sharing within the country as well as with the

Middle Eastern countries. Efforts should be made to reinvigorate the existing security dialogues and the exchange of intelligence information with countries such as Saudi Arabia, Iraq, Qatar, the UAE, Jordan, Egypt, Turkey and Israel. As a result, India needs to give considerable importance to its military security cooperation with the mentioned countries amid its Middle Eastern foreign policy that is heavily driven by oil, energy and commercial transactions. India should also go an extra mile in forging strong cooperation with the security establishments of the European countries and the US, which are also equally concerned with the rise of the ISIS.

India needs to adopt an inclusive policy in order to tackle the rising radicalisation of the Muslim youth in the country. In other words, the government and its security establishment need to build a strong rapport with the larger Muslim society in India, as a majority of it denounces the extremist thought process of organisations such as ISIS. As a part of the process, a strong channel of communication with the Muslim leaders in different parts of India should be established so as to understand their problems as well as their suggestions. In short, this should be done empathetically.

Finally, a robust cyber surveillance mechanism is the need of the hour, particularly considering the rising online campaign and advertisements used by terrorist outfits. There should be strict monitoring over the banking systems to prevent money laundering. Along with this, a closer coordination between different ministries, private corporations, security agencies, and most importantly, the local populace, should be promoted.

The Author

Alvite Singh Ningthoujam, is a Research Associate at the VIF. Earlier, he has served as a *Fellow* at the Begin-Sadat (BESA) Centre for Strategic Studies, Bar-Ilan University, Israel. He has published articles in the *Middle East Review of International Affairs (MERIA), The Diplomat, Asia Times, The Jerusalem Post, International Strategic and Security Studies Programme (ISSSP),* Bangalore. He was also a contributing writer for the magazine *Unmanned Flying Machines.* He is the author of the chapter titled “Iran” in P.R. Kumaraswamy (Ed.) *Persian Gulf 2014: India's Relations with the Region,* published by the Sage, New Delhi. Currently, he is also a final year Doctoral Candidate at the Centre for West Asian Studies, School of International Studies, Jawaharlal Nehru University, New Delhi.

*

END NOTES

1. For further reading, refer to Daniel Pipes, 'Caliph Ibrahim's Brutal Moment', *Middle East Forum,* 5 August 2014, http://www.meforum.org/4769/isis-caliph-ibrahim. Also see 'Abu Bakr al-Baghdadi: The Man who would be Caliph', *The Week,* 13 September 2014, http://theweek.com/article/index/267920/abu-bakr-al-baghdadi-the-man-who-would-be-caliph.
2. Zachary Laub and Jonathan Masters, 'Islamic State in Iraq and Syria', *Backgrounders,* Council on Foreign Relations, 8 August 2014, http://www.cfr.org/iraq/islamic-state-iraq-syria/p14811
3. 'ISIS Fast Facts', *CNN,* 6 September 2014, http://edition.cnn.com/2014/08/08/world/isis-fast-facts/
4. For a brief introduction to the Al-Nusra Front, see 'Al Nusra Front', *Mapping Militant Organizations,* 24 July 2014, Stanford University, http://web.stanford.edu/group/mappingmilitants/cgi-bin/groups/view/493
5. Liz Sly, 'Al-Qaeda Disavows Any Ties with Radical Islamist ISIS Group in Syria, Iraq', *The Washington Post,* 3 February 2014, http://www.washingtonpost.com/world/middle_east/al-qaeda-disavows-any-ties-with-radical-islamist-isis-group-in-syria-iraq/2014/02/03/2c9afc3a-8cef-11e3-98ab-fe5228217bd1_story.html
6. 'Multiple Kidnappings for Ransom, funding ISIS, Source', *CBS News,* 21 August 2014, http://www.cbsnews.com/news/multiple-kidnappings-for-ransom-funding-isis-source-says/
7. Rukmini Callimachi, 'Before Killing James Foley, ISIS demanded Ransom from U.S.', *The New York Times,* 20 August 2014, http://www.nytimes.com/2014/08/21/world/middleeast/isis-pressed-for-ransom-before-killing-james-foley.html
8. Josh Rogin, 'America's Allies are funding ISIS', *The Daily Beast,* 14 June 2014, http://www.thedailybeast.com/articles/2014/06/14/america-s-allies-are-funding-isis.html
9. Terrence McCoy, 'ISIS just stole $425 Million, Iraqi Governor Says, and became the 'World's Richest Terror Group'', *The Washington Post,* 12 June 2014, http://www.washingtonpost.com/news/morning-mix/wp/2014/06/12/isis-just-stole-425-million-and-became-the-worlds-richest-terrorist-group/
10. Ibid.
11. 'How Foreign Fighters are swelling ISIS Ranks in Startling Numbers', *CNN,* 14 September 2014, http://edition.cnn.com/2014/09/12/world/meast/isis-numbers/index.html?iref=allsearch
12. Helen Lock, 'How Isis became the Wealthiest Terror Group in History', *The Independent,* 15 September 2014, http://www.independent.co.uk/news/world/middle-east/how-isis-became-the-wealthiest-terror-group-in-history-9732750.html
13. Ibid.
14. 'ISIS Weapon Inventory grows', *Daily Sabah,* 3 July 2014, http://www.dailysabah.com/mideast/2014/07/03/isiss-weapon-inventory-grows
15. 'ISIS Propaganda Videos show their Weapons, Skills in Iraq', *The Washington Post,* 18 June 2014, http://www.washingtonpost.com/news/checkpoint/wp/2014/06/18/isis-propaganda-videos-show-their-weapons-skills-in-iraq/
16. Jeremy Bender, 'ISIS Militants captured 52 American-Made Artillery Weapons that cost $500,000 Each', *Business Insider,* 15 July 2014, http://www.businessinsider.in/ISIS-Militants-Captured-52-American-Made-Artillery-Weapons-That-Cost-500000-Each/articleshow/38437515.cms
17. 'Report: Islamic State may have taken Anti-Tank Weapons from Syrian Rebels', *The Washington Post,* 7 September 2014, http://www.washingtonpost.com/news/checkpoint/wp/2014/09/07/report-islamic-state-has-anti-tank-weapons-taken-from-syrian-rebels/

18. Dipanjan Roy Chaudhury, '40 Workers abducted in Iraq, Ex-Ambassador Suresh Reddy dispatched to Iraq; New Delhi seeks Help of US, Israel, Iran and Turkey', *The Economic Times,* 19 June 2014, http://articles.economictimes.indiatimes.com/2014-06-19/news/50710913_1_abducted-indians-iran-and-israel-northern-iraq. Also see Suhasini Haidar, 'Suresh Reddy is India's Crisis Manager in Iraq', *The Hindu,* 19 June 2014, http://www.thehindu.com/news/national/suresh-reddy-is-indias-crisis-manager-in-iraq/article6127462.ece
19. Harinder Baweja, 'ISIS unwilling to Negotiate Release of Indian Workers abducted in Iraq', *Hindustan Times,* 25 June 2014, http://www.hindustantimes.com/world-news/iraqonthebrink/isis-unwilling-to-negotiate-release-of-abducted-indian-workers/article1-1233311.aspx
20. 'Transcript of the Media Briefing by Official Spokesperson', *Media Briefings,* 4 July 2014, Ministry of External Affairs, New Delhi, India, http://www.mea.gov.in/media-briefings.htm?dtl/23559/Transcript+of+Media+Briefing+by+Official+Spokesperson+July+04+2014
21. Deeptiman Tiwary, 'ISIS has Designs on India: Experts', *The Times of India,* 9 June 2014, http://timesofindia.indiatimes.com/india/ISIS-has-designs-on-India-Experts/articleshow/36795859.cms
22. 'ISIS has 'Bigger Plans' for India in its Aim for Global Jihad, warn Experts', *Zee News,* 19 June 2014, http://zeenews.india.com/news/nation/isis-has-bigger-plans-for-india-in-its-aim-for-global-jihad-warn-experts_940975.html
23. "Thousands of Indian Muslims sign up to defend Iraq's Shrines", *The Times of India,* 26 June 2014, http://timesofindia.indiatimes.com/india/Thousands-of-Indian-Muslims-sign-up-to-defend-Iraqs-shrines/articleshow/37264170.cms
24. Deeptiman Tiwary, 'ISIS has Designs on India: Experts'. Op. cit.
25. Praveen Swami, "India among Jihad Targets of ISIS', *The Hindu,* 2 July 2014, http://www.thehindu.com/news/international/world/india-among-jihad-targets-of-isis/article6167595.ece
26. 'Pro-ISIS Stir a Disturbing Trend in Valley: Separatists', *The Times of India,* 2 August 2014, http://timesofindia.indiatimes.com/india/Pro-ISIS-stir-a-disturbing-trend-in-Valley-Separatists/articleshow/39450949.cms
27. 'ISIS uses Internet to reach Indian Youths to wage Jihad', *India Today,* 13 August 2014, http://indiatoday.intoday.in/story/isis-uses-internet-to-reach-indians-youths-to-wage-jihad/1/376788.html
28. For a brief report on the four youth, see Praveen Swami, 'Four Men from Mumbai believed to have joined Iraq Jihad, a Father appeals for Help', *The Indian Express,* 14 July 2014, http://indianexpress.com/article/india/maharashtra/four-men-from-mumbai-believed-to-have-joined-iraq-jihad-a-father-appeals-for-help/
29. 'Young Indians joining ISIS call for Jihad in West Asia', *Hindustan Times,* 6 August 2014, http://www.hindustantimes.com/india-news/kashmiri-youth-joins-jihad-in-syria-says-intel/article1-1248672.aspx
30. 'Kalyan youths may have gone to Iraq as Mercenaries', *The Times of India,* 19 July 2014, http://timesofindia.indiatimes.com/city/mumbai/Kalyan-youths-may-have-gone-to-Iraq-as-mercenaries/articleshow/38651842.cms
31. D.J. Walter Scott, 'Muslim Youths sporting ISIS T-Shirts cause a Flutter', *The Hindu,* 4 August 2014, http://www.thehindu.com/news/national/tamil-nadu/muslim-youths-sporting-isis-tshirts-cause-a-flutter/article6278285.ece
32. D.J. Walter Scott, 'Imam held for supplying T-Shirts with ISIS Slogan', *The Hindu,* 7 August 2014, http://www.thehindu.com/news/national/tamil-nadu/imam-arrested-for-supplying-

tshirts-with-isis-slogan/article6288657.ece

33. '"Supporting the ISIS Caliphate is Binding on All Muslims, ISIS fulfils Maulana Azad And Maududi's Aspirations for the Islamic Caliphate", says Jamaat-e-Islami Hind', *New Age Islam,* 26 August 2014, http://www.newageislam.com/radical-islamism-and-jihad/-supporting-the-isis-caliphate-is-binding-on-all-muslims,-isis-fulfils-maulana-azad-and-maududi-s-aspirations-for-the-islamic-caliphate,—says-jamaat-e-islami-hind/d/98745. Also see Prakash Nanda, 'Reviving the Sufi/Bhakti Tradition', *Uday India,* 13 September 2014, http://www.udayindia.in/english/content_13sept2014/right-angle.html
34. 'Nadwa Cleric asks Saudi Government to prepare an Army of Sunni Youth for Iraq', *The Times of India,* 26 July 2014, http://timesofindia.indiatimes.com/india/Nadwa-cleric-asks-Saudi-govt-to-prepare-an-army-of-Sunni-youth-for-Iraq/articleshow/39012903.cms
35. 'Come to Motherland of Jihad: Call to Arms from First Indian Group in Af-Pak', *The Indian Express,* 22 August 2014, http://indianexpress.com/article/india/india-others/come-to-motherland-of-jihad-call-to-arms-from-first-indian-group-in-afpak/
36. 'Tamil Nadu Man First ISIS Suicide Bomber from India?', *The Times of India,* 13 September 2014, http://timesofindia.indiatimes.com/india/Tamil-Nadu-man-first-ISIS-suicide-bomber-from-India/articleshow/42391955.cms
37. For a succinct account on the Jihadist movement in India, see Stephen Tankel, 'The Indian Jihadist Movement: Evolution and Dynamics: Analysis', *Eurasia Review: News and Analysis,* 10 September 2014, http://www.eurasiareview.com/10092014-indian-jihadist-movement-evolution-dynamics-analysis/
38. For a brief report, see Aman Sharma, 'Blasts in Narendra Modi's Patna Rally were Revenge for Gujarat Riots: NIA', *The Economic Times,* 11 September 2014, http://articles.economictimes.indiatimes.com/2014-09-11/news/53811431_1_gujarat-riots-charge-sheet-narendra-modi
39. For the report by NIA, see 'Bodhgaya Serial Blasts Cases', *Press Release,* National Investigation Agency, Ministry of Home Affairs, New Delhi, http://www.nia.gov.in/writereaddata/PressRelease11092014-2.pdf
40. Shishir Gupta, 'Crack the Whip on Indians joining ISIS, Centre may tell NIA', *Hindustan Times,* 14 September 2014, http://www.hindustantimes.com/india-news/crack-the-whip-on-indians-joining-isis-centre-may-tell-nia/article1-1263989.aspx
41. Ibid. Also see 'The Unlawful Activities (Prevention) Act, 1967', Ministry of Home Affairs, New Delhi, http://mha.nic.in/hindi/sites/upload_files/mhahindi/files/pdf/UAPA-1967.pdf.

2

International Terrorism Post 9/11: Emerging Trends and Global Response

Rohit Singh

Introduction

September 11, 2001 was a watershed in the manner in which the world acknowledged and responded to terrorism. The monstrosity of the multiple attacks which killed nearly 3,000 people in one planned strike brought universal condemnation for terror acts and the community of nations got together to formulate a collective response, in what came to be known as the 'Global War on Terrorism' (GWOT). However, the principle aim of the GWOT was to wipe out the al-Qaeda from its sanctuaries in Afghanistan, from where the 9/11 attacks had emanated. The prevailing atmosphere of outrage prompted even traditional archrivals like the US and Russia to close ranks, and Moscow's support was instrumental in facilitating the initial wave of the NATO air strikes in Afghanistan in October 2001 that dislodged the Taliban regime from power and forced the al-Qaeda into retreat. The US President George W. Bush saw the world divided into two camps—those who supported the war against terrorism and those who did not. The latter were considered enemies. The cooperation of countries like Pakistan which were reluctant to support the US-led campaign was coerced by the then US Secretary of State, Colin Powell, famously threatening to bomb the country into the Stone Age in case it was not willing to permit the use of its airspace and territory for the Coalition forces to enter Afghanistan.

In Afghanistan and Pakistan, over 1,200 al-Qaeda terrorists had been killed between 2004 and 2011, thereby greatly eroding the outfit's capacity to launch attacks on the US mainland. Thus, for the US, the broad goals of the GWOT had been achieved, considerably. Some of the important al-Qaeda leaders killed since 2001 include its leader, Osama bin Laden (2011), Atiyah Abdur al-Rahman (2011), Badar Mansur (2012), Aslam Awam (2012), Abu Ayyub al-Masri (2010), Abu Yazid (2010), Sheikh Fateh al Masri (2010) and Abu Zeid (2013). The degradation of the al-Qaeda's fighting core, the freezing of bank accounts and the pressure on different states to act against it eventually led to its de-centralisation. The surviving leadership realised that it had to morph into smaller entities and spread its tentacles to different parts of the world in order to survive the Western onslaught. While its small core remained intact in the Af-Pak region, many of its operatives, financiers and other supporters moved into lawless zones in West Asia, the Horn of Africa, the Middle East and the Caucasus. With a franchise-type operation, it developed a wide network across the world. The al-Qaeda's signature structure is small and the exposure of autonomous cells has little effect on the organisation as a whole. It has moved away from Arab leadership and is constrained to rely increasingly on non-Arab commanders.

International terrorism, post-2001, has become more diffused and widespread. The arc of Islamist terrorism has engulfed several countries in Africa and the Middle East in addition to assuming monstrous proportions in Afghanistan and Pakistan. In Iraq, the security situation has become far worse in the recent years with a wave of suicide bombings targeted at the Shias. The struggle of Sunni radical outfits to oust the Syrian government which is primarily led by Ahlawites is attracting Muslim fighters from across the globe, transforming Syria into a new symbol of the Global Jihad. The failure of the so-called Arab Spring has also given a new fillip to radicalisation and accentuated sectarian strife in the Muslim world. In the 45 months preceding 9/11, an average of 106 terrorist-related incidents was recorded every month across the world. Post-9/11, an average of 186 incidents has taken place every month and the number goes up to 284, if figures for Iraq are also included.

The terrorists inspired by the al-Qaeda have expanded the theatre of attacks and are looking for opportunities to target Westerners across the world. The Bali Bombings of 2002 and the London tube bombings in 2005 were carried out by terror groups loosely affiliated with the al-Qaeda or individuals inspired by its ideology. The victims of 9/11 included people from more than 90 countries, and 28 foreign nationals from 10 different countries were among the 166 people killed in the 26/11 attacks in Mumbai. The series of spectacular terrorist attacks all over the world since 9/11 point to the fact that despite the GWOT, the uncertainty and unpredictability of terror attacks remain very high. The Boston marathon bombings caught the security officials off guard as the attack was initiated by naturalised US citizens who had had no previous association with the terror groups.

So, why did the GWOT, which primarily remained focused on Afghanistan and Iraq not arrest the momentum of international terrorism elsewhere? For one, the International community has failed to even arrive at a universally accepted definition of terrorism with some member states of the UN stalling the passing of the draft comprehensive convention against terrorism. Advancing arguments such as first recognising the root causes of terrorism not only justifies violence perpetuated by the terrorists but also stymies a collective action against them. Selective action against some terror groups, while turning a blind eye towards the activities of others, ensures that terrorists retain their ability to strike anywhere in the world. The Jihadi terrorism post-9/11 has become more integrated and complementary in nature as the terror outfits across the globe have closely aligned under the broad al-Qaeda umbrella, willing to ideologically or logistically support each other for targeting their common enemies. For instance, the objectives of the Lashkar-e-Taiba (LeT), which carried out the attacks in Mumbai in 2008 were ideologically similar to that of the al-Qaeda and were in consonance with the latter's aim of targeting Westerners anywhere in the world. Documents recovered from bin Laden's Abbottabad hideout indicated that the al-Qaeda Emir may have had some knowledge of the Mumbai plot. Additionally, the role played by the members of the Pakistani state establishment in conceiving and facilitating the 26/11 attacks is well documented and underscores the deep linkages between the Jihadists and the deep state in Pakistan. Similarly, the most recent attack on a shopping mall in Nairobi, which also targeted citizens of different nationalities, was executed by Al-Shabaab, which is an affiliate of the al-Qaeda in East Africa.

Secondly, the inability of the UN Counter Terrorism Committee or the world community at large to impose costs on state sponsors of terrorism to deter them from nurturing Jihadist outfits, has provided them with physical space and access to resources to plot terror attacks worldwide. As a consequence, the terrorist groups have become stronger and more ambitious in their objectives; the sanctuary provided by the state has given them more immunity from state action. Maintaining proxies to carry out calibrated attacks on rival countries, has become an extension of state policy for some countries. Proxies like the LeT in Pakistan have become institutions in themselves and have expanded to other domains to include education, charity and health. While the United States recognises Iran, Cuba, Sudan and Syria as state sponsors of terrorism, and has imposed a host of economic and military sanctions against them, the dictates of geopolitics has allowed Pakistan to escape being designated a rogue state. In fact, it was declared to be a frontline ally of the US in the GWOT despite its continuance of overt support to the anti-India terrorist groups and the tacit backing of a few other groups active in Afghanistan. The diversion of financial aid meant for counter-terrorism to bolster its conventional military capabilities, the discovery of Osama bin Laden in a compound adjacent to the Pakistan Military Academy in Abbottabad and the involvement of terrorists of Pakistani origin or those who received some sort of training in that country in global terror plots even after 9/11, are only a few aspects which highlight the country's duplicitous role in the fight against global terrorism.

The countries which have borne the direct brunt of state-sponsored terrorism include India where more than 50,000 people have lost their lives in the state of Jammu and Kashmir in the violence directly perpetuated by Pakistan-based terrorist groups since 1989. The acts of terrorism sponsored by Pakistan have claimed nearly 1,500 lives and injured more than 4,000 in the Indian hinterland since the serial blasts in Mumbai on March 12, 1993. This number will be much higher if one takes into account the deaths attributed to the Khalistani groups and some North-Eastern insurgent outfits which received financial, training and logistical assistance from the Pakistani Inter Services Intelligence (ISI) from the 1980s onwards. Groups nurtured on Pakistani soil have also wreaked havoc in Afghanistan, killing thousands of innocent civilians since the 1980s.

Similarly, several states in strife-torn Africa have backed armed militias to gain control of resource-rich regions or capture territory plunging the continent into a permanent state of civil war where lakhs of people have died in the past century. Sudan was designated as a state sponsor of terrorism by the US for its support of Hamas and the al-Qaeda-inspired terrorist groups. The sectarian clashes in the Middle East have claimed thousands of lives, often at the hands of outfits backed by both Shia and Sunni countries. For instance, Iran and Lebanon are well known for their support of the Hezbollah, and Saudi Arabia for its financial backing of outfits like the Hamas in Palestine. The regime in Syria has been backing the Hezbollah for several decades and there have been instances of mass killings and use of brute military force by the state against its citizens.

Prior to 9/11, global Jihadists plotted major transnational attacks from safe havens in Sudan (bombings outside US embassies in Nairobi and Dar-e-Salaam, bombing of the USS *Cole* in Aden) and Afghanistan (9/11 attacks); today they have found new breeding grounds in Pakistan, Iraq, Syria and parts of North Africa and the Middle East. This, in conjunction with the widely dispersed cells in Europe, North America and South-East Asia, multiplies their capabilities to plan and launch more terror attacks. As the world approached another watershed period in 2014 when the international forces commenced their final phase of withdrawal from Afghanistan, the threat of international terrorism could become even more pronounced with the Jihadists re-gaining their traditional safe havens in the Af-Pak border region. The outward expansion of terror from this cradle of terrorism into Central and South Asia (with Jammu & Kashmir perhaps already in their cross-hairs) and increased radicalisation in the Muslim world from the Middle East to Bangladesh in South Asia, casts an ominous shadow on the prospects for peace post-2014.

With this background, the aim of this paper is to situate the main trends in the pattern of international terrorism post-9/11 and analyse the efficacy of the measures adopted by the world community to measure up to the threat. The paper will attempt to recommend some collective measures that need to be undertaken in order to combat the imminent threat of international terrorism.

PART I: EMERGING TRENDS IN INTERNATIONAL TERRORISM

Spatial Expanse

Post-9/11, International Terrorism, both in respect of stimulants and response, has undergone tactical changes. It has spread far beyond the traditional theatres of Palestine–Israel, Chechnya, parts of Africa, Sri Lanka and India. In fact, after 2001, more than 2,400 macro attacks (where more than 15–20 people have died) have taken place across the world, killing 37,000 people and injuring more than 60,000. Sixty per cent of the casualties have occurred in Iraq and Afghanistan and the two countries account for nearly 35 per cent of the total attacks recorded in the period 2001–11. Iraq, Pakistan, Afghanistan, India and Philippines are the top five countries laced with the maximum number of incidents during this period. The increase in the number of terrorist incidents has seen a jump of nearly 460 per cent since 2002. Since 2002, the impact of terrorism has been greatly felt in Iraq, Pakistan, Afghanistan, Yemen and Somalia.[1] In the year 2012, 11,000 deaths were reported in 6,771 incidents, of which the highest number of incidents took place in Pakistan (1,404), Iraq (1,271), Afghanistan (1,023) and India (557). Over 55 per cent of all attacks and 62 per cent of all casualties occurred in just three countries—Pakistan, Iraq and Afghanistan.[2] According to START, the US National Consortium for the Study of Terrorism and Responses to Terrorism, there were 5,100 terrorist attacks in the first six months of 2013, following the 8,400 attacks in 2012, which had killed nearly 15,400 people.[3]

The geographical expansion of terrorism into new theatres of Indonesia, Philippines and Thailand in South-East Asia, Afghanistan, Pakistan, India, the Gulf countries, Iraq and parts of Europe, North and East Africa, has also been accompanied by a shift in the pattern of attacks and tactics employed by the terrorist groups. In terms of casualties, the five countries which have borne the maximum impact of terrorism from 2002 to 2011 are:[4]

Countries	Fatalities
Iraq	22,000
Pakistan	9,000
Afghanistan	7,000
India*	5,000
Russia	2,000

The following terror outfits have been the major perpetrators of violence in this period, responsible for inflicting the maximum casualties:

Outfit	Country
Taliban groups & al-Qaeda	Pakistan & Afghanistan
Islamic State of Iraq (al-Qaeda affiliate in Iraq; previously known as AQI)	Iraq
Al-Shabaab	Somalia & Kenya
al-Qaeda in Arabian Peninsula (AQAP)	Yemen
Boko Haram	Nigeria
Lashkar-e-Taiba (LeT) & Indian Mujahideen (IM)	India
Al-Nusra (al-Qaeda affiliate)	Syria

Shifts in the Pattern of Attacks and Terror Targets

Due to hardening of targets by states, attacks are being majorly directed against soft targets, thereby increasing civilian casualties. The targets are selected to maximise impact and publicity. In the decade since 9/11, the bulk of terrorist attacks has been directed against civilians, unlike the previous years when the security forces and symbols of the government were primary targets. It has expanded the scope of targets for terrorists as it is much more difficult to penetrate the security apparatus in the government installations. There are numerous civilian targets and it is difficult to physically safeguard each and every infrastructure, mode of communications, public places, etc. The terrorists carry out a detailed reconnaissance of the prospective targets in order to identify loopholes in the security architecture before targeting them. Another shift in the pattern of attacks in the areas afflicted by insurgency such as Pakistan, Afghanistan, India (J&K) is the increasing frequency of targeted killings of members of a particular community, grass-root leaders, security force informers, etc., by a small group of terrorists. This is because of the depleting numbers of terrorists, and of operating in smaller numbers, which makes detection difficult.

The shift in the targeting pattern from government/military to civilian targets indicates that the terrorists are attempting to spread intimidation and create a permanent state of fear psychosis, leading to a disruption of economic activity and discouraging foreign investments in the target countries. The Western way of life and democracy are anathema to the Jihadists, therefore non-Muslim civilians are seen as legitimate targets for them. They also believe that economically bleeding a country is one way of gradually achieving victory over their enemies. Another reason for targeting more civilians is that the terrorist actions against security forces were receiving less attention and had become routine affairs occurring in far-flung areas, away from the media glare. Sensational attacks in big cities receive much more media attention than isolated incidents in peripheral areas of the countryside. The suicide bombings in major cities of Pakistan and Afghanistan and a larger number of attacks in the Indian hinterland with reduced incidents in peripheral states like the J&K are indicative of this trend.

Adaptations in Tactics and Technological Upgradation

The terrorist activities have transcended hijackings; the use of suicide bombers and Improvised Explosive Devices (IEDs) has now become the favourite weapon of terrorists across the globe. The terrorists have refined their tactical skills and the attacks are well calibrated and involve a careful selection of targets and meticulous planning over a long period before actually executing the attack. The IEDs are being fabricated in a much more professional manner and a host of innocuous looking daily use items such as pressure cookers, mobile phones, etc., are being used for preparing the IED. A lesser amount of explosive material is being used in a device which is packed with more sharpnel to maximise the impact of an explosion and cause casualties. The terrorists have reduced their dependency on military-grade plastic explosives like C4 and RDX due to stricter control and monitoring by the security agencies and rely more on commercially available materials like ammonium nitrate to fabricate the IEDs. Keeping pace with the advances in technology, there is an increased use of remote-controlled devices and mobile phones for the detonating IEDs.

There are reports that due to enhanced counter-measures and use of technology to detect explosives, female terrorists are being readied to conceal explosives in their body parts in order to avoid detection. Fewer amounts of explosives when detonated on an airline would be sufficient enough to cause an air crash. The terrorists arrested in the UK for plotting to blow the trans-Atlantic flights mid-air, had experimented with liquid explosives concealed inside the bodies of their wives. The attempted assassination of Saudi Prince Mohammed Bin Nayef Bin Abdul Aziz Al Saud on August 27, 2009 by Abdullah al-Asiri, and the failed attempt to blow up the Northwest Airline flight 253 by a Nigerian national owing allegiance to the al-Qaeda in the

Arabian Peninsula (AQAP) on Christmas Day the same year, were examples of ingenious attempts made by terrorists for attaching explosive devices to their bod parts. The explosive devices concealed inside printer cartridges recovered from two US-bound flights originating from Yemen on October 29, 2010 were also innovative methods to circumvent scanners at the airports. All these IEDs were believed to have been conceived by the Saudi-born Ibrahim al-Asiri, who was the chief bomb-maker of the AQAP. Interestingly, Ibrahim al-Asiri had himself detonated the IED concealed inside the rectum of his own brother Abdullah al-Asiri, using a mobile phone from his hideout inside Yemen. Ibrahim al-Asiri was killed alongside his mentor and the head of the AQAP, Anwar al-Awlaki—the US-born imam from Falls Church, Virginia, and the principal motivator of lone-wolf terrorists in a US drone strike in South Eastern Yemen—on September 30, 2011. The failed assassination attempt by the Taliban on Asadullah Khalid, the head of Afghanistan's intelligence wing, the National Directorate of Security, in December 2012 had also been carried out by a suicide bomber who had hidden explosives inside his rectum.

The terrorists are now found equipped with state-of-the-art navigation devices such as GPS and passive night-vision devices for navigation during the night. They have enhanced the use of cyberspace and satellite phones for communication, propaganda and online recruitment of prospective foot soldiers. Social networking sites like Facebook and online messaging tools such as Google Chat, Yahoo Messenger, etc., are being used for coded communications. In addition, 'Blackberry Messenger', 'WhatsApp', etc., also provide reliable platforms for communication. The al-Qaeda, in particular, increasingly makes use of pornographic sites for embedding messages. The handlers of the 26/11 attacks based in Pakistan communicated with the attackers on ground using Voice over Internet Protocol (VoIP) which was routed via servers located in a third country. A plethora of radical Jihadist websites have become a platform for recruiting terrorists and motivating and instructing self-motivated Jihadists for carrying out attacks. Almost all terror groups rely on cyberspace for communication and propaganda purposes.

The Fast Emulation of Successful Terrorist Practices by Other Groups

There is universality in the tactics adopted by various terrorist groups operating in different parts of the world although there may be no operational linkages between them. Terrorists easily replicate the tactics and modus operandi employed by a particular group in one theatre and it then becomes a worldwide trend. For instance, human bombings were an art perfected by the LTTE in Sri Lanka. Among Jihadists, this trend inspired by the al-Qaeda became widespread in Pakistan in the reprisal attacks that followed the storming of the Lal Masjid in Islamabad in June 2007. The Tehrik-e-Taliban Pakistan (TTP) has made widespread use of this method which was soon picked up by the Haqqani group in its strikes in Afghanistan. The human bombs have wreaked havoc in Pakistan and have been repeatedly used in sectarian incidents targeting places of worship as also to storm the fortified installations of security forces.

The use of Vehicle-Borne IEDs (VBIEDs) was maximised by the al-Qaeda in Iraq and it has now become common in all theatres of conflict though Iraq still accounts for the maximum number of VBIED blasts. Since 2012, nearly 50 VBIED blasts have been reported from Iraq every month.[5] Though car bombs have been used earlier in other areas but it was most successfully used in Iraq, thereby raising its preferability among the terror groups. Twenty-three people including the Iranian Cultural Attaché' were killed and 160 injured in a deadly VBIED explosion outside the Iranian Embassy in Beirut on November 19, 2013. The Abdullah Azam Brigade which has close links with the al-Qaeda, and is opposed to Hezbollah's presence in Lebanon, claimed responsibility for the incident. The use of vehicles for triggering explosions not only maximises possibilities for inflicting greater casualties but also has more publicity value and potential to generate perpetual fear in the minds of the people. The separatist Uighur Muslims belonging to the East Turkistan Islamic Movement (ETIM) detonated a car bomb at the Tiananmen Square in Beijing on October 28, 2013, attracting tremendous publicity. Similarly, the Indian Mujahideen (IM) had combined fire assault and detonation of an explosive device packed inside a car outside the Jama Masjid in New Delhi on September 19, 2010. It is another matter that the explosive device failed to detonate due to a technical fault, thus preventing major casualties.

The first prominent use of large vehicles like trucks for suicide bombings was also initiated by the al-Qaeda in the twin near-simultaneous explosions outside the US embassies in Nairobi and Dar-es-Salaam on August 7, 1998, which killed 223 people and wounded over 4,000. In Pakistan, a truck was used to ram through the entry gates of Hotel Marriot in Islamabad on

September 20, 2008. 54 people were killed and 266 injured in the devastating bomb attack.

The use of Integrated Chips to detonate the IEDs used in the Surat and Bengaluru blasts of 2008 was copied from the al-Qaeda manuals on bomb-making available on the internet. Similar circuits were used by the Jemaah Islamiyah (JI) in the Bali bombings of 2002 although there are no operational linkages between the IM and the JI. Prison breaks are emerging as a new tactic adopted by the Jihadist terrorists in order to free prisoners and bolster their fighting strength. This tactic originated in the Af-Pak region and was replicated by the al-Qaeda affiliate in Iraq. Some of the major prison breaks include the raid in Kandahar on April 25, 2011 which freed 500 prisoners and on the Bannu and Dera Ismail Khan Prisons in north-west Pakistan on April 15, 2012 and July 30, 2012 which led to the escape of more than 600 prisoners which included at least 40 hardcore terrorists. An outfit called the Ansar-al-Aseer has been especially formed to carry out prison breaks and consists of members from the TTP and foreign fighters of the Islamic Movement of Uzbekistan (IMU). The simultaneous raids on Abu Ghraib and Taji prisons in Iraq on July 21, 2013 by the group Islamic State in Iraq and Sham (ISIS) led to the escape of 500–1000 prisoners. Some of the freed terrorists were later found to be operating in Syria.

Another instance of the replication of tactics by unconnected groups or individuals was the use of a pressure cooker to carry out the Boston Marathon bombing in April 2013. Pressure cookers have been commonly used by the IM to execute blasts in India. The tactics of carrying out mass fire assault and simultaneously engaging multiple targets by the LeT in Mumbai on November 26, 27, 28 and 29, 2008 has become widespread in the Pakistan–Afghanistan region and several terror outfits have endeavoured to replicate the same. The attack on the Sri Lankan cricketers in Lahore in March 2009 was one example of this trend and similar attacks have been witnessed in the green zone of Kabul. In 2010, Western intelligence agencies pointed towards the likelihood of a 26/11 type attack on multiple cities of Europe.[6] In October 2012, the Indonesian Police arrested 11 individuals and claimed to have foiled a plot to carry out a series of attacks on the 10th anniversary of the Bali bombings. The multiple targets in Jakarta, Surabaya and Central Java province included the US Embassy, a shopping mall and the office of a US-based firm. A similar plot to assassinate the Indonesian President and simultaneously attack foreigners in hotels was uncovered in the year 2010.[7] The siege of the shopping mall in Kenya in September 2013 that killed over 60 people was eerily similar to the Mumbai carnage.

The terrorist groups are constantly evolving their tactics to keep one pace ahead of the security and intelligence agencies and to avoid detection by them. The phenomenon of the emergence of individual Jihadists would lead to new and unforeseen threats springing up. These individuals may not have sufficient access to resources and organisational support to mount a major attack but can generate scare by carrying out sensational attacks, involving acts of sabotage or targeted killings of prominent citizens. Knife attacks are quite common in the restive Xinjiang province of China and the knife attack in Kunming railway station that left 29 people dead and more than 150 injured took the authorities by surprise (the Kunming incident, however, appears to be a pre-meditated and organised attack and not perpetuated by unconnected individuals).

The Proliferation of Self-Motivated and Propelled Cells

Another universal trend in global terror tactics is the execution of attacks by small cells of self-motivated individuals who are based in the country where the attack is perpetuated. These individuals are often first-timers and easily evade scrutiny by the intelligence and security agencies. A minimal interaction with their handlers and the freedom of decision in the selection of targets and scale of attack also minimises the chances of interception of such plots. The terrorist groups which sponsor these attacks are content with small-scale attacks as carrying out strikes on the scale of 9/11 requires greater resources, time and activation of larger cells which have become difficult in the wake of enhanced international counter-terrorist actions.

The phenomenon of freelance terrorism is also on the rise. Individual terrorists are readily available to terrorist groups for carrying out reconnaissance and other logistical assistance for major plots. A classic example is that of Daood Gilani aka David Coleman Headley who first offered his services to the LeT for the Mumbai attacks and was later actively involved in the plot to target the office of a Danish newspaper in Copenhagen at the behest of Illyas Kashmiri, who had been associated with the Harkat-ul-Jihadi-al Islami (HuJI) and the al-Qaeda. Another illustration is that of Ahmed Omar Saeed Sheikh, a British national of Pakistani origin, who gained worldwide attention for his role in the beheading of the *Wall Street Journal* reporter Daniel Pearl in Karachi in 2002. The 9/11 Inquiry Commission also indicted Omar for transferring US$ 1,00,000 to Mohamed Atta, the leader of the group of 19 hijackers one month before the attacks. Previously, a student of London School of Economics, he had travelled to Bosnia to 'experience Jihad' and was arrested for the kidnapping of four Western tourists in India in 1994. In his global assignments, Omar had served the interests of multiple terror outfits like the Harkat-ul-Mujahideen, the al-Qaeda and the Jaish-e-Mohammed.

Additionally, it has become more difficult to distinguish between insurgents and terrorists as both complement each other in the methods employed and the terrorists have also enmeshed themselves closely in the ongoing insurgencies, greatly influencing their ideologies and targets.

The Lone Wolf Phenomenon

Several individual and isolated cells are believed to be present in Europe and North America. These cells may be modelled on the pattern of the Hamburg Cell whose members carried out the 9/11 attacks. Most individuals involved in such cells have either been self-motivated by watching radical Islamist propaganda material on the internet or have gotten brainwashed in mosques. Anwar al-Awlaki was a prominent figure who used to motivate self-made Jihadists through propaganda videos circulated on the internet. The AQIM due to its presence in areas contiguous to southern Europe also acts as a facilitator for plotting attacks in Europe. Algerians linked with the AQIM have been arrested for plotting attacks in France and London. The 2004 Madrid train and 2005 London bombings bore resemblance to the modus operandi adopted by the al-Qaeda. The London attack was claimed by an organisation calling itself 'The Secret Organisation of Al Qaeda in Europe'. And prior to the London bombings, the 'Abu Hafs a-Misri Brigades' had posted a message on several Islamist websites stating: "We ask all waiting Mujahideen, wherever they are, to carry out the planned attack".[8] The group had made reference to Mohammed Atef, al-Qaeda's Chief Operations Commander, who was killed in an US air raid on Kabul in November 2001. In the US, the phenomenon of self-motivated or individual "lone wolf" operatives (like the Boston Marathon bombers) is more pronounced, where between 1997 and 2011, 171 individuals (including the 19 hijackers who carried out the attacks on 9/11) have been charged for committing or plotting to commit terrorist attacks. Of these, nearly 47 per cent had received some form of training in camps in Afghanistan, Pakistan or Somalia. 38 per cent of these arrested individuals were directly associated with the al-Qaeda or the AQAP, 9 per cent with the LeT and 5 per cent with the Al-Shabaab. Nearly 54 per cent of those arrested were US citizens, most of whom were religious converts to Islam. The most common place of residence for the US-born accused was New York, followed by California and Virginia.

The impact of global terrorism has also led to incidents where the individuals impacted by radical Islamist propaganda and global events such as the US-led military interventions in the Muslim world have carried out attacks in their home countries even though they had no linkages with terrorist groups. For instance, a German national of Albanian descent shot dead two US Air Force personnel and injured another two outside the Frankfurt airport on March 2, 2011. More recent examples are the Boston Marathon bombing on April 15, 2013 and the beheading of a British soldier who had served in Afghanistan by two African Muslims in London on May 22, 2013.

Transnational Linkages of the Individual Jihadists

At least 7,000 foreign fighters from 50 countries, mainly from Europe and the Middle East but also from countries as far as Indonesia and Australia are believed to have joined the conflict in Syria.[9] This has not only strengthened the Al-Nusra and the Islamic State in Iraq & Sham (ISIS) involved in the sectarian conflict but also underscores the impact of radicalisation on the individual Jihadists to rally behind a common cause. Some of the battle-hardened Jihadists could pose a grave terror threat to their home countries. The transnational linkage to the terrorism in Europe is borne out by the fact that in almost all of the major terror attacks that were averted, some of the potential attackers had travelled to Afghanistan or Pakistan to receive training and additional indoctrination. Some Muslim youth from the UK have also travelled to Syria to join the fighting there. Similarly, the suspects in the Sauerland case in Germany which was busted in 2007 were linked to the Islamic Jihad Union (IJU) and had trained with the group in Waziristan reaching Pakistan via Syria, Turkey and Iran.[10] On December 10, 2012, an explosive device planted inside the Bonn train station failed to explode, highlighting the potent terror threat to Germany. The case of Frederic C. Jean Salvi who detonated a package explosive outside the Indonesian Embassy in Paris on March 21, 2012 is another indicator of the transnational threat of terrorism. Salvi, a French national, had rallied behind the cause of Islamist terrorists operating in Indonesia and was involved in a foiled terror plot in that country.

Terror Financing

Due to global efforts at identifying and freezing channels of terrorist funding, terrorists are relying heavily on narcotics and counterfeit smuggling. This has led to the growing nexus between criminal and terror groups. In 2010, a US Congressional Service Report indicated that the al-Qaeda had tapped into Dawood Ibrahim's smuggling and narcotics channels to fund its own activities. It is also a well-known fact that the D-Company is one of the sources of finance for the anti-India jihadist outfits. The Partho Burman kidnapping case is illustrative of the use of criminal networks to fund terror activities. Burman was kidnapped by a group led by Aftab Ansari, who was subsequently sentenced to death in the January 2002 attack on the American Center in Kolkata. It is widely suspected that the money which Omar Saeed Sheikh had transferred to Mohammed Ata, the 9/11 hijacker, had included a part of the ransom amount.

In addition, the terror groups are increasingly relying on mobile and internet banking facilities and 'hawala' channels to avoid detection by the intelligence agencies. They have also launched a proactive online campaign to seek donations from Muslims all over the world. The al-Qaeda's affiliates are advised to raise their own funds. The LeT in Pakistan collects a considerable amount of funds through donations especially during the month of Ramzan and by selling the hide of goats. Funding by Islamic charities to terror groups is also a common source of terror financing and they are increasingly receiving funding through the diaspora population residing in the Gulf and Europe to carry out terror attacks. Money is often transferred by sponsors via individuals residing in foreign countries to the bank accounts of their relatives in the destination country. The Western Union money transfer is a common channel for making such transfers. Though global intelligence agencies have succeeded in intercepting such money flows, the sheer magnitude of bank accounts makes it impossible to detect every transaction.

The freezing of bank accounts has restricted funding from the donors in Saudi Arabia and the clampdown on Osama bin Laden's private businesses has forced al-Qaeda to dilute its ideology to legitimise funding from other sources. Bin Laden had to issue several fatwas to justify raising money via the drug trade in Afghanistan as it violates the Islamic tenets. Similarly, several of al-Qaeda's affiliates in Africa generate funds through narcotics and smuggling of other goods, kidnappings for ransom, robberies, etc., which are not in consonance with the al-Qaeda's core ideology. The Taliban groups in Pakistan are also indulging in extortion and kidnappings for ransom for financial purposes. For instance, the Taliban is known to appropriate taxes and seek donations from the Pashtuns residing in Karachi who dominate the city's transport business.

The Intertwining of the Political Agenda of the Radicals and Terrorists

The multiple blasts on July 7, 2013 in Bodh Gaya in India, which is the most revered shrine for Buddhists in the world, is illustrative of the global nature of terrorist threat being encountered today. Several Jihadist outfits including the al-Qaeda and the TTP had vowed to avenge the killings of the Rohingya Muslims by the Buddhists in Myanmar. That the bombings were carried out by the Indian Mujahideen through its sleeper cells is indicative of the global agenda of the primarily India-centric terror outfit. It demonstrates the extent to which the pan-Islamic Jihadist groups are willing to adopt each other's goals and ideologies, even though the Indian Muslims are not directly affected by the violence in Myanmar.

Most Sunni terrorist groups by and large identify with the common aim of establishing the Islamic Umma under a Caliph and transform the Dar-ul-Harb, the house of war or house of the West (Dar-ul-Garb) into Dar-ul-Islam (abode of Islam). They consider democracy to be un-Islamic. This commonality of interest is evident in the political sermons of al-Qaeda's Ayman al-Zawahiri, TTP's late Hakimullah Mehsud or LeT's Hafeez Mohammed Saeed. The al-Qaeda, TTP and LeT were among several Jihadist groups that had vowed to avenge the persecution of the Rohingya Muslims in Myanmar though none of these groups had any presence in that country. This is just one recent example of the global and pan-Islamic agenda of the Jihadists and their attempt to infuse their radical breed of Islam across the Muslim world. The Indian intelligence agencies have evidence to suggest that the LeT which has already spread its tentacles in Maldives and Sri Lanka is now attempting to recruit Rohingyas from Myanmar into its fold.[11]

A grouping of Islamist terror outfits which includes the LeT, HuJI-B and Jamaat-ul-Mujahideen of Bangladesh (which carried out a series of coordinated bomb blasts across Bangladesh on August 17, 2005) have come together under the banner of Difa-e-Musalman Arakan in Myanmar to expand the arc of terror to that region. The enmeshing of global Jihadist elements has also been corroborated by the intelligence reports of an al-Qaeda bomb-making expert having gone to Bangladesh earlier this year to train the Rohingya Muslims and two members of a radical outfit calling itself Rohingya Solidarity Association (RSO) returning to the Arakan from London in January 2013, allegedly to conduct terrorist activities.[12] The exodus of people from Mumbai, Pune, Hyderabad and Bangalore to their homes in North-East India in 2012 was caused due to propaganda e-mails, online and mobile phone messages generated mostly from internet servers based in Pakistan and the Gulf countries, thereby establishing the global origins of this subversive design. Therefore, transnational terrorism has become more interlinked and the boundaries between various groups have been blurred due to the sharing of common ideologies, motivations, tactics and the need for complementing each other's efforts in the face of the global onslaught against terrorism.

Impact of Radicalisation and the Arab Spring

Jihadist radicalisation has increased in the decade following the West's counter-terrorism efforts, which after gaining initial support even from Muslim countries, led to a backlash due their disproportionate use of drones, collateral damage increasing civilian casualty and racial profiling. Even though the extent of collateral damage caused due to drone strikes may have been limited, the successful propaganda measures adopted by the Jihadists fostered an anti-West environment among the Muslims. It also had a ripple effect in instigating the populations in the Arab World to demand the ouster of pro-West regimes though economic discrimination and lack of employment avenues, with their corrupt and autocratic practices being the primary driving factors behind the uprisings.

The flight of several first-generation Saudi al-Qaeda commanders from Afghanistan after the US invasion aided the stoking of Jihadist radicalisation in the Middle East. This was compatible with the al-Qaeda's initial aims of overthrowing the pro-Western governments termed as "apostate regimes" in the Gulf. The al-Qaeda first initiated sectarian clashes in Iraq, while simultaneously establishing cells in Egypt, Lebanon, Jordan and North Africa. The US withdrawal from Iraq was termed as a victory by the al-Qaeda and it urged Muslims in other countries to overthrow their "apostate regimes". It had a very little role to play in instigating the so-called Arab Spring which erupted as a popular movement against the oppressive pro-West monarchical regimes and social causes such as unemployment, but it embedded itself with the post-revolution dispensation that emerged in Libya and Egypt. The Muslim Brotherhood leadership in Egypt was infiltrated by al-Qaeda sympathisers which led the military to dismiss the government, though it had presided over the ouster of President Hosni Mubarak due to an overwhelming public outcry against his regime at the Tahrir Square. The strength that the Jihadist elements acquired in Egypt is evident in the militarisation of the pro-Muslim Brotherhood supporters and large casualties that have occurred in clashes between the radicals and the military. The aftermath of the Arab Spring has led to a debate as to whether democracy is compatible with political Islam or not. Seeking an answer to that question is beyond the scope of this paper, but suffice it to say that the post-revolution political system that emerged in these countries created favourable conditions for the hard-line Salafist groups to get entrenched.

Egypt, which is the home country of the al-Qaeda Emir Ayman al-Zawahiri and the fact that many top al-Qaeda commanders including Osama bin Laden were products of the Al Azhar University in Cairo, has immense symbolic value for International Jihadism represented by the al-Qaeda. It is also a belief of the Salafists that the final battle of the Jihad waged by them will take place in Sham or the Levant, thereby attracting foreign fighters to Syria.[13] The rising tide of Islamic fundamentalism in the Arab World if left unchecked will have a devastating impact on world peace. In addition to Egypt, the Salafists have gained ground in Iraq, Lebanon, Libya and now in Syria. The proliferating network of Salafist and Wahhabi mosques has become the nerve centre for radicalising the traditional discourse of Islam that has been prevalent in these countries for centuries. Flush with Saudi money, they are able to source recruits and followers, especially in regions which have a large proportion of poor and unemployed Muslims. In the past decade, a large number of Wahhabi mosques and madrasas funded by Saudi Arabia have mushroomed all over the world, especially in South Asia. Since then, nearly 800 Ahl-e-Hadith madrasas have been established in the Kashmir valley alone.[14] The extremist Wahhabi ideology is popular among the al-Qaeda inspired Islamist terrorist groups and has increased the killings of non-Wahhabis including Shias and moderate Sunnis in parts of the Middle East and South Asia. All other Muslims who do not profess the Wahhabi faith are considered as non-Muslims, and killing them is justified. In fact, one of the virulent diatribes of the Wahhabis goes as such, "We will kill you so that you are re-born as a better person".

A devastating consequence of extreme radicalisation is the sharp escalation in suicide bombings. Post-9/11, the phenomenon of suicide attacks in Afghanistan, Pakistan and Iraq has been on an upward trajectory. Suicide attacks were virtually absent in these countries before the US-led invasion and subsequent civilian deaths in air strikes and drone attacks provided an alibi to the fundamentalists to whip up passions of the people by portraying the Western occupation as a danger to Islam. Among other things, a suicide bomber requires a tremendous amount of motivation and indoctrination which can be easily enthused in him/her in a religiously surcharged atmosphere created by increased radicalisation.

In India, the frequency of suicide attacks peaked in the period 1999–2002, particularly in the state of Jammu & Kashmir. The bulk of the suicide attacks was carried out by Pakistani and Afghan cadres of the LeT when insurgency in J&K received a fillip in the aftermath of the Kargil war. The number of 'fidayeen' attacks declined after 2002, and between 2006 and 2013, there have been only three such attacks in J&K. The attacks came down due to the fatigue factor among the terrorists and the LeT could no longer afford to lose a large number of cadres in fidayeen attacks. The Jihadists' preoccupation in Afghanistan and Pakistan and the unpopularity of these methods due to increased civilian casualties could also be some factors for a decline in the number of suicide attacks. But this situation could reverse once the Jihadists re-focus their energies on J&K and the Indian hinterland after the withdrawal of US forces from Afghanistan in 2014. Radicalisation among the population in J&K has increased in the past decade and its manifestation was seen in the civilian unrest from 2008–10. Therefore, increased radicalisation of the youth of the state may become a repository for re-introducing suicide attacks, as has happened in Pakistan, Afghanistan and Iraq. The IM, which closely mirrors the al-Qaeda in its ideology, has also been attempting to carry out suicide attacks. This was revealed in the interrogation of Yasin Bhatkal and his associate Asadullah Akhtar aka Haddi, the latter was being trained for carrying out a suicide attack. Earlier, there were also reports that Atif Ameen, an IM terrorist killed during the Batla House encounter in Delhi in September 2008, was also being trained in fidayeen tactics. This could be a dangerous trend as the Indian Muslims (with one exception in J&K in 2000) till date have not participated in suicide attacks or bombings. The fact that terrorist handlers and ideologues are able to motivate even some IM members for this purpose is worrisome and shows the extent of indoctrination and radicalisation that these Muslim youth have undergone.

A rise in radicalism among the growing Muslim population in several European countries has increased the threat of terrorism in Europe, especially in the UK and Germany. Salafist-funded mosques and extremist political organisations have become the primary pools for brainwashing the minds of even the educated Muslim youth for taking to extremism. In the recent past, there has also been a rise in the number of converts to Islam in the UK, indicating the popularity of extremist ideology in some sections of the society. The unraveling of several terror plots in the UK indicated one to bomb the Trans-Atlantic Airlines between London and New York with the bombs disguised as soft drinks in 2006 or the recent one in Birmingham to use eight rucksacks packed with explosives. Stuart Osborme, the Deputy Commissioner of Police in London, said, "On an average, we've probably had about one potential attack planned with an intent to create something similar to July 7 every year".[15] In Spain, though considerably weakened, the domestic terrorist group Basque Fatherland and Liberty (ETA) continues to recruit individuals and plot terror attacks. The influence of the al-Qaeda affiliates like AQIM is also growing in Spain.

PART II: GLOBAL RESPONSE TO TERRORISM AFTER 9/11 AND ITS EFFECTIVENESS

Till the attacks of September 11, 2001, the global response to terrorism was dominated by the leading world powers selectively defining international terrorism, by viewing violence in countries that did not affect them as domestic terrorism, insurgencies or even 'freedom struggles', thereby providing legitimacy to terrorist groups indulging in such acts. One major shift that 9/11 brought about was characterising terrorism as an unacceptable 'tactic' to achieve political or ideological objectives that was to be opposed irrespective of the underlying causes. Post-9/11, the international community, led by the US, largely gave up this discriminatory approach and promised cooperation to present a strong and united front against terrorism. This principled position notwithstanding, much was left to be desired in practice. Yet, the horror and magnitude of the 9/11 attacks had created a universal wave and abhorrence for terrorism and its brutal methods. This environment and anger against terrorism not only led to the cementing of an international opinion in favour of the US-led operation in Afghanistan but also allowed some countries like Sri Lanka to brutally crackdown on terror groups such as the LTTE with the world turning a blind eye towards the methods adopted by the state in wiping out the outfit and the resultant collateral damage it caused.

Let us now examine some of the major collective counter-terrorism measures adopted after 9/11 by the international community.

Operation Enduring Freedom

The US-led military operation in Afghanistan in the immediate aftermath of the September 11 attacks ousted the Taliban government and decimated the al-Qaeda core. Several hundred Taliban and al-Qaeda fighters were killed in the immediate assault in 2001–02. This eroded its capability to plan and mount attacks globally and the US, in particular has so far remained unscathed by any major terror attack since 9/11. Afghanistan was symbolic of the fight against terrorism as the 9/11 attacks were planned on Afghan soil with the attackers themselves receiving some form of training in that country. However, the remnants of the al-Qaeda including Osama bin Laden found refuge across the Durand Line in Afghanistan where it subsumed itself into the TTP to mount a war against the Pakistani state. The Jihad in Pakistan, accentuated by the lackadaisical attitude and half-hearted measures adopted by the Pakistani state, was to soon assume monstrous proportions, further enabling the al-Qaeda to revitalise itself and bring more Islamist groups under its ideological sway. The US diversion to Iraq in 2003 allowed it to re-group on both sides of the Durand Line and once again plan attacks outside the region.

Though the 13-year-long ISAF military mission in Afghanistan was successful in wiping out the al-Qaeda and eroding to a considerable extent the military capabilities of the Taliban; those very elements are today on the verge of making a comeback post-2014 with the winding up of the ISAF mission. This has been partially due to the faulty counter-insurgency strategies adopted by the Coalition forces and more importantly, due to the state support enjoyed by the Taliban in Pakistan which ensured that it was never completely destroyed. The mounting war costs in the backdrop of a declining US economy and increasing troop casualties leading to a sharp fall in popular support for the war back home also led the US to focus more on preventing terrorism on its home soil. With little appetite left for the war, the US refocused its efforts from counter-insurgency to counter-terrorism, targeting only the al-Qaeda and its affiliates. Its recent policy of engaging the Taliban in dialogue to cut its losses and present a semblance of victory before exiting Afghanistan, is further indicative of its selective approach whereby it is less worried about the negative impact of terrorism on other countries. It is hopeful of shielding itself from the blowback of terrorism which is on the verge of once again taking strong roots in the region by maintaining a limited counter-terrorism capability in Afghanistan–Pakistan (drones, special forces, etc.), incentivising Pakistan and extracting assurances from the Taliban that it would not allow the al-Qaeda to train on Afghan soil. Therefore, while Operation Enduring Freedom coupled with the US covert operations and drone strikes in Pakistan mounted severe operational losses on the al-Qaeda, the long-drawn campaign failed to achieve a desirable end-state in Afghanistan where the conditions are still ripe to keep the threat of Islamist terrorism alive.

Counter-Terror Legislations

While terrorism in various hues and shades has existed over the past half-century or so and this was addressed by various UN conventions, it took the absolute mass barbarity of the 9/11 attack to spur the world community to usher in Resolution 1373 by the UN Security Council (as against the General Assembly) as a right to self-defence. The UN Security Council Resolution 1373 adopted unanimously on September 28, 2001, calls upon the member states to implement a slew of measures intended to enhance their legal and institutional ability to counter terrorist activities. It obligates all states to criminalise assistance for terrorist activities, deny financial support and safe haven to terrorists and to share information about groups planning terrorist attacks unlike the counter-terrorism conventions and protocols which bind only those states which are party to them.

The Patriot Act (Providing Appropriate Tools Required to Intercept and Obstruct Terrorism on October 28, 2001) and the Homeland Security Act in the US and the Anti-Terrorism Act in the UK were some of the robust counter-terrorism legislations which strengthened the resolve and ability of some countries to combat terrorism. These legislations have been useful in enabling the security and intelligence agencies to monitor and resolutely act upon the terror threats. The strict and time-bound judicial processes resulting in faster convictions in some Western countries also act as a deterrent against terrorism.

New Global Counter-Terror Institutions

Post 9/11, other than INTERPOL, new global institutions such as the UN Counter Terrorism Committee (CTC), the CTC Executive Directorate, the 1540 Committee, the Al Qaeda and Taliban Sanctions Committee and the Counter Terrorism Implementation Task Force (CTITF) formed to criminalise terror financing, freeze terror related bank accounts, improve information-sharing between governments and assist in terror investigations between them, have come up. The CTC directs stringent steps both at the national and international levels. But except for monitoring sanctions, these UN bodies have no mandate to penalise member countries for not following the UN resolutions, thereby greatly eroding their effectiveness. For instance, the UN Global Counter Terrorism Strategy (GCT) adopted in 2006 to increase the legitimacy of UN counter-terrorism actions and bodies, earned little attention from member countries. Only eight UN member countries are signatories to all 16 treaties on counter-terrorism and even ratification does not mean a total compliance from them.

Nevertheless, these bodies have been instrumental in freezing the flow of terror finance through legitimate bank accounts by first proscribing terror outfits and providing a platform for the member countries to detect and close down their bank accounts. The Al Qaeda Sanctions Committee of the UN Security Council under the resolutions has proscribed 64 groups and 223 individuals associated with the al-Qaeda. The sanctions make it incumbent for member states to:[16]

- Freeze without delay the funds and other financial assets or economic resources, including funds derived from property owned or controlled directly or indirectly.
- Prevent the entry into or the transit through their territories.

- Prevent the direct or indirect supply, sale, or transfer of arms and related material, including military and paramilitary equipment, technical advice, assistance or training related to military activities, with regard to the individuals, groups, undertakings and entities placed on the Al-Qaeda Sanctions List.

Some of the other international bodies include the Financial Action Task Force and G8's Counter Terrorist Action Group which was formed in 1989 to counter money-laundering. Multilateral organisations such as the European Union (EU), the African Union and the Association of South East Asian Nations (ASEAN) have outlined shared commitments to counter-terrorism, but all except the EU lack funding and capacities in order to be effective.

Limitations of CTC

The CTC was created to monitor the implementation of Resolution 1373. However, it suffered from some inherent flaws which made the UN Resolution 1373 non-implementable in totality. The CTC recognised that all states have different capacities, and therefore, the CTC will work separately with each state towards the implementation of the resolution. Thus, each state is at a different level of implementation of resolution and not being chased to implement any target date and is being assisted and therefore not coerced to implement the Resolution 1373. The CTC, thus by not targeting individual states and not condemning them while focussing on their technical capacity building, garners support from all member states.

The other deficiency is that while a UN Security Council Resolution created the CTC, it did not provide guidance to its role in combating terrorism. More prohibitive is that the 'terrorism act' continues to be undefined. Resolution 1373 does not define terrorism, in order to avoid controversy. So, even though the Resolution entails heavy consequences upon the states which do not review their domestic laws and practices to ensure that the terrorists cannot finance themselves or find safe havens, Resolution 1373 and CTC suffer at the implementation level for not being able to define terrorism. This is especially true in the Indian context, where Pakistan blatantly gives spin to the definition of terrorism, and feigns an inability to combat terrorism due to various factors. On the other hand, most member states through the amendment and enactment of new legislations in criminal law, criminal procedure and immigration law have rapidly implemented the resolution. In the European Union, the anti-terrorist legislations and countermeasures were harmonised between states. As the measures against terrorism fall under the provision of the EU treaty relating to the common foreign and security policy, the Resolution was enforced by EU regulations on June 13, 2002.

Milestone Declarations and Limitations

The World Summit 2005 and the Millennium Declaration 2005 are important developments in recognising the need to identify terrorism as a global scourge and threat to international peace and security. However, as is evident in the statement by Ambassador Masood Khan in his address to the UN on October 7, 2013, in his capacity as a Permanent Representative of Pakistan to the UN, the Pakistani propensity for doublespeak and putting spins on the definition of 'terrorism' and the state's incapacity to fight terrorism, are all too evident. "The use of drone (by the US)...is detrimental to our efforts to eliminate extremism and terrorism...the international community must address the root causes of terrorism including unresolved conflicts...denial of the right to self-determination".

Enhanced International Counter-Terror Cooperation and Intelligence Sharing

The major world powers increased cooperation and intelligence-sharing at the tactical level to combat terrorism post-9/11. The US Central Investigation Agency (CIA) and the Federal Bureau of Investigation (FBI), in particular, became greatly energised for expanding their assets worldwide and to cooperate with other intelligence agencies of the world. Joint Working Groups on intelligence-sharing have been formed between several countries to collectively combat terrorism. Intelligence-sharing has been very useful in nabbing terror suspects and in preventing attacks. The enormous technical assets of the US intelligence agencies with eyes and ears in most corners of the world have increased the flow of intelligence to other countries, leading to the neutralisation of terror cells in the recipient countries. The US, in turn, has also benefitted from the information provided by other countries in eliminating the terror plots aimed at the US. The intelligence-driven operations and covert actions to neutralise terror cells have achieved the desired results which is borne by the killing of a large number of al-Qaeda and other terror group leaders worldwide. But despite an increased cooperation, the selective or partial sharing of information has had disastrous consequences. If specific information on David Headley (who was an informant for the US DEA and FBI)'s activities in India had been shared timely with the Indian intelligence agencies, the entire plot of 26/11 could have been foiled.

The US expanded its financial and technical assistance to weak nation states and to governments in the countries wreaked by terrorist violence. Financial aid coupled with investment in building up of democratic institutions in countries of Africa, Middle East, South-East Asia and South America strengthened the capacities of these countries to neutralise the terror threat. The US Special Forces have helped to train and equip security forces and militias in several weak nation states in order to combat insurgents and terrorists. Similarly, the US has provided military equipment, financed security agencies and invested in economic and human resource development programmes to provide alternate employment avenues to the people and lift them out of poverty. This would in turn wean them away from terrorist propaganda. More vigorous international cooperation in the fields of counter-narcotics, money laundering, etc., have also benefitted the fight against terrorism and vice versa, as there are now common linkages between terrorists and criminal groups at the tactical level.

Technology as a Key Enabler

An enhanced technical surveillance by governments to monitor extremist behaviour among the population and detect terrorist communications has also proved effective. The busting of the Sauerland Cell in Germany in 2007 due to electronic snooping is one such example. The employment of improved scientific methods and forensics for investigations and use of technology for bolstering physical security measures has been equally effective and made it more difficult for terrorists to plot attacks and smuggle explosives. Electromagnetic rays, full body X-ray scanners for detecting explosives, voice sampling and artificial intelligence methods have helped in enhancing physical security and in identifying terror cells. By one estimate, at least 90 per cent of the weapons and equipment is neutralised even before it is used. The use of robots for detecting and defusing explosive devices has reduced the risk to human life for conducting such operations. Similarly, a plethora of devices and methods aided by technology is employed by security agencies to physically strengthen their defences against the use of heavy explosives and suicide bombers. Some of these enablers are door-frame metal detectors, reinforced concrete materials, bullet-proof, blast-resistant structures and vehicles to withstand the impact of explosives, electronic sensors, frequency jammers, close-circuit television cameras (CCTV) for early warning, radio frequency and satellite monitoring devices, etc.

The use of force multipliers in the form of drones for surveillance as well as targeting, satellites and other technical means to monitor telephonic communication and internet traffic have come to the aid of the security agencies. In fact, electronic interception has led to the uncovering of a large number of terror cells worldwide, forcing the terrorists to rely on human couriers to pass their messages across. Technological enablers have cast a vast surveillance web on the terrorists, keeping them constantly on the run and degrading their capacities to strike. On the flip side, technology has greatly encroached upon the privacy of citizens due to increased physical security measures and technical snooping by state agencies, but it is a cost worth paying in the fight against terrorism.

Weak Nation States

The fight against terrorism has been marred due to weak systems of governance and continued civil war conditions prevailing in the African continent. Weak systems in some countries like Somalia, Nigeria and Mali allows terrorism to proliferate in these regions. Often governments in these strife-torn countries sponsor and maintain armed militias to further their political and territorial interests. The al-Qaeda and its affiliates have infiltrated these countries, taking advantage of the political vacuum and feeding on the existing ethnic strife to establish safe havens and weapon stockpiles. These areas then provide a platform or secure base for the terrorists to plot attacks all over the world. The UN and African Union Peacekeepers in the continent are playing their part to prevent the civil wars from engulfing the region and provide breeding grounds for the al-Qaeda. The US, UK, France and Italy are particularly impacted by the developments in Africa and continuously provide military and financial assistance to the weak nation states to stem the rising tide of internecine conflict and terrorism in the continent. The US, for instance, has several partnership arrangements in Africa to enhance the capacities of the local governments to counter terrorism and facilitate cooperation between these governments and the US partners for countering extremism and marginalising the terror organisations. Two such groupings are the Trans-Sahara Counter Terror Partnership (TSCTP) in the Saharan-Sahel region (Mauritania, Mali, Chad, Niger, Nigeria, Senegal and Burkina Faso) and its counterpart for East Africa called The Partnership for East African Counter Terrorism (PREACT).[17] The French intervention in Mali in 2012 was timely in preventing the country from being overrun by Islamists linked with the al-Qaeda. In the recent decades, China, due to its economic clout has emerged as a major player in Africa but needs to play a more positive role by actively combating the terrorists and insurgents rather than investing economically and providing financial assistance to the weak nation states that support militias and terror groups.

The Way Forward: Steps to Effectively Counter International Terrorism

A Common Definition of Terrorism: The menace of international terrorism cannot be dealt without first defining 'terrorism'. A problem cannot be tackled without first recognising it. The Draft 'Comprehensive Convention against Terrorism' in 2005 came close to stipulating a globally recognised definition of terrorism but disagreements on part of some member nations thwarted the efforts. Violence in any form that targets civilians to achieve political aims or independence should be squarely defined as acts of terrorism. The definition of terrorism cannot be diluted by first addressing the root causes of violence as is being desired by some member states of the UN. Political grievances, whether genuine or manufactured by outside forces, cannot justify violence or the taking up of arms by a group of individuals or organisations to achieve their stated ideological goals. For instance, can acts of terrorism perpetuated by foreign terrorists in a geographical area which they purportedly are claiming to 'liberate' from the stranglehold of 'occupation forces', be passed off as a right to self-determination or freedom struggle by that foreign terrorist organisation or people inhabiting the region? How can a foreign terrorist organisation which is based in a different country champion the cause of those very people it is persecuting? These are some fundamental questions which countries that propagate the root causes of terrorism and espouse genuine grievances of the people who take to the gun need to answer.

Passage of the UN Resolution: The UN urgently needs to evolve a consensus and pass the draft convention against terrorism which has been stalled for many years now. Once operational, the convention will become a common reference point for all the UN member states to adhere to its charter and implement measures in their own countries for countering terrorism. The clauses in the treaty must be made binding on the member states and leave no ambiguities for them to forestall actions against the banned foreign terrorist organisations operating from their soil.

The Effectiveness of the CTC: The CTC should be made more powerful by vesting it with rights and powers to verify and monitor activities of groups which are designated as terrorist organisations by the CTC. Member states can share intelligence on the activities of terror groups in a different country with the CTC which should have the powers to make these countries accountable for the actions taken by them against the terror groups. For all this, suitable amendments in the charter of the CTC will have to be made under the mandate of the UN Security Council.

Monitoring Activities of Rogue States: In addition to accounting for the measures undertaken by the rogue states or states suspected of harbouring terror groups to strengthen the anti-terror legislations and strengthening financial networks being manipulated by terrorist groups, the CTC or a suitable UN body must have powers to investigate whether the state institutions in these countries are involved in providing material or ideological support to the proscribed terror groups. Such a body must have the right to dispatch UN inspectors to locations in these countries where the terrorists are suspected of receiving support from the state institutions for fomenting terror. The same principles which are adopted for despatching UN weapons inspectors to Iran, North Korea, Iraq or more recently to Syria for investigating the use of chemical weapons must be adopted with regard to the state sponsors of terrorism or those countries that plead their inability to counter the activities of terror groups due to lack of capacity.

List of Rogue States: The UN CTC or a new body as discussed in the preceding paragraph must also periodically review the list of nations declared as rogue or state sponsors of terrorism. In addition to implementing sanctions against the existing rogue states, such a body should maintain a list of countries which are suspected of providing institutional support to terrorists or are complacent in taking action against them.

All member states of the UN must share regular evidence on that state's complicity in harbouring terror groups or turning a blind eye towards the blatant activities of terror groups. On the basis of such inputs and verifiable evidence of a terror attack originating from its soil, that country, after being given an adequate warning period to undertake corrective measures, must be declared a state sponsor of terrorism by the UN Security Council. Providing material, logistical, financial or infrastructural support to the banned terror organisations and their overground entities, the involvement of state institutions or individuals in imparting weapons and training to the terrorists, facilitating their movement within and outside the country, permitting their overt and visible activities for recruitment, propaganda and fund-raising, etc, are few parameters which can be used for designating a nation as a rogue state.

Imposing Sanctions against the State Sponsors of Terrorism: It should be the duty of the UN CTC to monitor the implementation of economic and military sanctions imposed on a state suspected of harbouring banned terror outfits. A case for the imposition of sanctions must be made against the states where there is direct and undeniable evidence of their role in sponsoring the terror attacks on another nation state or a glaring inaction in taking preventive actions against groups launching an attack from their soil, despite the overwhelming evidence or prior intelligence inputs shared with them. The CTC must monitor the volume of evidence accumulated against a country over a considerable period of time, making it a fit case for imposing sanctions.

Military Action against the Proscribed Terror Groups: The UN Security Council should allow an affected nation state or permit a collective grouping of affected countries or states whose citizens have been killed in a terror attack even outside their territorial borders to undertake military action against terrorist hideouts or leaders based in a third country. The UN should provide legitimacy to such military action by the states which are victims of a major terror attack or mobilise an international force under the UN to take action against the terror groups based outside the target country (where the terrorist attack has been executed) on the basis of a solid and verifiable evidence of an individual terrorist's role or a facility in that country being used for planning/ executing the attack. The UN should also permit a country which has been subjected to terror attacks from a country over a sustained period of time and that country's inability to check the activities of terror groups on its soil to take requisite military action against the sanctuaries of terror in that country. A country must have the right to undertake actions even beyond its territorial borders if it is constantly being subjected to attacks launched from across its territorial borders to effectively safeguard its citizens against terror strikes. In case a country expresses its inability to check the activities of banned terrorist organisations on its territory or territory under its military control on political/ideological grounds or cites inadequate capacities to tackle their activities, a collective international force under the UN must be permitted to assist that country or take independent military actions against the sources of terrorism in that country.

Economic and Military Aid to Weak Nation States: More stringent measures should be adopted by the international community in providing aid to the weak nation states. Robust safeguards and sufficient guarantees on part of recipient states that military or economic aid will not be diverted/leaked/siphoned off to terrorists must be made. The donor countries should be held accountable in case the aid provided by them is indirectly or directly misused for launching a terror attack. Strict pre-conditions and verification mechanisms must be in place to ensure that the aid is utilised only for countering terrorism and not diverted for conventional military use. Only those types of equipment which are employed in counter-insurgency campaigns must be supplied. For example, main battle tanks, fighter aircrafts and radars have very little utility against terrorists holed up inside population centres. Donor countries should exercise due caution in providing military aid to the weak nation states which lack the capacities to safeguard equipment and state institutions from terror attacks or countries that are vulnerable of being militarily overwhelmed by non-state actors. On the other hand, the international community under UN auspices must extend all possible financial, institutional and infrastructural assistance that aids in building up state capacities to combat terrorism and provides education, medical and economic benefits to the people affected by violence. There is also a case for strengthening systems and defensive security measures all over the world. Even in the decade after 9/11, airport security is still a grey area in several small countries. Similarly, major vulnerabilities exist in the mechanisms of coastal defence and port security in several countries which could be exploited by the terrorists to launch attacks on a different country.

Actions to Check Nuclear Proliferation: The nuclear non-proliferation regime led by the International Atomic Energy Agency (IAEA) needs to be more proactive in monitoring the proliferation of nuclear material by the state as well as non-state actors. With increasing instability, the spectre of use of small nuclear devices in the form of 'dirty bombs' or even short-range nuclear-tipped warheads of a weak nation state by terrorists cannot be entirely ruled out. In addition to striving for more safeguards and guarantees against accidental launch of nuclear warning by states whose nuclear stockpiles are prone to fall into the hands of terrorists, these countries must be made aware of the counter-actions that can be taken against them in the event of a nuclear launch from their soil by the state or non-state actors. It is the larger responsibility of the world community to strive for the goal of nuclear disarmament and in the interim, discourage and dis-incentivise weak nuclear nation states where the security situation is particularly precarious, from expanding their nuclear arsenal.

Adequate leverages must be created to deter such nation states from accelerating production of nuclear material and also on those states that are actively transferring nuclear technology and material to such nations for military use. A case in point is China's nuclear assistance to Pakistan. China, which itself is at the receiving end of Islamist terrorists active in Xinjiang and who receive training in Pakistan, should realise the implications of such actions. It is a moral obligation of the world community to dissuade Pakistan from a possible development of the short-range Tactical Nuclear Weapons (TNWs). A large stockpile of such nuclear-tipped tactical weapons compromises security in the storage of such weapons, alarmingly amplifying its propensity of falling into the hands of non-state actors. The UN must also initiate steps to draft a convention on the use of CBRN weapons by terrorist organisations which would be binding on all the member states for implementing safeguards and contingencies against the use of such weapons by the non-state actors.

Perception Management and Limiting Collateral Damage: It needs to be realistically assessed whether the use of disproportionate military force and heavy weapons in population centres in Afghanistan, Pakistan and Iraq actually led to a further complication of the insurgency problem. While the use of unmanned drones or precision aerial strikes on suspected terrorist hideouts are justified, due care must be taken to avoid or limit civilian casualties in these strikes. Though these methods provide limited tactical gains in the short run, they prolong the problem in the long run by validating the propaganda of terrorists in helping them win over more recruits. In the information area, wars are not lost due to wrong intentions or illegitimate aims of those pursuing them, but in the manner in which they are portrayed and perceived by the people. In today's networked environment, perceptions can be formed in seconds and messages beamed to a large audience across the world in no time.

Moral Issues: Even though the military campaigns in Afghanistan and Iraq were directed against terrorists and had genuine causes, a wide section of the population in those countries and also many of those who were not directly affected by the campaigns saw them as a military occupation by the foreign forces. In some ways, the military actions in Iraq and Afghanistan have perpetuated perceptions of a 'clash of civilisations' between the West and Muslim world as professed by Samuel Huntington. The military actions against terrorists have to be projected in the right manner by the countries engaged so that the propaganda value is not hijacked by the terrorists and non-state actors. Questioning the basic aim and purpose of a military campaign can be demoralising for the forces running it on ground and erode the international prestige and standing of that country in the world, thus forcing it to prematurely terminate the campaign without achieving its desired goals.

Effective Governance and Equal Access to Economic Opportunities: With the global downturn in economy and rising unemployment, a lack of access to economic resources and gainful employment opportunities for the people will provide the biggest fodder to terrorist organisations. The state, by means of effective governance and safeguarding the fundamental right of every citizen to life, liberty and employment, will limit opportunities for the terror groups to indoctrinate people. Ensuring justice and equal livelihood opportunities for all citizens without practising religious indiscrimination will create peaceful conditions that cannot be exploited by inimical groups. The state must also guard against doling out freebies or job opportunities on the basis of religious or minority quotas as such measures only widen the gaps in society, leading to an accentuation of social tensions between communities. Reforming the madrasa education system and making it more job-oriented and broad-based will go a long way in choking the recruitment base of terrorists. In the long run, Muslim students should be encouraged to seek education in multi-religious institutions where they can develop a more inclusive worldview. State institutions also need to invest more resources in countering radicalisation in society and checking the spread of radical madrasas from abroad, which aim to change the moderate system of Islam traditionally prevalent in a particular region. The harassment or defaming of a particular community for aligning with terrorists, punishing entire communities for wrongs done by few individuals and wrongful arrests of terror suspects should be avoided to the core and must form the cornerstone of a successful counter-terrorism strategy.

Monitoring Activities of the Radical Madrasas: In the past decade, thousands of Wahhabi/Salafist madrasas and mosques have proliferated all over the world. According to a US intelligence report, in 2005, the House of Saud had in 2005 approved a US$ 35-billion (Rs.1,75,000 crore) plan to build mosques and madrasas in South Asia. The governments in the respective countries need to monitor the activities of those madrasas and mosques which are suspected of routing funds for terror activities, sheltering terror suspects and involved in indoctrinating people for recruitment into terror groups. In some countries, sensitivities over disturbing religious practices of a community and other political inhibitions lead to the overlooking of nefarious activities by such organisations. State institutions should take Maulvis or preachers into confidence and make them stakeholders in checking illegal activities that may be channelled through their religious institutions.

Policing the Cyber Space: The terrorists are increasingly making use of the cyber space to communicate among themselves. The very open nature of the internet and inadequate legal protocols make it susceptible to wrongful use by individuals who can mask their real identities. Today, while states have capabilities to monitor the communication of terror groups in cyber space, there is an urgent requirement for introducing an international legislation which would enable the states to legally detect and disrupt communication channels including the social media being used for terrorism purposes and book individuals who carry out these activities.

Countering False Propaganda of OGWs and NGOs: The environment of irregular warfare is constantly evolving with the terrorists adopting new methods and tactics to further their activities. Over Ground Workers (OGWs) and sympathisers and NGOs which are ideologically connected to terrorist networks are playing a greater role in carrying out propaganda activities and the collection and distribution of funds to terrorists. They are also instrumental in requisitioning the services of sympathetic journalists to give a favourable slant to terrorism and gain sympathy and minimise condemnation for their acts. Monitoring and banning the activities of such NGOs and members of the third estate who have global inter-connections has been a grey area in countering international terrorism and the nation states must pay adequate attention to this aspect.

CONCLUSION

At the tactical level, the terror groups have become more un-structured and autonomous than before due to constant pressure and reverses suffered by them. The non-centrally controlled attacks are more difficult to prevent and account for. Smaller and more diffused terrorist cells easily entrench themselves in population centres and can be activated when the need arises. Collateral damage in military operations and negative perception of drone strikes also help terrorist groups to garner ideological support and recruits to their fold. In fact, today Iraq has emerged as an international training ground for terrorists where battle-hardened terrorists are spreading terror into neighbouring Syria and inspiring their compatriots in the Af-Pak region.

The shift in the targeting pattern of the terrorists due to a target hardening of the government and military installations puts in additional vulnerability in countering international terrorism. In today's fourth-generation warfare, the entire urban landscape has become a battle theatre and warfare has moved out of the trenches and military lines. To combat the hidden enemy which has unleashed asymmetric warfare, defeating the ideology that spawns terror groups has assumed vital importance. The indiscriminate targeting of civilians by terrorists is making them more unpopular and this factor should be exploited to galvanise the public opinion against them.

What is however worrisome is that despite the global efforts against terrorism, it continues to be a preferred low-cost option for some countries to further their foreign policy objectives. The case of Pakistan and some states in the Middle East are illustrative of this aspect. The use of proxies or non-state actors also provides a layer of deniability and strategic advantage to these states. A greater calibration of attacks with controlled frequencies and inflicting lesser casualties in one strike fails to evoke a strong reaction and outrage by the international community. Sadly, the global community has failed to gather consensus and resolve to raise the prohibitive costs on these countries so that state-sponsored terrorism becomes counter-productive to their interests.

The Global Economic Meltdown has weakened the fight against terrorism and accelerated the pace of the US withdrawal from Afghanistan. Prohibitive economic costs would make it difficult for governments to sustain the momentum of counter-terrorist operations overseas. The impact of increased lawlessness and security vacuum in Afghanistan after the thinning down of the ISAF will be felt across the world. Regional players in the Middle East, Central and South Asia need to situate the threat of terrorism emanating from Iraq, Syria, Afghanistan and Pakistan and pool their resources to meet this impending threat which will impact them more than anyone else. These players should also desist from furthering their own geopolitical interests by backing their respective proxies and recognise the collective threat of international terrorism. The al-Qaeda-backed terror groups have already become resurgent, operating out of strongholds in Northern Iraq (Mosul and Anbar), Syria, Pakistan (North Waziristan) and Eastern Afghanistan (Kunar and adjoining districts). Their further expansion from these strongholds and the seeking of new areas of influence or regaining old ones must be prevented at all costs.

The world has been witness to the counter-productive and destructive effects of the power games played out in Afghanistan from 1979 to 1990, and the major world powers would be ignoring security concerns at their own peril. The world must have safeguards and contingencies in place to address the security challenges that may re-emerge due to the increased destabilisation and lack of governed space in Afghanistan post-2014. It should strengthen regional powers and allow them to take actions to pursue their national security interests in the light of the deteriorating regional security environment and deter states which may become more encouraged in the absence of an international military presence in Afghanistan to intensify their disruptive activities in the neighbouring countries by using terrorists as proxies.

Finally, it must be understood that conventional military operations can achieve limited success against terrorists and will blunt their capabilities only for a limited period. The war against international terrorism is a protracted struggle. Therefore, we must shore up our defences and strengthen our resolve to fight our own battles with an offensive mindset to preemptively strike at the roots of terrorism. If the world is a global village for economic interdependence, then so it is to counter terrorism. After all, development and security are flip sides of the same coin. One without the other is difficult to envisage. Safety from terror is the watchword and the world can become safer only if we fight terror together and more importantly, define terror together.

The Author

Rohit Singh graduated in History (Honours) from Hansraj College, Delhi University. Additionally, he holds a post-graduate diploma in Electronic Media from Guru Gobind Singh Indraprastha University, Delhi and a Masters in Mass Communication from Guru Jambeshwar University, Hisar. He had been a Research Assistant and later Associate Fellow at the Centre for Land Warfare Studies (CLAWS) from February 2009 to December 2012, and a Senior Research Associate and Special Assistant to the Director at the Vivekananda International Foundation (VIF), New Delhi.

*

END NOTES

1. Global Terrorism Database maintained by the National Consortium for the Study of Terrorism and Responses to Terrorism (START) – A Study of Excellence of the US Department of Homeland Security at the University of Maryland & Institute for Economics and Peace, Sydney (Global Terrorism Index; released in December 2012).
2. US Country Report on Terrorism 2012.
3. Rohan Gunaratna, 'The Global Terrorist Threat: Set to Grow in 2014', The International Relations and Security Network, Zurich, accessed at http://isn.ethz.ch/Digital-Library/Articles/Detail/?lng=en&id=176020
4. Source: Global Terrorism Index 2012, Institute for Economics and Peace. In India, the high casualty figure is largely attributed to the people killed in Maoist violence accounting for 40 per cent of the total number of casualties.
5. Jessica D. Lewis, 'The Breaking of the Wall Campaign: Al Qaeda in Iraq Resurgent', Institute for the Study of War, 2013.
6. Ashis Ray, 'Alarm in Europe over 26/11 Type Plot', *The Times of India*, 30 September 2010, accessed at http://articles.timesofindia.indiatimes.com/2010-09-30/uk/28262971_1_threat-level-intelligence-agencies-eiffel-tower
7. http://www.thenational.ae/news/world/asia-pacific/indonesian-police-uncover-plot-to-kill-president
8. Global Terrorism Index 2012, op. cit.
9. http://news.antiwar.com/2014/01/30/us-intelligence-estimate-7000-foreign-fighters-in-syria/
10. Yassin Musharbash and Marcel Rosenbach, 'Sauerland Cell in the Dock', *Spiegel Online International*, accessed at http://www.spiegel.de/international/germany/sauerland-cell-in-the-dock-germany-prepares-for-homegrown-terror-trial-a-619381.html

11. Indrani Bagchi, 'Buddhist-Rohingya conflict in Myanmar spells trouble for India', *The Times of India*, 08 July 2013, accessed at http://timesofindia.indiatimes.com/india/Buddhist-Rohingya-conflict-in-Myanmar-spells-trouble-for-India/articleshow/20964208.cms?
12. Shishir Gupta, 'IM, Rohingya Outfit under Scanner for Bodh Gaya Blasts', *Hindustan Times*, 9 July 2013, accessed at http://www.hindustantimes.com/India-news/Patna/IM-Rohingya-outfit-under-scanner-for-Bodh-Gaya-blasts/Article1-1089415.aspx
13. Joe Cochrane, 'Indonesian Militants join Foreigners fighting in Syria', *New York Times*, 31 January 2014, accessed at http://www.nytimes.com/2014/02/01/world/asia/indonesian-militants-join-fight-in-syria.html?_r=1
14. Asit Jolly, 'The Wahhabi Invasion', *India Today*, 23 December 2011, accessed at http://indiatoday.intoday.in/story/saudi-charities-pump-in-funds-through-hawala-channels-to-radicalise-kashmir-valley/1/165660.html
15. 'Terrorism plot Size of 7/7 Attacks 'Foiled Every Year', *BBC News*, 21 March 2013, accessed at http://www.bbc.co.uk/news/uk-21878867
16. Al Qaida Sanctions List, UN Security Council Resolutions 1267 (1999) and 1989 (2011), accessed at http://www.un.org/sc/committees/1267/aq_sanctions_list.shtml
17. Country Report on Terrorism, 2012, US Department of State.

3

Maoist Insurgency: Escalation and Dimensions of the State's Armed Response

Lt Gen Gautam Banerjee

PREVIEW: THE GATHERING OF A STORM

Resurgence of Maoist Violence

Since mid-2011 or so, the intensity of Maoist insurgency had somewhat been less spectacular as compared to the preceding years. Indeed, there had been many Maoist–Police encounters during this time, mostly in Jharkhand and Chhattisgarh, but the frequency of such incidents had shown a definite downslide. More than that, these encounters had not been so one-sided in favour of the insurgents as it had been the case in the past, though the insurgents still retained an upper hand as evidenced by the casualty ratios, loss of police weapons and the acts of unencumbered assembly, attack and dispersal that the insurgents were able to perform without much difficulty.[1]

No doubt, this period of relative downtrend in armed engagements was rooted in the caution exercised by the government after it was chastised by a series of massacres perpetrated upon the inadequately prepared police forces that were set out to rein in the insurgency in its bastions. Subsequently, the police forces became cautious and selective in their 'Anti-Naxal' operations while they modernised, equippped and trained. At the other end, the Maoists, being conscious of the inevitability of escalation of armed confrontation with the forces of the Union, decided to utilise this period to strengthen themselves organisationally, financially and militarily. Meanwhile, they also undertook to marshal their armed strength to prevent the state from intruding into the areas of their established domain.[2] Thus there was little doubt that with both the contestants in consolidation mode, the statistical dip in Maoist-related violent incidents was but illusionary; the signs of escalation were already in evidence.

To those initiated in Maoist methods, the notional slowdown in the rebels' armed activities was a standard deceptive ploy, adopted to consolidate and prepare for the inevitable showdown once the police forces had, by and large, completed their modernisation and expansion. Besides, most of the states had been going slow in proactive counter-Maoist operations either due to political reasons or to allow a preparatory time to the police. Thus, while the frequency of clashes had reduced, the Maoists had a free run in imposing their will upon the inhabitants, the business community and the state functionaries of the affected areas. No doubt, the state authorities responsible for controlling the Maoist menace were conscious of this anomaly, but bereft of a better alternative, had, in all earnestness, opted to accept it, albeit temporarily.

That was the situation that prevailed till May 2013 when the period of ominous inactivity was shattered by the ambush of the Congress Party convoy in *Sukma Hills* in the Chhattisgarh–Odisha region. Till the end of 2015, there had been some more Maoist attacks, including the most distressing event of targeting a passenger train in *Jamui* in the Bihar–Jharkhand region. Notably, all these incidents took place in Maoist-dominated areas—the Maoists' 'domain'—which they have explicitly committed to defend against the state's 'intrusion'. To that extent, the escalation in acts of violence at this stage was, most certainly, aimed at keeping their sanctuaries off-limit to their declared enemies. The renewal of terror may also have been motivated by the need to retain hold over the cadres and to reaffirm their organisational power. The insurgents' plan to gear up to be able to stand up to the impending state offensive having hit a plateau in terms of its fiscal sustainability, was another reason for the Maoists to start flexing muscle. Whatever be the case, after some reduction in the years 2011–2013, some escalation in Maoist violence and incidents of Maoist–police encounters were anticipated in 2015. That the acts of violence have presently remained somewhat under control, is attributed to firstly, the undertaking of selective police actions after due preparation; secondly, fruition of the police modernisation schemes; thirdly, the Maoists' having to focus on retaining their motivation, cadre base and territory and four, the insurgents' inability to rise over their financial crunch.

Indeed, there is nothing to indicate any possibility of reconciliation between the Maoist hard line and the sanctified ordinations that the Indian state is obliged to uphold. It is therefore prudent for the Central and the affected state governments to prepare for a looming flare-up in confrontation with the Maoist insurgents. The adoption of deliberate and comprehensive measures to respond effectively with force to disarm the insurgents was, and continues to be, one distinct part of that preparation. As stated, such preparations are underway, though the pace is slow on the account of logistic complexities, and more than that, on the account of a mix of banal hope, manipulative interests and complacency among the regional politicians and their committed state functionaries for whom the Maoist insurgency is a 'fruit tree'.

The Scope and Layout of the Paper

The State's response to the Maoist rebellion has multifarious dimensions. To retain focus, the discussion in this paper has been confined solely to the aspects of the State's armed response to the Maoist insurgency. In so doing, certain experiences gained in the conduct of counter-insurgency operations across the globe, as relevant to the present situation in Central India, have been taken cognisance of. The issue is proposed to be discussed in four parts.

In the first part, the government's current strategy to control the Maoist insurgency has been touched upon. It has also been argued that this strategy may be better reinforced by the enunciation of a 'Grand Policy' that covers the limitations of the government's existing strategy. Part 2 elaborates upon certain 'Executive Measures' which play a catalytic role in weakening the stronghold of the Maoists and so to reinforce the hands of the forces of the Union that are deployed in counter-insurgency operations. In a similar vein, certain 'Tactical Measures' that help the Union's forces in undertaking their charter with better results, have been discussed in Part 3. At the end, in Part 4, a mention has been made of certain 'Legal Measures' which may be thought of to empower the State in denying the impunity that is enjoyed by the organised violators of the Indian Constitution.

PART 1
THE STATE'S COUNTER-INSURGENCY STRATEGY

The Government's 'Action Plan' and Impediments

In 2011, after nearly two decades of procrastination and pussyfooting, the policymakers finally woke up to the need to preserve the integrity of the State against the rising spread of Maoist intransigence. That charter is sought to be met by the adoption of a well-articulated 'Integrated Action Plan' (IAP)—a 'two-pronged' policy—so to say. One prong of this policy envisages improved governance and economic development to ameliorate the causes of the rebellion, while the second prong aims at strengthening the police forces for them to be able to defang the Maoist's armed wing—the 'People's Liberation Guerrilla Army' (PLGA). It was so that nearly two years after the process of modernisation and training of the counter-Maoist police forces was vitalised, police actions, selective and limited in scope, commenced in 2014 in selected areas of Jharkhand, Chhattisgarh, Bihar, Maharashtra and West Bengal, and to some extent in Odisha. In these operations, the police forces were able to clear the insurgents' presence from certain designated areas so as to provide space for the government-sponsored socio-economic schemes to commence. Yet, even as the government's counter-Maoist action plan slowly gets into steady gear, there are reasons to be circumspect regarding the escalation of violence in the coming years.

The government's 'two-pronged' policy is but an indigenised version of the 'stabilisation' strategy adopted by the International Security Assistance Force (ISAF) in Afghanistan. This is a plan to 'clear, hold and develop' that hinges upon the execution of progressive socio-economic schemes for the state institutions to gain the people's confidence and thereby upstage the latter's backing of the Maoists. However, typical of the affected states, what few schemes have been undertaken have been marred by tardy planning and languid execution. Besides, the implementation of many schemes has been virtually taken over by the Maoists to strengthen their grip over the local beneficiaries at the government's expense. It would therefore be simplistic to expect the Maoist support base to dissolve any time early. In any case, the local inhabitants are in no position to repudiate the Maoists' rulings which are invariably made under an implicit threat of summary retribution. This situation, when seen in light of the fact that arrogated by their success, the Maoists have no intentions to come to terms with what they refer to as a 'decadent state', the escalation of armed confrontation between the state and the insurgents may well be anticipated.

The confrontationist situation is exacerbated by the compulsions of a developing, over-populated and poverty-ridden nation. The people's mounting demands for economic betterment leaves no choice to the government but to sustain progress that must be contingent upon the expansion and accelerated exploitation of the primary reservoir of natural resources. Conversely, a galloping consumption of raw materials can be met only by a massive churning of the forests and mineral-rich plateau lands, which in turn would cause a large-scale displacement of the inhabitants, besides inflicting environmental degradation having serious, long-term consequences. Given the State's track record of rehabilitation of either the people or Nature—or rather its callous disregard—this is a vicious cycle that has strong potential to mar any hope of harmonious management of national progress. The societal tension and confrontations, based on demands that are genuine or impractical, spontaneous or instigated, may therefore be expected to boost the Maoist rebellion in large parts of India. It may not be possible for the government to have enough forces to suppress the turmoil of that scale in one stroke, or even to 'hold' against the return of the rebels, all of those areas which might have been 'cleared' once. Thus in the overall context, it would be obligatory for the government to operate with what forces it may be able to muster. And that obligation would have to be met either against the agitations of the people or their non-cooperation that might either be instigated by the Maoists or imposed under their threat. This aspect adds to the complexity of the successful undertaking of the 'clear-hold-develop' policy.

Indeed, notwithstanding a brave and encouraging articulation of intent, the fact is that the state has neither the forces to 'hold' with any degree of permanency, the expanse where the Maoists operate, nor the institutional mechanism to carry out a development work at that scale. Obviously, the rebellion may be brought under control only after a long period of sustained commitment that is bereft of political and fiscal chicanery.

The Decree of Armed Response

There is no doubt that in order to implement the 'clear-hold-develop' policy, the government has to adopt comprehensive measures to be able to control a heightened condition of state-versus-insurgent confrontation that is expected to break out sooner than later. Indeed, an ability to competently respond to the violence perpetrated by the Maoists' armed insurgency is imperative for the IAP to bear fruition. On the other hand, when tested against the lessons of past insurgencies of similar characteristics all across the world, it transpires that the current framework of the state's armed response may not be adequate to meet that end when pitted against a continuously strengthening Maoist insurgency. It would therefore be prudent for the Central and the state governments to take a step further in devising a more *wholesome policy* to govern the conduct of counter-Maoist operations, even if it must be minimalistic in terms of force application, that the Union's forces are destined to undertake sooner than later.

Thus apart from the planning and implementation of socio-economic and legislative measures to reclaim the people's confidence in the institution of the state, comprehensive measures need also to be instituted to upgrade the capability of the Union forces in disarming the insurgents. Appropriately, these exclusive measures may encompass two aspects of extreme sensitivity. One, it must empower the forces with adequate operational capabilities as well as bureaucratic back-up and so facilitate the conduct of counter-Maoist operations with a higher efficiency as compared to what had been seen so far and two, the policemen must be saved, by a better cultural education, from falling prey to attitudinal insensitivity against the locals. The second aspect needs particular attention in view of the established fact that a visible expression of empathy from the representatives of the State plays a positive role even when certain discomfitures may have to be perforce imposed upon the inhabitants during the counter-insurgency operations. Cultural understanding thus saves the State from further alienation of the local inhabitants.

In continuation with such support measures, a substantive upgradation of the tactical and logistic policies has also to be devised, defined and formally incorporated into the afore-stated *wholesome policy*—a '*Grand Policy*' to wit—in order to disable the insurgency. Finally, it would be wise to cover within the scope of that Grand Policy, such measures as are necessary to deal with the anticipated escalation in the State–insurgent conflict. Provisions for such wherewithal that the forces may need to deal with the extreme situations which the Maoists may aggravate in their desperation, should therefore form part of the proposed Grand Policy. Affected with foresight, these steps would obviate the need for the Union's forces to pause or retract their operations in order to prepare better and that would deny to the Maoists another breather to recoup, as has been the case earlier. Of course, all of the three decisions to be taken at the political level—that is, the *extent* to which armed force is to be applied in controlling the Maoist violence, the delineation of the *ambit* of police action and its intended *end goal*—would have to be formally promulgated by the government in power.

It may be worthwhile to discuss the aspects that the afore-stated Grand Policy—to reiterate, a policy to govern the *state's armed response* in containing the Maoist violence—may cover. The intent here is to see that by learning from past experiences, no repetition of the state's armed capability falling short of the challenges posed, may take place. Indeed, there is no need to wait for a foreseen escalation to descend and then to suffer the obligation of conceding ground to the Maoists, offering another opportunity for them to consolidate and build up. No doubt, at this juncture of the Maoist rebellion, the ordained decree upon the state is to go proactive in its preparation to rein-in the violent insurgency.

Three Aspects of a 'Grand Policy'

Drawing parallels with somewhat similar situations that prevailed in the post-World War II era and its sixty-odd long roll of insurgencies, the emergence of certain well-established conventions is observable. In so doing, it becomes apparent that the Indian security community has been rather smug in 'reinventing the wheel' over and over again, and that only after being hit badly enough to elicit loud cries of nationwide dismay. Even then, rather than devising, planning and rehearsing appropriate responses to the challenges *before* taking the plunge, the trend is to hurriedly engage in a sequence of trials and errors under a minimalist approach, a sort of blindfolded groping so to say, and thus failing to apply diligently enough to the complex nuances ahead, until slapped to senses. The decimation that the State's institutions, including the police forces, have been subjected to at the hands of the Maoists over the past decade or so, bears to that conclusion. May be, the governing establishment can do better this time.

If one were to summarise the lessons culled out of past armed insurrections across the globe since the past six decades, there would be three notable conclusions. These are:

- One, the *insurgent's intelligence superiority and logistic backbone are broken when it is divested of their captive public;*
- Two, the *insurgents are reduced to helplessness when their main strength, that is, the intimacy with the terrain, is broken by forcing them to displace from their known environs;* and,
- Three, the *insurgency is defeated when a free movement of its armed groups is deterred* by the means of cleverly sited check posts, blocks, traps and ambushes.

Further, there is one vital lesson that emerges loud and clear, that is, just the achievement of physical control over the violence perpetrated by the armed insurgents is not enough to secure lasting peace and social stability; to achieve that end, the entire organisational structure around which the insurgency thrives—command, logistic chain, funding and propaganda set-up—needs to be dismantled. In other words, the process of *dismantling the organisational structure of the insurgency must be inherent in the State's armed response* to the Maoist violence.

That being so, one may venture to define the proposed Grand Policy under three distinct heads—namely, the '*Executive*', '*Tactical*' and '*Legal*' *Measures*.

The first step for the government to comprehensively defeat the Maoists' armed assault upon the institutions of the Indian State would be to unequivocally demonstrate to the people, the resolve to best equip the Central and state forces for that task. As a corollary, that resolve is best articulated through the initiation of certain steps that would pave the way for the Union forces to effectively deal with the impending State–non-State confrontation. These are the steps that may be classified under the terminology of '*Executive Measures*'.

PART 2
THE EXECUTIVE MEASURES

Definition

The Executive Measures under discussion here are those which, would contribute in controlling the insurgency. In other words, these are meant to back up those aspects of the State's efforts which involve the articulation of its armed forces in reining-in the rebellion. Appropriately, these are civil measures which fall within the ambit of standard administrative mechanisms, albeit with an added emphasis on firm implementation and continuous monitoring—the aim being to close those avenues which the Maoists exploit to garner armed muscle and exercise to attack the State. The enforcement of these civil measures do not call for any extraordinary use of force, that is, more than what is usual at normal times. However, even if many of these Executive Measures may have certain commonalities with other social, economic and political initiatives that might be undertaken by the government under the first 'prong' of its strategy—that is, to remedy the root causes of the rebellion—it is necessary for the state functionaries to distinguish between the two. This is so because as past experience reveals, unless applied exclusively and freed of peripheral linkages, such measures tend to get entangled in contradictions that might be thrown up by inter-departmental priorities, procedural and fiscal hurdles and motivated opposition.[3] The State's effort to rein-in the insurgency thus gets diverted. As a result, the very purpose of the adoption of measures gets defeated, much to the insurgents' advantage.

Experience also shows that these measures, even if apparently mundane, offer out-of-proportion advantages in weakening the violent arm of a rebellion within a short period. Therefore, by customising the lessons learnt from the past insurgencies of similar nature outside as well as within India to the situation created by the current Maoist insurgency, it is possible to identify some of the 'Executive Measures' that could play a catalytic role in disarming the rebellion.[4] A brief discussion over the fundamental ones among these measures would therefore be in order.

Fundamental 1: Effective Law Enforcement

It is known that all kinds of criminal activities—even those which are normally not considered as anti-national *per se*—contribute in strengthening the anti-

State rebellion in some manner or the other. Conversely, when engaged with insurgency, the State's law enforcement mechanism becomes inhibited, and that permits the criminals and outlaws to enter into a mutually profitable nexus with the anti-national rebellious groups. The cultivation and trade of opium and other contraband, smuggling, kidnapping for ransom, '*Rangdari*' taxation (extortion against dispensation from arm-twisting), land-grabbing, bulk theft from railway wagons and government store yards, local gun manufacturing, diversion of industrial explosives and detonators, etc., are such illegal activities which promote that kind of mutually beneficial nexus. At some stage, many of the state functionaries, while closing their eyes to law-breaking which in any case they are obliged to do against the pain of violent death, acquiesce to join the bandwagon to make some extra money. The development of such loops of nexus allows the insurgency to take advantage of, one, the criminals' information network; two, the information leakages from the governing establishment; three, a widening of the 'catchment area' for the collection of funds, and four, illegal gunrunning. Therefore, a zero tolerance of all illegal activities must engage the attention of the affected states while engaging in the counter-insurgency operations.

In this context, the recent tightening of the law-enforcement mechanism in Bihar and Maharashtra provide encouraging examples. In these states, it has been possible to subdue the intensity of insurgent activities by a better administration of law, order and governance. Conversely, with the State administration laid low in a condition of asphyxiation, the situation is exactly the opposite in Jharkhand, and to some extent in Odisha too. To illustrate, there is no doubt that a concerted enforcement of mandatory laws, for which the government has always been adequately equipped, would make it possible to dismantle the industry of illegal arms manufacture that flourishes because of the dual clientele of the criminals and the Maoist insurgents. Helped by an energised system of criminal justice, it would also be possible to arrest a widespread diversion of industrial explosives and agricultural chemicals to the making of Improvised Explosives Devices (IEDs), just as it would be possible to clamp down on a collection of 'levy' by the Maoists. Most crucially, by tightening screws on the criminals on the fringe, the flow of tactical information would be reversed in favour of the State. In short, a better enforcement of common laws would dampen the free run that the Maoists enjoy today.

Fundamental 2: The Empowerment of a 'Lead Agency'

The Maoist insurgency flourishes in four states—Chhattisgarh, Jharkhand, Odisha and Bihar—while sustaining itself in another three—West Bengal, Madhya Pradesh and Maharashtra; meanwhile, the rebellion continues to harbour in Andhra Pradesh and Uttar Pradesh. To deal with the insurgency in each of these states, there have been deployed a number of armed police battalions from the Centre as well as some other states, referred to under the generic nomenclature of the 'Central Armed Police Forces' (CAPF). The intelligence functions are undertaken by the state's own internal intelligence set-up as well as the Centre's Intelligence Bureau (IB). Besides, within each state, the policy of 'clear-hold-develop' requires the conjoined participation of many state government departments: health, education, civil supplies, public works, revenue, etc., for example. Thus, there is a crowd of inter-departmental functionaries who have to join hands in countering the rebellion. The lessons of the past reveal that under such situations, it is imperative to devise a common set of political directives and enforce these through a *joint* command, control and executive mechanism.[5] However, notwithstanding the Home Ministry's rote, an adoption of standard policies and common approach to planning and coordination of inter- as well as intra-state counter-insurgency operations remains yet in half-cock. Similar is the case with the institution of an empowered controlling headquarters to tackle the rebellion at the inter-state level. The result is that in many instances, the requirements posed by the police department to its health or public works counterparts within the same state—the provision of which might help in controlling the Maoist activities—have been repudiated by the latter departments over partisan considerations. This attitude is even more visible when matters of inter-state assistance come up. Further, the divergence of goals is no less marred by the incessant politics of Centre–state wrangling.

The situation prevailing is that the political leadership of the various affected states and the officials of the various administrative departments within each of these states continue to articulate their own priorities and compulsions. Though engaged to a common purpose, diffused thinking prevails even among the various police organisations, notwithstanding the tenuous existence of 'unified headquarters' in some of the affected states. Granted that exclusive concerns among the various arms of governance may have some real, if contradictory, substance, these may, no doubt, still be accommodated within a unified set up provided there is the will to rise out of petty rivalries. That, however, is not the case, and a unification of effort to control the rebellion seems elusive even as the insurgency enters its third decade. Indeed, such a state of affairs cannot be the prescription to control an anti-State armed rebellion—not to the requisite extent that would make a difference for the better. This is a severe flaw in the overall situation; it needs to be corrected if the commitment to suppress the insurgency is to be secured with a minimal loss of life and the least disruption in societal stability. Indeed, an empowered *Lead Agency* to deal with the Maoists' war upon the state is wanted—and soon. It could be a 'joint command', an 'empowered committee', a 'coordinating headquarters' or whatever, as long as it is able to maintain the singularity of purpose.

Fundamental 3: The Regulation over Trade

The imposition of regulatory mechanisms on the trade of certain crucial commodities that the Maoists would find themselves to be at sea without, may be another aspect of the Executive Measures. It needs no elaboration that even a soft clampdown over the insurgent's supply chain for dry rations, kerosene oil, dry cells, medicines and clothes would hit them hard. Similarly, effective surveillance—as against the present practice of exchanging bribes to look the other way—over the bulk tailoring of the PLGA uniforms, treatment of cadres by private medical practitioners, diversion from public distribution ration shops and under-the-counter sale of fertiliser chemicals may cause severe difficulties to the rebels. However, for these steps to bear fruit, the overall standard of administration would have to be improved. A stringent enforcement of discipline to promote accountability and curb graft among the government functionaries and a dynamic enforcement of the existing laws would be necessary to achieve that end.

In this context, it may be pointed out that in terms of law enforcement establishments, each state is well equipped to clamp down on the underworld business; it just needs the political will to do so. This fact is reiterated by the success of control mechanisms—even if limited—as instituted in Bihar, Chhattisgarh and Maharashtra.

Fundamental 4: The Denial of Rebel Sanctuaries

It is no secret that the townships located in the areas of Sonebhadra, Balaghat, Sambalpur, Aurangabad, Chaibasa and Bankura are used as sanctuaries by the Maoists to recoup, seek medical treatment, procure provisions, broadcast propaganda, carry out fiscal transactions and interact among themselves. It would therefore be an effective measure to disrupt such activities—the result would be very rewarding indeed. For such measures to fructify, priority has to be accorded to the assignment of intelligence and law-enforcement agencies in 'internal security surveillance' and the marshalling of traditional human intelligence resources including municipal workers, chowkidars, petty criminals, wheeler-dealers, part-time informers, etc., to that purpose, from where these might have been diverted for political expediency over the years.

Fundamental 5: Alacrity in Decision-Making

It is needless to emphasise that faster decision-making over issues directly related to the control of the insurgency is the need of the hour. The issuance of timely rulings on matters related to organisational strengthening of the police forces, prosecution of rebels and their accomplishes, impositions of trade and movement restrictions, location and construction of well-protected police posts, etc., could choke the logistic supply line of the rebellion and forestall the Maoists from expanding their areas of influence. Similarly, a quick response over the provision of security to development and commercial projects could prevent the rebels from widening their extortion base and raise a higher 'levy', while a faster pace of the finalisation of equipment procurement cases and recruitment procedure could quicken the pace of modernisation of the police forces. Conversely, to mention just a few instances of scoring self-goals, an inertia in decision-making has already stonewalled for over half a decade, the recruitment and training of the State police constabulary and raising of special counter-insurgency police battalions—even if these schemes had been unanimously endorsed. Such a languid approach to decision-making needs to be corrected.

A quick and credible response to the ever-changing situational dynamics would also be needed to prevent the return of the insurgents into the areas cleared by police action, emergence of subsidiary factions of intransigents and indulgence of mass corruption among public servants, as it usually happens when the conditions are tenuous. An alacrity of the government's response mechanism is a condition that is fundamental in assuring the common citizens of their safety against the Maoist retribution, just as it is to redress the current impracticality of the 'surrender policy' that remains impotent in protecting the reformed cadres. That kind of credible assurance would in turn lead to the dismantling of the insurgents' life-line, that is, a fear-induced network of human surveillance and forewarning.

Comments

As past experience suggests, the implementation of *Executive Measures* as discussed above would strangulate the logistics of food, funds, firepower and forewarning network of the Maoists. That would have a cascading effect in discouraging the organised intransigence of the rebels; to fall back to the oft repeated simile, it would drain out the 'pond' of people's cooperation and thus stuff out the life-line of the Maoist 'fish'. Indeed, the adoption of Executive Measures would be the most visible sign of the government being serious in countering the armed insurrection. Indeed, no less important than the actual use of force, it would offer all-round advantages in dealing with the Maoists' war upon the State.

A scrutiny of the situation on the ground reveals that the affected state governments are wary of enforcing the right measures for fear of provoking a socio-political backlash that could topple them from power. Further, in an ostrich-like mentality, the political parties in the affected states are happy to gloss over the festering wounds inflicted by the Maoist activities upon the democratic administration; they are wary of even admitting to the anarchy that prevails for fear of exposing their incessant machinations to divert the people's attention from the real issues while jockeying for power. The other functionaries of the State, bureaucracy and industry for example, on their part, are smug with the status quo, wallowing in lethargy and corrupt practices, even gaining from them, and leaving those hapless policemen—those who cannot manage to avoid being sent to their *gulag*—to do what they can. This situation has to change if the State is really committed to root out the Maoist menace.

PART 3
THE TACTICAL MEASURES

The Tactical Tenets of Counter-Insurgency Operations

Taking advantage of the Executive Measures to clamp down over the Maoist rebellion, it is yet necessary to disarm the insurgents—by force, obviously. But then that is easier said than done, particularly when the insurgency is active over four-score areas of varying sizes and spread across nearly a seventh of the country's land mass; the forces and the logistic resources at the State's disposal would never be enough, particularly because the counter-insurgency task is manpower-intensive. Therefore, that end would have to be achieved by the following initiatives:

- Strengthening the quality of the forces in terms of training and equipment
- Raising the sanctioned establishment of police personnel
- Recruitments to fill up the vacancies accumulated over the years
- Raising more units of armed constabularies
- Dynamic deployment of the available forces after due planning and preparation.

Some tenets of counter-insurgency operations, proven over the past, may offer some practical options in an effective mustering of the forces to undertake the extensive task of clearing out the insurgents from areas so vast in extent.

Tenet 1: The 'Cluster Clearance' Method

Past experience indicates that *displacement from their known environs* and *disruption of their free movement* are the two most effective weapons in debilitating the strength of an insurgency. Frequently forced displacements to unfamiliar areas causes dismay and frustration among the insurgent cadres and robs them of their strength—an intimate knowledge of the tactical attributes of the terrain and a self-confidence borne out of territorial dominance—thus severely weakening the insurgency. The 'Tactical Measures', therefore, must be built around the purpose of exploiting these two vulnerabilities of the Maoist insurgents. Considering the wide spread of the rebellion and the tangible forces at hand, it may be wise to group the Maoist affected areas into distinct '*clusters*' and concentrate forces to clear these one after the other. Operations directed over a finite area would permit the deployment of overwhelming forces and oblige the insurgents to flee their remote PLGA bases and camps to relocate to unfamiliar areas. Such displacements would also entail the abandonment of the insurgent stocks of scarce material resources. Thus, even if the 'search-and-engage' missions do not lead to an infliction of high casualties or capture of the armed cadres, as it invariably be so at the beginning, the insurgency would still be seriously affected by the need to establish new camps and devise new networks of supply and surveillance. The most damaging effect upon the insurgents' cause would be the loss of tactical advantages borne out of their terrain familiarity and the confidence enjoyed by the cadres while operating on home turf. Above all, being chased out of their domain would inflict an embarrassing dent upon their inflated self-estimation and over-publicised bravado.

Obviously, the clearance of one such cluster would cause the insurgents to shift base to other areas over which they have been exercising control. As the Union's forces are redeployed to operate in the next targeted cluster, the exodus would be repeated, thus causing the insurgent groups to scatter once again; some groups would even come back to a cleared cluster and try to reclaim the ground lost earlier. There is really no straight solution to this ritualistic cycle of 'chase-and-scoot' but to position some force in occupation of the cleared clusters, the purpose being to prevent the insurgents having a free hand in reclaiming these. Indeed, this is a tough call which has to be taken even at the cost of depleting the forces to clear the remaining clusters.

At the end, a repeat of the 'cluster-clearance' operations is to be undertaken after the first round is done with. Even if these perambulations may seem tedious to the bureaucratic controllers of the Union's forces, actually however, as past experience suggests, the insurgency's backbone is broken, more or less, after the first round of cluster-clearance is affected. Indeed, it is also seen that the insurgency meets its final doom at the early stages of the second round of such clearance operations—of course, when undertaken without a break.

It therefore makes sense to adopt this strategy in the context of the Maoist insurgency in Central India. Of course, the considerations of terrain, resources at hand and insurgent habits would dictate the size and location of the designated clusters. The clusters could either be contiguous or separated, as dictated by the terrain, the forces available from time to time and the overall clearance plan. The clearance of one cluster after another in tandem may follow, and as stated, repeated till the insurgency is suppressed. Obviously, the time needed to get the situation somewhat under control would remain a function of the strategic articulation of the tempo and spread of the operations and the forces that may be available for that purpose.

Tenet 2: The Denial of Free Movement

Alongside the process of 'cluster clearance', the movement of the Maoist squads within the designated clusters may be rendered tedious and risky by a dynamic siting of blocks, traps and day-and-night ambushes. These tactical initiatives have to be exercised in a manner so as to take the transiting insurgents by surprise, or at the least, limit their elbow-room for uncontested movement. Further, the proven tenets indicate that to be able to effectively perform the above-mentioned missions, the best practice is to establish the networks of well-protected, self-contained and logistically sustained 'outposts'. These 'outposts' are sited according to tactical considerations and interconnected in terms of communications as well as transport links relative to time and distance. Effective 'security grids' are thus activated to perform the functions of 'operating bases' for the forces to dominate a designated area. The resultant imposition of movement restrictions and infliction of casualties, even if occasional, fosters a sense of claustrophobia and frustration among the insurgents and thus plays havoc with their psychology.

Tenet 3: The Application of Force

As indicated in the figure below, the insurgencies having similar characteristics to the Maoist problem have flourished from three distinct kind of areas: '*liberated*' bases in remote jungles, rural *'intermediate'* areas of control and urban *'constituencies'* of influence from where come ideological support and funds. Past lessons also indicate that counter-insurgency operations have seen best results when they have made good progress in the 'intermediate' areas before inching into the 'liberated' ones.

Stage II LIBERATED/BASE AREAS	**Stage I** INTERMEDIATE/RURAL AREAS	**Stage III** INFLUENCE/URBAN AREAS
- Search, - Dislocate, - Destroy (**Military Action**)	- Tactical intelligence, - Security of movement, - Choke rebel logistics, - Grid-based deployment, - Domination of space, - Clear & Develop, - Assure inhabitants. (**CAPF + Police Action**)	- Internal Intelligence, - Law Enforcement. (**Police Action**)

Further, invariably in all successful cases, the clearance of the 'intermediate' areas have almost entirely been executed under the aegis of the police forces, sometimes with the elements of the army in a back-up role, while the offensive into 'liberated' base areas have been led either by the regular army or special para-military forces that are structured in the manner of the army.[6] Notably, the confrontation more or less ends as control is wrested from the grip of insurgency from these two areas, whereafter, with its umbilical cord snapped, the urban 'constituencies' either shrink to hibernate or dissolve altogether. The Indian State's counter-insurgency effort may be devised accordingly to reap the benefits of that lesson.

Another notable lesson from the past experiences is that the counter-insurgency operations, when conducted intermittently, tentatively and with inadequate forces, tend to stagnate or even fail. That encourages societal rejects, outlaws and the unemployed to ally with the rebels. Larger and larger areas are thus lost to the rebellion. Thus while more and more people are intimidated into extending their cooperation and support, the rebellion gets strengthened. Therefore, there are strong reasons to save the Indian State from repeating the mistakes it has made in the past in Assam in 1992 and Kashmir in 1999.[7]

Having discussed the lessons from similar counter-insurgency scenarios that have occurred in the past the world over, it may be appropriate at this stage to examine the tactical situation which is seen to be unfolding in the context of the Maoist insurgency in Central India. Such a situational scan would be relevant in delving further into the Tactical Measures which may yet have to be adopted.

The Scene Unfolding on the Ground

Starting from the later part of the year 2011, certain small parts—mainly around Latehar-Palamu in Jharkhand, Sukma-Malkangiri and Bastar-Bijapur in Chhattisgarh and Odisha and Gadchiroli in Maharashtra—were reclaimed slowly but inexorably from the clutches of the Maoists. Following the right practice, the police forces continued with a clearance of such selected areas, howsoever small, that they were able to tackle the enemy even as the envisaged build up and modernisation of forces got underway concurrently. The purpose was to create a secure space in the areas usurped by the insurgents for the State to find its feet and commence the socio-economic development schemes. These nascent efforts apparently did not cause much concern among the Maoist leadership, as evidenced by the half-hearted resistance that was put up to discourage the police from intruding into their realm. May be, having dealt with, and decimated, such attempts before, they did not consider the situation to be so alarming as to call for the diversion of their then current thrust towards strengthening the rebellion in terms of funds, weaponry and cadre base. It was therefore possible for the State to reclaim certain limited territories and kick-start the development schemes in these areas.

As the police forces gained in experience, training and modern equipment, an appropriate *tactical policy*—many times referred to as the '*Tactical Counter-Maoist Campaign*' (TCMC)—was devised around a four-legged operating principle, viz, '*Key Area Domination*', '*Intelligence Based Operations*', '*Night Operations/Ambush*' and '*Clear-and-Hold*' assignments. Indeed, the enunciation of this tactical policy conformed to the lessons of the past insurgencies as discussed above. Accordingly, the police forces commenced operating according to this policy in certain selected areas. Better fortified posts or operating bases were occupied in order to establish security grids and area-dominating exercises were undertaken with a steady frequency. Not used to such deliberate challenges, the Maoists seemed to have stirred in alarm at the inexorable advance of the State's authority. By the closing month of the year 2012, this alarm had manifested in the outbreak of fierce encounters when the insurgents started contesting, with extraordinary vehemence, the police forces' 'intrusion' into what they claimed as their exclusive domain.

As evidenced by the ambush of the Central Reserve Police Force (CRPF) column in Latehar and the firing at the Air Force helicopter in Sukma on the one hand, and the infliction of high casualties on the insurgents by the Maharashtra state's C-60 Commando Police Force in Gadchiroli on the other, the contest could be seen as fast turning into a serious confrontation. Thus, while the police forces are gradually catching up with the PLGA's tactical superiority, the Maoist Area Commanders have panicked enough to resort to booby-trapping the bodies of police casualties, with the idea of instilling terror among the police ranks. As more police outposts were set up in conformity with the security grid, the frequency and coverage of '*gherabandi*' missions increased and as the envisaged night operations to ambush insurgent movements commenced, there was no doubt that the Maoists found the noose tightening around their armed activities. The Maoists knew this and prepared feverishly to withstand that challenge. This trend was evidenced since January 2013 and goes to indicate that both the contestants are upping the ante. The Maoist attack on the Congress convoy in *Sukma*, followed by interception of a passenger train in *Jamui* are therefore the manifestation of an intense conflict ahead. As to how far the insurgents would really be able to operate with the abandon that they were used to in the past when the police forces had been reduced to mere sitting ducks, would be a matter to watch over in the coming days.

Whatever be the case, a new phase of escalated and long-drawn armed confrontation may be expected.

The Response to the Escalation in Maoist Violence

There is no doubt that in imposing their reign, today the Maoist rebels do not have the kind of absolute freedom that they had been enjoying earlier. Similarly, the police forces are no more the sitting ducks that they had been when the insurgents could decimate them in a one-sided contest. There is also no doubt that pitted against the power of the Indian State, finally, the Maoists will not be able to overrun the state through the kind of armed revolution that they have set their eyes at. However, for the next few years, even if the State manages to push the insurgents out of certain affected areas, the marginal loss of territorial control would not cause any substantial weakening of the insurgency. In effect, the Maoists would use their armed strength to preserve their control over many of the areas in which they have established themselves and thereby continue to sustain their cadres by extortion under threat or acts of violence. Further, it is certain that as the State proceeds to harness more and more mineral-rich areas to sustain the nation's economic growth, the instances of instigation of local people's resistance as well as the imposition of 'levy' upon venturing entrepreneurs and industries, backed up with armed attacks, murders, abductions, destruction of plant and equipment or plain issuance of threat, would increase.

Thus, in reiteration of the conclusions discussed in the preceding paragraphs, as both sides gear up to proceed in conformity to their compulsions, it is certain that the conflict will escalate in pace as well as in intensity. Therefore, to be ready to deal successfully with the escalation of violent impositions from the Maoists, the State's counter-insurgency forces have to attend to certain tactical imperatives; the earlier the process starts, the better it would be. A discussion over the tactical aspects that are considered necessary for the coming escalation in the armed confrontation would therefore be in order.

The Imperatives of Tactical Upgrades

It may be necessary at this stage to take the discussion to the next level, that is, as to what better the security forces could do to reinforce their armed response to the Maoist insurgency. To do so, it would be appropriate to discuss the broad nuances of certain reinforcing tactical initiatives that may be applied as the contest gains pace and intensity.

Field Craft: An analysis of the present trends in conduct of the clearance operations indicates that among the police forces, there is more to be honed up with regard to the skills of field craft and minor tactics. Such upgradation is necessary in order to avoid being overwhelmed by Maoist ambushes as much as to stay clear of IED attacks. Each task has to be planned exclusively in terms of routes and timings, tactical formations for movement and employment of scouts and reconnaissance teams. In so performing, the urge to overlook the minute nuances of field craft, so prevalent among the police ranks, needs to be rooted out. Similarly, the skills of tactical deployment for engagement and employment of crew-served weapons, including small calibre mortars and illumination rounds, needs to be sharpened further. Presently, these are the weaknesses which allow the PLGA to come out with a relative success in tactical engagements.

Field Intelligence: For any kind of operational information, the forces deployed in a counter-insurgency role are almost entirely dependent upon the state and Central intelligence agencies, whereas these agencies are actually not equipped to gather 'tactical intelligence' which could be relevant to the planning and execution of actionable missions. Even the newly formed CRPF intelligence wing is not up to that task yet. This is a major weakness in the counter-insurgency intelligence system because of which the jungle patrol search-and-clear missions tend to turn into 'groping-in-the-dark' rather than 'stealth-hunt' operations. The effect is that the forces are instilled with tense apprehensions rather than assured confidence. Further, with their widespread network of embedded surveillance and early warning elements, the insurgents always remain a step or two ahead of the forces and that permits them to set up engagements according to their choice. Under such situations, the necessary tactical intelligence has to be collected by a combination of observation, probes and reconnaissance. Obviously, these exercises have to be tactically launched, both in strength and by stealth, from suitably established operating bases. Considering that these kind of intelligence collection operations have to be carried out over undefined areas, and that the inhabitants would not cooperate with the police while sheltering Maoist informers, 'area familiarisation'—the term here implies terrain as well as population familiarisation—must be the first priority field intelligence task. For example, in deep jungles, the knowledge of sources of water and jungle trails would point to the location of PLGA camps. The knowledge of the terrain would also reveal a fair picture of the existence of the Maoist surveillance and logistic networks which may then be effectively disrupted. Finally, population familiarisation leads to the building up of rapport with the locals and that is the first step in the establishment of the channel of information.

Minor Tactics: The most fundamental weakness, as seen in the CAPF operations, has been over somewhat a shallow understanding of the nuances of tactical manoeuvres. It has to be appreciated that a deployment either in smaller teams or larger groups must depend on the terrain and mission rather than to find safety in numbers. Similarly, it needs to be understood that the practice of out-manoeuvring calls for securing static, dominating positions to catch the adversary on the move and therefore is exposed to destruction in detail. In effect, with better adherence to the basics of field craft and minor tactics, and by tuning up an effective system of field intelligence and terrain familiarisation, the conduct of search-and-destroy missions against PLGA camps would not appear daunting; the instances of walking into insurgent ambush traps, wariness of operating in small numbers or in the dark and the inability to pursue fleeing cadres would become rarer. Next, at some stage, the counter-insurgency operations may have to be enlarged in scope from just the clearance and reaction operations to proactive initiatives. For example, the assembly stage of 'swarming attacks' on vulnerable targets not being easy to hide from an alert policing system, the entrapment of the attacking cadres may be contrived with good prospects of success. Similarly, even with a nascent information network, the vulnerability of the insurgent groups coming out to engage under the Maoist version of 'mobile warfare' may be exploited to apprehend these. The point to appreciate from the past experiences is that even if most of such attempts do not yield tangible results, the exercise in itself poses enough threat to the insurgents in order to make them anxious and jittery. A success in such actions, even if few and far between, would give to the cadres a taste of their own medicine and spell a decimation of the core of the insurgency.

Logistics: The last two years have seen much improvements in the logistic support system of the forces deployed in counter-insurgency operations. Now, supplies are provisioned on a weekly basis over picketed roads, outposts are better stocked and secured with protective works, inter-communications are well-networked and helicopters are more readily available to deal with emergencies. However, the logistic resources that are presently committed seem to have hit the limit of force-sustenance. As the conflict escalates to the next stage, these resources would prove to be inadequate to support the higher force levels that must operate over a larger spread and deeper into the remote areas. There is therefore, good reasons to start the process—rather lengthy as it is—of the acquisition of a larger logistical wherewithal, particularly so in terms of the construction of metalled roads, location of secure intermediate logistic nodes relative to the 'security grid', execution of protective works for operating bases, provisioning of transportation fleets and in strengthening the helicopter back-up.

Force Management: Needless to emphasise, in seeking the ends discussed above, the present system of deployment of forces and turnover of personnel may have to be modified; this would be necessary in order to foster a sense of semi-permanency, as against transiency, and to promote a higher expertise as well as situational awareness. Unless enforced regardless, that would not be easy to accomplish against the policemen's urge to avoid deployment in the Naxal-affected areas. Further, the traditional structure of police leadership may be competent to handle the operational dynamics of counter-insurgency only upto a point. Therefore, even as the level of training of the platoon and company commanders is raised, at a certain stage of escalation, this structure may need to be reviewed—and reinforced—with a tactical leadership of the army kind.

The Role of the Army

Many times in the past, whenever there had been some incidents of massacre of policemen by the Maoist insurgents, the issue of deploying the Indian Army to counter the rebellion has been discussed in the government circles. Better sense has however prevailed and that drastic step has been avoided—apart from moving a brigade once for training exercises to the PLGA's forests bastion of *Narayanpur*—simply because this rebellion is not of the kind that may be suppressed by the use of brute force; the use of military power of the State against a mass-backed uprising would be counterproductive in many ways. In any case, the conditions when the Army has to be called out to protect national integrity do not exist yet—there is no secessionist agenda, nor any sponsorship from external adversaries—neither has the state finally failed to control the insurgency even after committing all its police forces.

Notwithstanding the above argument, there are two situations which might necessitate the Army to pitch in. This is so because there is no other force that is competent in undertaking set-piece surgical attack operations to destroy an organised, ground-holding force that fashions itself on military lines. One situation could be that deviating from their current policy, should the Maoists choose to precipitate the situation by disrupting, for a length of time, the transportation of crucial minerals, including coal to generate power across the country, there would be no option left for the government but to recapture the ground through a deliberate offensive action. The other case could be when it becomes necessary to establish contact with and then overrun the remotely located PLGA bases. In either situation, the only organisation that is competent to undertake such missions is the Army. It may therefore, make sense to keep the Army sensitised to its possible role.

The Aspects of Recruitment, New Raisings and Training

It is well appreciated that with the existing availability of the force level, the policy of 'clear-hold-develop' would succeed only in part. As areas are cleared and a part of the force is committed to hold these on a long-term basis, the forces available to further expand the operational coverage would gradually deplete. That the area affected by the rebellion is no less than one-seventh of the vast Indian land mass, renders the charter even more demanding. Accordingly, recruitment to fill up the existing vacancies in the constabularies—substantial as these are—is underway, albeit at a snail's pace on account of the usual charade of 'job-politics' played by rival political groups. Besides, between two to four new battalions, manned by ex-servicemen, police volunteers and dedicated recruits, have been raised by the state governments in Bihar, Jharkhand, Chhattisgarh and Odisha. Purportedly raised for the purpose of counter-insurgency, the employment of these units has, however, been haphazard and devoid of professional touch.

The stranglehold of systemic inertia is also reflected in the fact that it took nearly half a decade for the Central and state governments to finalise the paperwork related to the raising of specialised police units in four of the worst affected states, viz, Jharkhand, Chhattisgarh, Odisha and Bihar; it remains yet a guess as to when the promised allocation of Rs 280 crores would bear fruition. However, even if these matters hereafter progress with alacrity, the major hurdle lies in training new recruits and the transferees—the training infrastructure is not geared to handle larger batches of freshly inducted trainees without compromising on the quality of the training. It may therefore, be prudent, firstly, to pace the expansion of the counter-insurgency operations to newer areas in relation to the build-up of the forces; secondly, to make formal arrangements for the employment of ex-servicemen as instructors as well as members of the specialised forces and thirdly, to create an additional training infrastructure, even if temporary in nature.

Comments

Factoring past experiences with the situation as seen on the ground, it becomes clear that there is the need to instill a distinct ethos among the counter-insurgency forces. A painstaking adherence to the fundamentals of minor tactics must be the plank of that ethos. Besides, the forces have to be educated on the unfamiliar nuances of local culture and inhabitant sensitivities, so as to promote mutual understanding and empathy. Definitely, such understandings are important factors for success in the counter-insurgency scenario.

Finally, there is no gainsaying that in preparing the forces to arrest the Maoists' propensity in indulging in ruthless armed attacks upon the society, the need of the hour is to free the matter of the State's armed response from the usual systemic labyrinth that causes procrastination, half-measures and distractions. The fact to be recognised by the polity is that for the forces engaged in counter-insurgency operations, the charter is no less than a 'war'—an extraordinary challenge that is not just confined to disarming a well-entrenched armed banditry over the areas desolated, but what requires a defeat and scatter of a clandestinely structured, cunning and ideologically violent organisation. The Maoists are an organisation that repudiates outrightly any suggestion for reasoned negotiations, and seized by idealistic, if actually diabolic, vision, is intent on forcing the State to capitulate to its absolute dictatorship. Indeed, the cause of nation's internal security would be better served when that entire organisation is comprehensively dismantled; half-measures would not do. But that kind of undertaking may require an adoption of certain legal measures.

The examination of the legal provisions that may be directly related to the prevention of illegal armed actions that target the state in an organised manner is beyond the scope of this paper. However, certain aspects, as propagated among those knowledgeable who have the feel of affected societies—and not just the policemen alone—may call for a brief discussion.

PART 4
LEGAL MEASURES

The Context

Admittedly, the rebellion has not yet fully blown into terrorism *per se*. However, experiences of the recent decades across the world show that insurgents are increasingly adapting to terrorist methods to advance their cause. This trend indicates that as the Maoist insurgent–police confrontation heats up, there is a distinct possibility of that situation dawning in India too. It is also clear that in dealing with the Maoist insurgency, the societal sanction is in favour of the 'criminal justice approach' rather than that of the 'war model'.[8] Therefore, there may be a case to prepare the ground for the institution of certain legal measures to strengthen the hands of the forces if and when the need arises to do so. In so doing, care has to be taken to prevent the transgression of accepted norms of democratic dispensation by the over-provoked State functionaries.

Experts opine that there are adequate provisions under the existing laws to deal with the constitutional intransigence of the Maoist rebels; the lacunae are in implementation. The first and foremost consideration, therefore, must be to put on rail a process of efficient prosecution of the outlaws and their accomplices and a judicial disposal of the cases related to the insurgency. The issue is rather well known and hence needs no elaboration. The point to learn from past experience is that it has proved to be advantageous to have a judicial process that is seen to be benevolent, yet firm. In the Indian context, while the burden of prosecution is afflicted with severe weaknesses, the credibility of the judicial system remains quite strong. An application of effective judicial dispensation therefore, when focused specifically upon a vigorous prosecution of the Maoist outlaws, may not be too difficult to administer.

Legal Considerations

There are two issues which stare at the sanctified edifice of the State; these need to be examined beyond the usual rhetoric. One is that even if the Maoists' armed assault upon the State and its citizenry—who have the right to be protected under the rule of law—has been going on for more than two decades past, there has been no demonstrated legal conviction of the outlaws. The second fact is that the Maoists, who have so far been intimidating the citizens by their acts of brutality, have recently began to show signs of degenerating further into adopting terrorist methods—torching property, celebrating murder of dissenters and booby-trapping dead bodies, for example.

In adopting terrorist methods to wage war upon the society, the Maoist insurgents are unencumbered by the pristine norms of accountability. It may be time therefore that delinking from the rhetoric of 'freedom' and democratic 'rights', the State and its citizens find some measures to distinguish between a *nihilist* engaged in digging out the foundation of the nation and an *innocent Indian*. Shades of this concept being already in force in the form of special provisions of law and the institution of arbitrary authorities, the following facts may deserve consideration:

- Unlike the forces of the Union, the Maoists are not bound to stake their lives for public good. They operate clandestinely, attack innocent and defenceless targets at the time and place of their choosing, escape at their convenience, take shelter among intimidated civilians and carry out murders with the sole purpose of terrorising the people. Therefore, *having repudiated their societal obligations, the Maoists may not lay claim to the same rights that the law-abiding citizens, including the forces, are entitled to*. Therefore, some minimal differentiation in terms of special laws may be called for to deal with the insurgency gnawing at the roots of our nationhood.
- Further, being free of the tedious impositions of the constitutional sanctions that the forces must submit to, the insurgents are always well in the lead while the latter have to struggle getting past the starting point. Therefore, these special laws may be instituted well in time to permit the forces to catch up with the handicap of a late start. There is also the good possibility of deterring a conflagration of the confrontation if such special laws are enacted without making it a matter of political wrestling.

At the executive's as well as the common citizen's levels in the Maoist-affected areas, there is much support for the idea of defining the Maoist 'accomplishers', 'activists', 'financiers' and 'cadres'. Knowledgeable sources among the affected lot articulate that the parameters of such classifications are readily definable with an adequate degree of certainty and in a manner that would stand legal and moral scrutiny. Once categorised as such, there would be certain limits imposed upon the activities of the individuals who are identified as such, and that would restrict their opportunities of abusing the democratic system. Indeed, an imposition of such categorisation is permitted under the existing laws, though it might be necessary to subject these provisions to certain amplifications. However, this is a matter that must be left to the legal luminaries to examine.

The Constitutional Application of Federal Provisions

Finally, accepting the fact that in the coming dispensation, the growing assertiveness of the state governments and a possible fractured electoral mandate at the Centre could continue to restrain the federal government from exercising the latter's constitutionally valid option of forceful intervention in such matters that the state administration sees as its turf. This is particularly relevant in the case of the Maoist insurgency which many of the state governments prefer to view as a law and order issue, and therefore, their sole prerogative to handle. On the other hand, there have been many instances of state politics influencing such measures that could turn out to be detrimental to the nation in the long run—caste, religion and muscle-based politics for example. Notwithstanding the sensitiveness of this issue, there may be a case for strengthening the federal provisions, may be as a one-time exception, to deal with such an extraordinary situation that the Maoist rebellion has brought about. If the Finance Commission, Planning Commission, Telecommunication Regulatory Authority, etc., could be empowered to override the majority assertions, and the states feel no hesitation in demanding a Central intervention to bail them out from crisis situations, there is no reason to be chary of extending that concept to protect the edifice of the Indian state.

CONCLUSION: THE COMING OF THE STORM?

At the present juncture, it is clear that both the police forces and the Maoists are engaged in an exercise of what may be termed as a 'testing confrontation'. This is an arrangement in which the State is engaged in a slow and incremental clearance of few selected areas to be able to execute the development projects and provide better governance. Conversely, the Maoists are contesting the police forces who are attempting to intrude into their bastions while protecting, even expanding, their catchment areas of fund extortion. Indeed, at this moment, this is an incremental contest that is exacerbating in slow motion.

It appears that presently, the unstated purpose of the states seems to be to 'push out' the Maoist insurgents from certain selected areas, rather than to engage in an all-out decimation of the rebellion's organisational structure. In this effort, the model applied by the 'Grey Hound' police forces in Andhra Pradesh is sought to be replicated. Notably, that model was successful in expelling the insurgents to other states, but not so in destroying the organisation completely. That may have been a practical policy when dealing with one particular state in isolation, but the future recourse would have to be decided based on two different kinds of options, described as under:

- One option could be to prevent any further spread of the insurgency, while nibbling at the Maoist assets. Reposing hope in a gradual realisation of societal wisdom among the Maoist support base over time, the rebellion may be pushed towards stagnation, atrophy and irrelevancy in due course.
- The second option could be to adopt all-round measures to destroy the organisational structure of the rebellion. That would involve overrunning the insurgents' bases as well as arresting the rebels' activities in the rural and urban areas. Presently, the political decision seems to favour the exercising of the first option.

Indeed, at the present juncture, the choice of a restrained use of force is an appropriate one, given that time is needed to establish the grid of security outposts, perform the cycle of cluster-clearance, hold areas cleared of Maoist domination and to tire out the rebellion. Should however, either to meet its commitment in expanding mining activities or due to the growing impositions of the Maoists, the State is forced to stamp out the menace for good, there are two cardinal facts based on past experiences and as discussed in Part 3 above, that may be taken note of. These facts are:

- The first fact is that offensive action to destroy the insurgents' bases in the 'liberated' areas requires the deployment of the army or a force similarly organised, trained, led and motivated.
- The second fact is that just defeating the insurgency would not stamp out the menace; the entire structure of the rebellious organisation would have to be *uprooted* to ensure lasting social stability.

Whatever be the recourse the state adopts in dealing with the Maoist rebellion, there would be the need to institute executive, tactical and legal measures that would empower the forces in tackling the insurgency better. Meanwhile, the polity has to remain resolute and patient over a long time that a situation of this kind needs to master.

*

END NOTES

1. In this paper, the Maoists' armed activities are referred to as an 'insurgency', while 'rebellion' is the term used to point at their overarching anti-national activities.
2. Capital 'S' has been used to refer to the constituent 'States' of the Union of India, while small 's' has been used to point to the larger definition of the 'state'.

3. For example, it is the 'criminal-election-politician' alliance that shelters the illegal arms industry against its eradication.
4. Various governments, mostly the democratic ones, have, at one time or the other, taken recourse to the measures described here to curb insurgencies: the American government in Korea (1951–52 & 1953–54); the British in Malaya (1948–55); the French and the American in Indo-China (1950s & 1960s); the French in Algeria (1956–57); the British in Northern Ireland (1970–2005) and in Spain (1970s), Greece (1970s), Columbia (since 1964), Chechnya (since the 1990s), Sri Lanka (1983–2009), Waziristan in Pakistan (since 2004)—the list is long.
5. The diversities in local concerns being so strong, there is no doubt that in the Indian context, the idea of a 'unified' set-up of command and control has failed to function in its true sense. There is, therefore, a case to consider redefining the mechanism for the management of counter-insurgency operations in its totality by the means of what may be termed as a 'joint' headquarters in which all the stakeholding departments and establishments are bound.
6. Most countries prefer to avoid projecting a war-like situation by deploying their regular army; the raising of police units that are under the control of the interior ministry but structured, trained and manned on the lines of the army, is preferred. The examples are: France's *Grandarmerie*, Italy's *Carabinieri*, Germany's *GSG9*, Russia's *Venutrenniye Voiska*, Sri Lanka's *Ranger Force*, the United States Central Investigating Agency's *Special Activities Division*, United Kingdom's *Quick Reaction Alert Force*, etc. In India, there are the *Rashtriya Rifles, the Assam Rifles* and *National Security Guard* which function on the lines of the Indian Army.
7. In 1992, the Assam Government chose to suspend the Army's operations (Operation Rhino I), to control the armed secessionist activities of the 'United Liberation front of Assam' (ULFA); after that, the insurgency was brought to its knees. The *coup de main* was withheld in the hope of bringing about a change of heart among the weakened rebels. The hope was belied while the rebels took the opportunity to recoup. Soon, the Army was obliged to restart the counter-insurgency operations (Operation Rhino II). Similarly, post-Kargil War, Army units were withdrawn from the counter-insurgency grid in the Kashmir Valley to bolster up defences elsewhere. This gave a fillip to the Pakistan-based terrorists and their Indian cohorts. The violence, which had been well controlled, revived and it took another phase of intense operations to repair the damage.
8. Considering the limited wherewithal the Maoists have to undermine the Indian State, and the restraining influence enjoyed by the vociferous groups of the nation's conscience-keepers, there is neither any need, nor the possibility of adopting the draconian 'war model' of tackling the insurgency. Should however, the Maoists choose to seek assistance from inimical external forces, that restraint may undergo revision. The Maoists know this.

4

Terror Financing and the Global CTF Regime

Abhinav Pandya and C.D. Sahay

How do Terrorists Finance their Operations and Supply their Funds?

Finance and movement of funds are crucial to any terrorist organisation. Regular sources of finance are as important as ideology and the ready supply of recruits. The Former US Secretary of State Colin Powell had rightly asserted that "money is the oxygen of terrorism".[1] This paper examines the sources of financing terrorism, movement of terror funds and finally, evaluates the effectiveness of the global Anti-Money Laundering/Countering Terror Finance (AML/CTF) regime. This paper primarily focuses on pan-Islamic terrorist groups like the al-Qaeda (AQ). In the final section, it analyses India's response to terror financing. The analysis brings forth the lacunae in the strategy and proposes a set of recommendations on the establishment of a robust CTF regime. This paper draws heavily upon the research work of Juan Miguel del Cid Gomez, Aimen Dean, Edwina Thompson, Tom Keatinge, Michael Freeman, Moyara Ruchsen, Dr Sanghmitra Sharma, Ramanand Garge and Vivek Chaddha.

Sources of Financing Terror

Terrorist organisations need funding for the following purposes:

1) Specific operations
2) Structural and maintenance costs which include travel costs, recruitment, subsistence, propaganda, communications, training and indoctrination, vehicles, weapons and surveillance material purchasing and charity work (to get social legitimacy—Lashkar-e-Taiba (LeT) and Jamat-ud-Dawa (JuD) do a lot of it).

Affiliate groups of transnational organisations like the AQ generally raise their own funding. These primarily comprise newly radicalised militants who form local cells and have loose and vague linkages with the parent organisations. They neither depend on the centralised authority nor are they directly linked to it. They share fundamental objectives with the AQ but in operational matters and fundraising, are quite independent of the parent organisation.

Fundraisers

Since its beginning, the AQ has used a core of fundraisers to solicit money from a range of donors. Their donors were mostly from the Gulf area, principally Saudi Arabia, but also existed in other parts of the world. Sometimes, the donors are aware of the final destination of their money and sometimes, they are not. The funds also come from the corrupt employees of charitable organisations in the month of Ramazan. Fundraisers often approach the Imams during Ramazan and since the Quran has specific instructions to do *zakat* (money donated for religious works), the fundraisers get a good amount from mosques. Fundraisers have used legitimate charitable organisations, front organisations and even legitimate businesses to provide cover for their activities. The AQ has been able to create a sophisticated financial network with the help of fundraisers throughout the Muslim world and in foreign diasporas. With the spread of awareness about the global Islamic movement through the social media and a rapid increase in the *Tablighi* activity, the zakat donations have increased across the globe, including the hitherto un-approached and remote places like the small villages of North India.[2]

After the UN Security Council sanctions, many original fundraisers like Khalid Sheikh Muhammad, etc. have been arrested. The funds, businesses and assets of known fundraisers have been seized, but still, they continue to operate under other names. In many cases, the AQ has been able to replace fundraisers with yet unknown individuals, organisations and front business ventures, which highlights the loopholes in the existing AML/CTF regime.

Charitable Organisations

Charitable entities enjoy the confidence of the public and have significant access to cash. These also have a transnational presence which enables them to use their infrastructure for national and international transactions. These are subject to limited or no regulation, and no background checks on the employees are made. No initial capital is required to start these and because of their presence in the social sector, they enjoy good linkages among the political, bureaucratic and economic elites of the countries of operation. Further, the Quran facilitates collections as it is mandatory to do zakat (2.5 per cent) of the savings and voluntary *Sadaqah*. Most Muslims pay these contributions to the mosques for humanitarian and social causes, so it is easy to deceptively divert the money to terrorist activities. The AQ often infiltrates the local-level employees of charities to divert funds from humanitarian work towards its own illicit activities. Further, the AQ has its own charitable organisations. Some prominent examples of charitable organisations involved in terror financing include the International Islamic Relief Organization of Jeddah, the Al-Haramain Islamic Foundation of Saudi Arabia and the Revival of Islamic Heritage Society (RIHS) of Kuwait.

The Al-Haramain and its subsidiaries funded the operations of the AQ, Jemmah Islamiyah, Egyptian Islamic Jihad, and LeT. According to a 2009 report of the Pakistani Police, Al-Haramain contributed 15 million dollars to Tehreek-e-Taliban, responsible for suicide attacks and the assassination of Benazir Bhutto. The RIHS has been accused of lending financial and logistic support to the Lashkar, an organisation linked to the AQ and involved in the 2006 train attacks in Mumbai and the 2001 attack on the Indian Parliament (reportedly, the Parliament attack was planned and executed by the Jaish-e-Mohammed (JeM)). The RIHS also funded the Bangladeshi terrorist organisation Jamatul Mujahidin Bangladesh (JMB).[3] Despite the freezing of the accounts of the said charities, these continue to function using the same locations, using bank accounts and resources in the name of third parties.

Offshore Companies

The AQ has used commercial companies to finance itself as well as to transfer funds. Bin Laden used Barakaat, a network of companies, which in 2001, had a foothold in 40 nations operating in telecommunications, money transfer, construction work and cash exchange services from US and Somalia, for cash transfers. Bin Laden had invested in its telecom network. Barakaat also managed, invested and distributed funds for the AQ. These funds were linked with transfers made in the name of Non-Government Organisations (NGOs) like the Al-Haramain and the International Islamic Relief Organization. Another Somalian group, Al-Itihaad Al-Islamiya led terrorist training centres and raised money from its followers in Europe and the Middle East. The said group financed its activities with commercial operations like the export of coal to the Middle East, the provision of transport, security and telecom services, running hawala, agriculture and hotel companies.

The use of fictitious companies and offshore fiduciary companies to protect the identity of the individuals and organisations indulging in terrorist financing present great difficulty for those trying to regulate business transactions. These are companies, funds, entities or business registered in the extra-territorial financial jurisdiction. An example of this are the International Businesses Corporations (IBCs) which are used to create complex financial structures. They do not have to publish accounts. The residents of financial centres can act as fictitious directors or shareholders to hide the real directors or owners. These types of companies are very attractive to the investors as they provide anonymity to conduct illicit activities and safety from official scrutiny.

Drug Trafficking and Common Crime

The Taliban practices extortion at various points in the heroin business in Afghanistan: taxing poppy farmers, drug laboratories and traffickers. The Taliban also taxes the legitimate businesses in Afghanistan to finance its activities. Even though the AQ has diversified its activities to finance jihad, it too indulges in common crime like kidnapping, ransom, contraband and drug trafficking in Mauritania, Mali and Algeria. It makes it difficult to differentiate terrorist financing activities from common criminal activities like money laundering. The terrorists also have links to drug dealers of Latin America. Cocaine is brought to the West African coast and from there, is transported to Europe via Egypt and Libya.[4] Drug trafficking groups operating in North African enclaves of Ceuta and Melilla send profits from hashish smuggling to finance Islamic terrorist groups. In India, in the Malda district (WB), drug trafficking is emerging as a source to finance jihadi terrorism. Drugs are also smuggled by Pakistan's Inter Services intelligence (ISI) into Punjab where the addiction rate is as high as 70 per cent in the males and the revenue is used to finance the proxy war against India.

Moroccan radicals have also specialised in robbery and resale of modern information technology gadgetry like GOS, smart phones and electronic diaries. Spanish investigations revealed that a Salafist group, viz. the 'Group of the Truth', sells designer watches, gold bracelets and emerald necklaces to finance its operations. These days, the Islamic terrorists are also using stolen credit cards to buy GPS systems, night-vision goggles, sleeping bags, knives and telephones from various websites. These items are sent to jihadists in Iraq. Various stolen credit cards and hacked bank accounts were used to buy web-based services in the US and Europe and to create an online global network for the jihadists to exchange information, recruit and plan attacks. Pakistani-origin radicals in Spain have close links with radical cells in the UK which specialise in stealing credit cards. Such cards are cloned and sent to Spain where they are sold by certain business owners for 1000s of Euros, and then used to transfer money to the radical organisations after deducting their commission. The INTERPOL has also confirmed linkages between intellectual property crimes and terrorist financing. Some terrorist groups indulge in production and sale of fake items and divert profits to finance attacks.

Tajheez Al Ghazi

This is the most common method of contributing to the jihad. It is sanctioned by the Quran. It literally means fitting or arming a soldier, which allows those who cannot or will not join the jihad physically to attain a similar honour and reward which a jihadi gets. With the rise of jihadi theaters around the globe, local individuals, clerics and fundraising cells organically emerge to collect the funding for *Tajheez*. The funds are collected in cash and handled by local cells and sympathisers, as a result of which no banking transactions are involved. Since the jihadi terrorist groups are local, there is no requirement for international or national banking transactions. The *Tajheez* relies on thousands of outlets whether they are clerics or coordinators spread over several countries and has no central authority or any organised structure. Thus, it becomes almost impossible to track these activities. Hence, it is very important to make the local level HUMINT (Human Intelligence) effective and sharp. The use of cash and network of clerics, followers, coordinators and contributors, based on goodwill and secrecy, enables the jihadi groups to retain anonymity and thus escape any scrutiny from formalised national and international CTF/AML regimes.

State Sponsorship and Counterfeit Currency

In the cases of India and Afghanistan, the ISI has been sponsoring jihadist groups for nearly four decades now. Some reports have even suggested that the development and military aids which Pakistan received from the US, have also been diverted to radical and extremist activities. In Kashmir, every year, 250 to 300 million US dollars are being pumped in to fund the protests, civil unrest, stone-pelters and terrorist activities through the hawala networks. Further, the ISI has also pumped in huge amounts of fake Indian currency to fund terrorist activities and destabilise the Indian economy through Nepal, Bangladesh and Sri Lanka.

The Movement of Terror Finance

Cash Couriers

Often, when the borders are uncontrolled and the State is constrained in resources to keep a strong vigil over the borders, couriers are used to carry cash across the border. The cash is normally concealed in vehicles, luggage or anything that can hide large amounts. It is the simplest and the oldest way of moving value.[5]

The AQ is known to have used cash couriers before 9/11. According to a 9/11 Commission monograph, the AQ used money changers to transfer US$ 1 million from UAE to Pakistan and then the couriers were used to transfer the funds in cash into Afghanistan. For the 9/11 attack itself, Khalid Sheikh Mohammed delivered US$ 120,000 in cash to Abdul Aziz Ali in Dubai who then used the cash to wire funds to the hijackers in US.[6] The foreign fighters traveling to Iraq to join the AQ in Iraq (AQI) often brought cash with them. Overall, the cash transfers made 70 per cent of the budget of the AQI which highlights the importance of this mechanism for both raising and moving funds into the organisation.[7]

Likewise, the Jemmah Islamiyah also used cash couriers as the primary method of moving funds in the Bali bombings. For terrorist networks, security is an important criterion when using cash couriers. Only trusted personnel are used. Between the Middle East and South Asia, money couriers moved funds using indirect flights between the places of origin and destination, with a large number of couriers and frequent exchanges of money. This method could be more expensive than a simple transaction, but it leaves no trace even if the courier is detained since the origin and final destination of the cash might not even be known to him or her. However, the transfer in this mechanism is a bit slow, and with the tightening global CTF regime, it also requires complex coordination.

Informal Transfer Systems

Several kinds of informal financial networks have been existing before formal banking networks started in various parts of the world, for example, hawala/*Hundi* in the Middle East and South Asia, *Feich'ien* in China, *Phoe Khan* in Thailand and, 'Door-to-Door' in the Philippines. These networks have been functioning traditionally and have strong ethnic ties, operating in places where formal banking systems are poorly developed. They are popular in countries populated by émigrés and refugees, who use this system to remit money to their families in the home countries to avoid paying exorbitant bank charges. These informal global remittance systems are estimated to be worth US$ 500 billion. In the simplest method to settle accounts, the hawaladars wait for the similar value of transactions to move in the other direction, but they also periodically balance their books by money service businesses, smuggling high-value commodities or false trade invoicing transactions to transfer funds.

Before 9/11, the AQ used a group of trusted hawaladars in Pakistan, Dubai and the Middle East to transfer funds. Besides the AQ, the LeT used hawala networks to move funds before their 2000 Red Fort attack in Delhi. Likewise, Dawood Ibrahim (the Karachi-based Indian fugitive), transferred funds with hawala networks before the 1993 Mumbai serial bomb blasts.[8] In India, the hawala networks are extensively used for moving funds for financing terrorist operations. More recently, these networks were used to transfer US$ 4,900 to the would-be Times Square bomber Faisal Shahzad by the handlers in Pakistan. The hawala networks and other informal transfer systems are fast (happen within hours), and relatively anonymous as there are no standard book-keeping methods among the hawaladars, and even if there are, these are very complex to decipher. These methods are cheap as they charge 1–2 per cent as transfer fees and are very convenient, especially for areas which are underserved by banking institutions like Afghanistan, Africa, Iraq and parts of South Asia. Most of the countries have legalised hawala networks as it is easier to police them if they are registered, but many hawaladars continue working illegally without getting registered because of the complex registration process, to keep anonymity (by not providing the identity of the remitters and beneficiaries) and to avoid heavy licensing and registration fees. In the US, informal networks are required to register with the FinCEN. In the UAE and Afghanistan also, state agencies have made efforts to regulate the hawala network, but the adverse topography and weak state institutions make the task difficult.[9] Most of the other countries have not paid enough attention to regulating these informal banking institutions; rather, they have unsuccessfully tried to prohibit such informal institutions.

Money Service Businesses (MSBs)

The Bank Secrecy Act (BSA) defines money service businesses (MSBs) as "currency dealers or exchangers, check cashers, issuers [or redeemers] of traveler's checks, money orders, or stored value cards; and money transmitters".[10] The MSBs generally follow the same regulations and laws as banks and are subject to regulatory audits. However, unlike the formal banking sector, they do not follow the 'Due Diligence Care' (identification, record-keeping and report of suspicious transactions) and 'Know Your Customer' (KYC) procedures very strictly. The banks conduct business with the customers who have accounts in the concerned bank, and those account-holders must provide relevant personal information when they open the account, but the MSBs do not require the customers to have an account. The customers just have to produce a valid ID card.

Most MSBs, in particular the established ones such as Western Union, transfer funds quickly to most locations and they are quite inexpensive for transfers larger than US$ 1000. The omnipresence of MSBs is very helpful. One can find the MSBs mushrooming in the petty towns of Pakistan, and even in India, one witnesses their spread. The risks of detection are very low, especially if the MSB is unregistered. The suspicious transactions can hardly be noticed as they get lost in traffic of numerous legitimate remittances. The specific terrorist operations generally do not require large amounts of money, and the small amounts of transfers are difficult to detect. In 2013, a Federal jury convicted four Somali immigrants of conspiring to fund Al-Shabab, a terrorist group in Somalia.[11] These funds were being sent from the MSBs located in St. Louis, Missouri, and Minneapolis, where there is a sizable Somali immigrant community. The MSBs operate in those regions and communities where there is a huge diaspora community. In the case of India, states like

Kerala have a huge diaspora community of workers in the Middle East who use MSBs. Such MSBs have a fertile ground for operating in places where the Bangladeshi immigrant communities reside.

The AQ made a wide use of MSBs in its financing of the 9/11 attacks. An AQ financer, Ali Abdul Aziz, deposited US$ 120,000 at two MSBs in Dubai: the Wall Street Exchange Center and the UA Exchange Center. Then, the money was transferred to the hijackers' US bank accounts through the MSBs correspondent accounts with the RBC (Royal Bank of Canada) and the Citi Bank, respectively. Even though the MSBs in Dubai required identification, Ali Abdul used aliases and his transactions appeared unremarkable among the millions of MSB transactions flowing out of that area.[12] Before 9/11, the MSBs were not much under the radar of regulatory bodies and could escape detection, but of late, the CTF regime has tightened its hold and monitoring of the activities of the MSBs. These are being subjected to external audits by regulatory agencies and many MSBs in North America are finding it difficult to establish accounts with formal banks which avoid additional risks.[13] In India, a general increase in religiousness or rather radicalisation as a result of proselytising by the *Deobandis* has been accompanied by a mushrooming of the MSBs, mostly functioning between the Middle East and India.

Formal Banking

The formal banking sector includes depository financial institutions (DFIs)—banks, saving and loans and credit unions—which are the sole entities permitted "to engage in the business of receiving deposits and providing access to those deposits" through a payment system of cheques, electronic networks, credit and debit cards and bank-to-bank transfers.[14]

The banks can become a vehicle for criminal financing in myriad ways. Banks which do not ask any questions about the identity and business practices of the customer are the ones most preferred for moving funds for terrorist financing (for example, the Al-Madina Bank of Lebanon). Further, there can be dishonest employees at the lower level or even at the senior level who could facilitate a laundering and movement of funds. Besides, the banks can be used for criminal activity by way of correspondent accounts or payable-thorough-accounts of the correspondent bank, as was the case with HSBC-US.[15] The Lebanese Central Bank was involved in financing the activities of the Hezbollah. The Al-Madina bank facilitated the laundering of funds by Saddam Hussein's regime, conflict diamond dealers, Russian mafia groups and an arms dealer for the Hezbollah.[16] For the 9/11 attack, the AQ used the formal banking sector as its primary method of moving and storing funds. Out of the total of US$ 300,000, US$ 130,000 of the funds that the hijackers used came through bank-to-bank transfers including MSB correspondent account at banks, and the rest was deposited as cash. Once these funds arrived in the US, these were deposited in accounts at the Union Bank of California and the Sun Trust Bank in Florida. The hijackers accessed their accounts with debit cards and ATM cards. The main reason for not being able to detect these funds was their small size (US$47,000 was deposited in the overseas banks; US$ 9600 in the Saudi British Bank in Saudi Arabia and US$ 30,000 in the Standard Chartered Bank branch in Saudi Arabia).

The formal banks are under the strict eye of regulatory agencies and financial intelligence agencies, so there are higher risks of detection. The AQ, however, overcame these drawbacks by utilising bank branches in the UAE and Pakistan, which then lacked advanced regulatory oversight. The formal banking sector is safe and convenient, and large amounts can be easily transferred, but it can be expensive. With the recent emphasis by the global CTF regime on KYC procedures and customer due diligence, it has become riskier for terrorists to operate in the formal banking sector. The formal financial institutions are required to submit Suspicious Activity Reports (SARs) to financial intelligence agencies and other regulatory agencies, but still there are many loopholes as the sheer volume of SARs makes it difficult to scrutinise the huge amount of data. Besides, the Financial Intelligence Agencies' approach towards such activities is to catch money-laundering activities, but a nuanced analysis will show the thin demarcating lines between simple money-laundering activities which are criminal in nature and terror-financing activities. The details will be discussed in the later section.

In a synergy with other mechanisms like offshore companies, the formal financial system can still provide terrorists with enough cover to carry out operations and launder crime money. The sheer volume and the speed at which large sums of money pass through the computer-based international financial system, render the CTF regime ineffective and inefficient. The global AML/CTF regime still needs to catch up with the speed and complexity of the international financial transactions.

International Trade: This system is also vulnerable to abuse by terrorist and criminal organisations. The enormous volume, complexity of transactions and payment methods makes it immensely difficult to detect individual transactions. The custom agencies have limited resources because of which, in the absence of case-specific additional intelligence, it becomes extremely difficult to detect illegal transactions.

International trade is used for hidden transfers of money by techniques like false trade invoicing. It is one of the most involved methods of laundering which make it extremely difficult to detect. This is the reason why it is extensively utilised by organised criminal gangs and terrorist groups to move funds internationally. It is done through over-invoicing or under-invoicing. For example, if a US-based terrorist group purchases some American honey and then exports it to Yemen, it could overprice the shipment by, say, US$ 70,000 without attracting much attention. When the Yemeni importer pays for the overpriced honey, some of that goes into the pocket of the US honey producer. The additional US$ 70,000 goes right into the pocket of the fellow terrorists in the US. This happened in case of the 9/11 attacks. False trade invoicing may not be simple and be very time-consuming, but it can be highly convenient if the group already has front companies to conduct the transactions. Traditionally, the detection has been low, but with the establishment of TTUs (Trade Transparency Units) around the world, the risk of detection is rising. The TTUs assist port security and search for unusually priced transactions. With this method, it may not be possible to catch falsely-invoiced transactions in real time but the paper trail related to the discovered transactions can be immensely helpful in investigating money laundering and terrorism-financing cases.

Because of the involvement of multiple parties and complex payment methods (personal and bank cheques, transfers, payment orders, banking remittances and credits), the observance of due diligence procedures is very difficult. Additionally, international trade is also vulnerable to the use of falsified documents for money laundering, terrorist financing and avoidance of international embargoes. The terrorist organisations use front companies which make it even more difficult to track these transactions. The international trade in services or commodities is used for complex money laundering schemes like the peso exchange black market, hawala and carousel fraud.

High-Value Commodities: Gold is a very reliable form of transportable payment during strife or when fiat currencies are heavily devalued or not convertible. Besides, gold can be smelted easily into any shape and disguised. Its weight, quality and price can be easily determined, and its origin is almost impossible to trace. Additionally, in Middle East and South Asia, it is used in dowries and has a lot of cultural significance. So the movement of large amounts of gold jewellery is not suspected. The AQ and Taliban pay gold to would-be jihadists.

The Hezbollah has a hand in the diamond business as a large Lebanese diaspora involved in the African diamond trade helps the organisation. Douglas Farah of the *Washington Post* brought to light the use of conflict diamonds by the AQ and later, the FBI investigations confirmed it. After the 1998 East African embassy bombings, the Clinton Administration froze more than USD 220 million of assets belonging to the Taliban and the AQ. The organisations needed to convert their assets into something convertible which could not be easily traced or seized. Diamonds fulfill these criteria.[17] Diamonds and gold are easy to carry, hide and convert into cash, but they are difficult to obtain from the source like African mines. Further, they need to be transported by hand which increases the chances of theft or seizure.

Other Methods: These include prepaid phone cards, online payment services, virtual money that is exchanged in the form of gold, silver and other metals and most recently, mobile phone payments.[18] Prepaid cards are frequently used as an alternative to cash. They can easily be obtained with complete anonymity and easily transported. One type of these cards can be used to withdraw money from ATMs throughout the world. There is no requirement of having a bank account and the users do not have answer all the rigorous questions of the bank employee regarding the former's identity. These cards can also be used for shopping. These cards can be topped up by a member of a terrorist group in one country and be used by the other member in another country, thereby making the task of countering terror finance even more challenging. The vulnerability of these cards lies in the way they can be obtained. They can be bought on the internet, by fax and in those shops which do not require identification from customers.

The online payment services like Paytm, PayPal, etc. are used by people without bank accounts or credit cards to make purchases over the internet. The people who use these services can first use their bank accounts, credit cards, electronic transfers or prepaid cards or simply cash to open an account with an online intermediary who will then carry out the payments. It is difficult to know the client's identity if the service provider has no strict requirement for the proof of identity or is willing to accept cash or giro transfers on opening the account.

The payments via mobile phones are another alternative to the use of cash and formal banking systems. The money sender buys a prepaid phone card which is 'topped-up' anonymously with funds which are subsequently transferred to another person's card. This person can withdraw money from an ATM cash-point using a prepaid card. The sender and receiver, both remain anonymous.

But still, the use of these new payment methods (NPMs) remains unpopular with the terrorists. A 2008 report lists several examples of criminals using NPMs like digital currencies (bitcoins), SVC (stored value cards) and mobile payments, but lists only a single example of a terrorist selling a phone card to raise funds.[19] However, in future, with the rapid pace technological advancement in the cyber world and rigid surveillance of regulatory and intelligence agencies over conventional methods, the terrorists are likely to use NPMs.

The Need for a Robust CTF Regime

Funding is crucial to any terrorist organisation. Personnel records seized from the AQI reveal the minutest detail of the management of finances, spreadsheets, receipts, expenditure reports, etc. This information has invaluable importance for the intelligence agencies as the money trail can lead to the core planners and executioners of the terrorist organisations and prevent an attack with a timely warning. So far, the evidence found in the AQ's Manchester manual has indicated that financial prudence is highly important for the AQ.[20] It divides its finances into funds to be invested for monetary gains and the remaining to be used for operations. The funds are divided amongst the members of a cell to avoid detection and protect the sources of financing. Given the crucial importance of terror finance not just for a terrorist organisation but also for the investigative and intelligence agencies, it becomes essential to examine the effectiveness of the CTF apparatus created after 9/11.

The Global CTF Regime

The White House within 100 days of 9/11, hailed the CTF as a great success, reporting that assets of more than 150 terrorists, their organisations and backers had been frozen by the US. 142 countries have issued freezing orders and as a result, more than US$ 33 million in terrorist assets were blocked inside the US, and more than US$ 30 million dollars were blocked outside the US by the global partners under the CTF.[21] The then UK Chancellor, Gordon Brown, hailed the importance and success of the CTF in the following words in his speech to the Chatham House:

> "What the use of fingerprints was in the 19th century, and DNA analysis was to the 20th century, so financial information and forensic accounting have come to be one of today's most powerful investigative and intelligence tools available in the fight against crime and terrorism".

However, the story is not all about an unblemished success. On the one hand, if policy experts like the former Treasury Secretary of US John Snow have praised the global CTF, then on the other hand, AML experts like Dr Demetis have labelled the entire CTF effort as a 'farce.' A study undertaken for a 2011 IMF report has found the global AML/CTF programme disappointing, and poor on compliance and implementation.[22] Despite whatever claims are made about the success of the CTF regime, its true assessment must emanate from Osama bin Laden's October 2001 interview with a Pakistani newspaper in which he said that the AQ's financiers were as "aware of the cracks inside the Western financial system as they are aware of the lines on their hands".[23]

Over the years, a big ideological divide has emerged in the CTF regime between the proponents of the "asset freezers" and the people who want to focus and tighten the movement of terror funds. The question arises that whether the state should focus on the 'cracks in the system' as stated by bin Laden or it should address the root sources of terror finance? The present focus of the CTF regime is in the financial services industry which includes the formal banking sector and The MSB community. The formal financial sector is being subjected to harsh regulatory measures and monitoring which includes an array of practices like customer due diligence and KYC. One of the most ardent critics of the CTF regime is the Somali MSB community based in the UK and the US.[24] It has complained that it is being forced to follow stringent operating procedures and compliance systems under the threat of loss of its bank accounts. For the financial services industry, it is a balancing act between, on the one hand, the blind compliance with regulations for the fear of reputational and financial damage caused in the case of being labelled as non-compliant, and on the other hand, the increasing cost of implementing AML/CTF (250 million pounds in the UK and over USD 1 billion in the US).[25]

Recent trends show that in the case of the MSBs and the NGOs, they defray the costs of compliance with AML/CTF by terminating relationships with even the legitimate clients who are not able to meet the stringent customer due diligence requirements. In other cases, financial service providers try to escape the net of regulatory burdens and costs by closing down 'correspondent banking services' and the provision of banking accounts to the so-called 'politically exposed persons.' Further, increased regulation also leads to higher transaction costs as a result of which the customers prefer cheaper means of moving their money, which means the use of informal and unregulated channels. As a result, it becomes even more difficult to monitor the flow of funds. The existing CTF is leading to financial exclusion which is exactly the reverse of what the CTF regime is trying to achieve, at least in its policy papers.

Further, the formal financial sector is required to submit SARs (Suspicious Activity Reports) or STRs (Suspicious Transaction Reports, in India) to the national authorities. Such reports are submitted by banks and other financial services in bulk. There is no special focus on targeting those activities which are linked to terrorism. When such reports come in bulk, the law enforcement and regulatory authorities either lack the technical expertise to analyse such reports (more so in the case of developing countries) or are too inefficient or corrupt to process the majority of reports that are made. Hence, the follow-up actions are missing on the STR filings.[26]

The Financial Action Task Force (FATF)

After 9/11, it was realised that the transnational nature of terrorist operations and organisations would require a globally coordinated and multilateral effort to counter the menace. Especially with regards to the sources and movement of terror finance, the investigations post-9/11 have revealed the complex and global nature of such activities. Hence, for the development of the CTF regime and the enactment of best practices at a global level, the authorities turned to FATF which was originally established in 1989 at the G7 summit in Paris to lead the fight against criminal money-laundering, especially from drug-trafficking. However, after 9/11, it quickly became the nodal authority for knowledge development and for spreading the best practices in CTF across the world community.

The FATF published its nine special recommendations on terrorist financing, supported the UNCTF (United Nations Counter-Terrorism Committee)'s efforts under UNSCR 1267 and 1373. It included calling upon the countries to criminalise terrorist financing and to freeze the assets accordingly, aim to set up international standards for cooperation, report suspicious transactions and regulate and control the NGOs, wire transfers and cash transfers.

The FATF regime was primarily designed to address the issues of criminal money laundering, particularly from drug trafficking. Although, it has helped in developing an advanced CTF regime but, developing the CTF regime in the armour of the FATF ignores the fundamental differences between criminal money laundering and terrorist financing. Terrorist financing originates from a variety of sources like state sponsorship, individual donations and petty crimes, not just drug trafficking. Secondly, contrary to most money laundering practices, terrorist financing is not done for a profit motive.[27]

Further, philosophical assumptions underlying the FATF's nine recommendations are flawed and need a serious review. the FATF regime assumes that the individual nations have a degree of control which in reality is 'often lacking'; that information is easily available in each nation it visits; that the first world standards apply in the 'Global South'; and that complying with its recommendations is as high a priority for all the countries as it is for the FATF's sponsors. It is often not the case 'where greater existential social, economic and security issues deserve the most urgent attention of the government'. For example, in the case of Somalia and other North African nations, the financial systems, law enforcement machinery and regulatory bodies are simply unequipped, understaffed and unskilled. Even in a fairly functioning democracy like India, it becomes difficult to implement the best practices. In other cases like Saudi Arabia and Kuwait, the WikiLeaks US government cables revealed in 2009 that it was a 'challenge to persuade Saudi officials to treat terrorist-financing emanating from Saudi territory as a strategic priority'.[28] Pakistan has also been reluctant to take action against anti-India terrorist outfits like the LeT and JeM, based in and operating from its territory and under the control of the ISI. Pakistan has failed to take any action even against the money-laundering activities of Dawood Ibrahim. Furthermore, the state supports the non-state actors against India through counterfeit currency. In an article published in *The New Yorker*, Lawrence Wright informs that the Pakistanis have diverted American aid to fund the terrorist activities of the Taliban.

The tightening of the AML/CTF regime has led the banks to withdraw from services deemed too risky, as noted earlier in this paper. Besides, the stringent compliance measures of the CTF regime have led to several unintended consequences, like excluding legitimate businesses and consumers from the financial system.[29]

Over 2.5 billion people in the world do not use a formal banking system because of the cost, travel distance and amount of paperwork.[30] They rely on informal mechanisms like hawala especially for diaspora remittances in hard-to-reach places. Among the Muslim communities, the use of hawala is traditional and very useful in the difficult terrains of Afghanistan and the interiors of Iraq and South Asia (also because the formal financial sector is not well-developed there). In such a milieu, if the AML/CTF regime leads to a further exclusion and marginalisation of the legitimate customers, then it becomes a self-defeating exercise. In such a scenario, the CTF regime will be able to keep track of the small portion of terror financing which operates through formal channels, leaving the unregistered and informal sector vulnerable to abuse. Further, the diaspora communities settled in the Middle East and the Western nations might feel frustrated by their inability to transfer funds and in the process might get radicalised. Hence, broadening financial inclusion must be the key element of a robust CTF regime.

Conclusions

Although the US Treasury Department was graded 'A-' by the Public Discourse Project in 2005[31] for its global CTF efforts, it seems that the AML/CTF regime has been effective only in freezing assets vis-à-vis tracking the movement of terror funds. Further, efforts have been commendable in generating policy papers, best practice guides and recommendations for a globally coordinated action, but the ground-level implementation and compliance has been poor. In assessing FATF compliance, it appears that the countries and financial institutions are more interested in 'box-ticking' rather than the effective implementation of the global standards—some of which are irrelevant or almost impossible to implement given the country's situation and capabilities.[32]

Hence, it can be stated that throughout the early phase of modern jihad during the Soviet invasion of Afghanistan, money was moving freely through formal and informal channels like banking, cash couriers, and hawala, without scrutiny. Post-9/11, with the tightened AML/CTF regime and advances in fraud detection and prevention technology like biometric passports, ID cards and 'chip' and 'pin' technology, the transnational terrorist groups like the AQ have faced increased challenges. However, as the governments and regulatory authorities have become sophisticated in countering terror finance, the terrorist groups have adopted simpler and mostly under-the-radar technologies which can escape detection. Hence, they avoid electronic means of communications like emails and phones between the leaders and ground-level operatives. They are placing more emphasis on human element for the movement and exchange of money, messages and information.

The strict regulatory and governmental pressure on formal and informal financial services sector has led the terrorist organisations to seek unregulated channels for terror financing and the movement of funds. It has further led to negative consequences like financial exclusion and use of new sources like kidnapping-for-ransom, sale of antiquities and sale of oil (in the case of the ISIS). To conclude, it seems reasonable to argue that most of the terror financing takes place outside regulated channels and the increasing checks and regulatory burden on the formal financial sector makes is a wasteful exercise, leading to dissipation of resources in the wrong direction.

Recommendations

Aimen Dean, Edwina Thompson and Tom Keatinge have provided the following recommendations for a robust AML/CTF regime in their article published in *Perspectives on Terrorism*:

1) **Dialogue**: Broadly, the relationship between the financial service providers and those administering the AML/CTF regime has been confrontational. The formal sector finds the pressing demands of the AML/CTF regime very costly to put in practice. Mostly, it complies out of the fear of loss of reputation. The relationship in the case of the informal sector is the worst, characterised by rigidity and

unwillingness on the both the sides. It must be realised that the informal channels like hawala have been operating in almost all parts of the world for centuries. In South Asia, Afghanistan, Iraq, and Africa, they are still very relevant and useful for the common people because of their familiarity, cheap rates, user-friendliness, cultural factors, illiteracy and lack of banking facilities. Therefore, multilateral institutions and national authorities need to engage them in a constructive dialogue to chisel an effective regulatory regime. Openness and dialogue will result in a better awareness and understanding of the informal channels, and better capabilities to formalise their activities. The regulatory authority's interaction with such informal actors might supply them with the necessary intelligence and critical cooperation required to check the terror finance without annoying the legitimate customers of such informal sectors. In fragile countries like Somalia, where there is a lack of sufficiently developed formal banking sector, such informal channels play an important role for diaspora remittances. When the attitude or multilateral institutions is confrontational and inflexible, then the terrorist organisations like Al-Shabaab get an opportunity to control the nuts and bolts of such informal services, and in the process, gain goodwill among the local residents. Hence a constructive dialogue is necessary, and the approach should be to bring such unchartered terrains of money movement under some kind of engagement process or surveillance. Secondly, better information-sharing is also needed between the regulators and the banks, and the intelligence should be shared. The bank staff do not have sufficient understanding of the phenomenon of terror finance. Therefore, the STR filings are vague, general and bulky. They need better guidance and support. Given the right guidance and collaborative approach, the financial industry can provide higher quality and valuable data to intelligence authorities. Any sound and effective CTF regime must develop this connection on collaborative lines.

2) **FATF Reform:** In 2011, the IMF characterised the FATF's assessment policy as comprehensive, inflexible and general, without reflecting the local realities and requirements of the individual countries. The best practices and compliance model imposed by the FATF on businesses and nations seem like more of the paperwork which is cumbersome, complicated and costly. The FATF must take a more

nuanced approach which takes into account the local requirements of the individual countries shaped by their specific cultural, social and political factors. For instance, imposing the idea of cashless economy in a country like Afghanistan is certainly going to be counterproductive.

3) **International Cooperation**: A 2010 study of the FATF mutual evaluation data by the AML/CTF group revealed that 80 per cent of the countries were not meeting the most basic standards, i.e. ratification and implementation of the UN instruments and a freezing and confiscation of terrorist assets. This is due to a range of factors like lack of technical capability where identity verification is not possible, and the lack of cooperation between ministries and political parties that makes the passing of laws difficult. But the most important reason for most of the nations is that the relevance of the CTF for them is unclear, and it is seen as a Western-sponsored initiative. Some countries have not shown enough enthusiasm to control terrorist organisations because of their internal dynamics, ideological affinities and the social-political clout of extremist and terrorist organisations in their domestic politics. Therefore, strong and systematic efforts are needed to secure international political support. The sponsors of international CTF regime must demonstrate that their efforts are effective in reducing crime and terrorism. The non-complaint states must be made to realise that the CTF efforts are as important as the other existential social and security issues for stability and peaceful economic development.
4) **Financial Inclusion**: A systematic and apolitical effort is needed to devise ways for cost-effective and efficient ways of transferring funds to the poorest people who lack access to banking and more formalised channels. A focused effort is needed to address the issues of diaspora remittances and humanitarian aid. Most of the diaspora remittances are genuine, and the zakat donations are also for humanitarian objectives. Hence an effort is needed to develop a nuanced CTF regime which can isolate the cases of terrorism from genuine ones and even develop an effective alternative for the genuine cases of transfer of funds. An effort is also needed to bring the marginalised sections from traditional and informal fund transfer systems into the ambit of modern and formal systems like banking sector and 'mobile money.'

5) **Cashless Systems:** The monitoring and policing of cash couriers, transfer of high-value items like diamonds and gold and use of charitable services for health and welfare by the terrorist organisations is a very difficult task and in some situations, almost impossible. Once cash leaves the bank counter, it is very difficult to track its movement effectively. The clandestine activities of charities that bank with the formal sector are difficult to detect. A charity might use the cash for helping jihadis or building clinics for jihadis in a deceptive manner, under the cover of its legitimate operations. Hence, money transfer companies working with diaspora remittances must convert their operations to cashless systems. This would involve collaboration with telecommunication companies at global and national levels. Though it might be an abstract idea to implement the perfect cashless financial system, even if the larger cash flows are prevented, it can be immensely helpful in checking the terror-financing activity.
6) **Prevent Terrorism at the Source:** Post-9/11, many efforts have been made to target the legitimate and illegitimate funding of terrorists by closing NGOs, Informal Value Transfer Systems (IVTS) and implementing UN and FATF resolutions and best practices, but still the CTF regime has not been able to starve the terrorists of funding due to their deceptive and dispersed style of operations. Furthermore, there are thousands of zakat and *Tajheez* coordinators, individual donors and facilitators. It is not possible to trace and arrest all of them and even if they are arrested, new ones will emerge.

With the tightening of the CTF regime, even the terrorists have moved to criminal fundraising methods like kidnapping, smuggling, bank robbery, cyber fraud and new payment technologies that remain outside the scrutiny of regulators. Nowadays, with spread of jihad at the grass-roots level, the model and modus operandi of the terrorist operations have changed. There is no central command and control structure. All one finds is a loosely connected web of the terrorist network. The terrorists have moved to domestic sources of funding, thus bypassing the risk of international transfers and complex processes. Locally based organisations, working with domestic funding sources make the entire operations highly cost effective. The new phenomenon of lone-wolf terrorism hardly requires any large-scale planning of terrorist operations, collection and movement of terror funds. The said phenomenon presents a very serious challenge to the entire counter-terror apparatus.

Hence to starve the terrorists of funding, the authorities need to focus on the source i.e. donors need to be dissuaded/prevented from providing their support. Therefore, strong steps must be taken to check the sympathetic ideology which exists in society for jihadi causes or even extremist ideas. Some sects preach a puritanical version of faith which might not be directly related to terrorist operations, but it lays the fertile bed for radicalisation and jihadi terrorism. Donations to such puritanical schools must be checked, and their networks busted. Further, oppressive regimes, denial of basic rights, social misery, and squalor in society also generate sympathy for such ideological groups and charities. Poor economic conditions provide the fertile ground for dual-use charities to operate and recruit cadres for jihadi causes without detection. Therefore, efforts must be taken for providing satisfying and fulfilling livelihood sources, economic development, educational development and representative governments. One of the best ways to 'check at the source' is to generate awareness among the donors that their money might be financing terrorist operations. The common people must be encouraged to explore and find out about the charities and coordinators with hidden jihadist sympathies.

Since 9/11, terrorist organisations and terrorist operations have evolved in structure, operations and financing activities. However, the CTF strategy has remained stagnated. A lot has been done to track the formal sector by international agreements, monitoring and the spread of best practices. But the compliance remains poor at the ground level. And the efforts so far have covered a very small part of terror funding lying in the formal sector and that too not without unintended negative consequences like financial exclusion as discussed earlier in the paper.

Hence to conclude, the CTF strategy needs a serious rethinking and intensive research. It must reflect the changes that the terrorist organisations have undergone. The CTF regime must be developed in a nuanced manner rather than as a comprehensive approach. An area, culture and country-specific approach must be adopted for establishing a robust CTF regime. Last but not the least, without goal-setting, benchmarking and continuous evaluation at the local, national and international levels, the CTF regime will not be able to zero-in on the right targets and generate the desired objectives.

India: Evaluation of the CTF Regime and Recommendations

The investigating agencies and research analysts have found that the Indian scenario is characterised by a distinct linkage between crime and money laundering in terror financing. It is also evident that a three-stage progression of terror financing—state-sponsored, privatised and globalised financing of terrorism—has been in operation in promoting and sustaining terrorism in India. In financing terror groups operating in India, Pakistan has used the trinity network of globalisation, privatisation and criminal activities in tandem.[33] Because of the said intricacies, combating terror finance has become a daunting challenge for India. Based on its long experience of dealing with terror financing, India has identified the following major sources of terror financing: funds/resources flowing from organisations outside India including foreign Non-Profit Organisations/NGOs; funds provided by state entities (read ISI); induction of counterfeit currency and funds generated through a variety of criminal activities such as drug trafficking and extortion (*AGP*, June 25, 2010).

Since the publication of the Mutual Evaluation Report on June 24, 2010, India has been reporting to the FATF on a regular basis on the progress made in the implementation of its Action Plan to strengthen India's counter-financing and money-laundering system. India has particularly focused its attention on:[34]

- Amending nearly all of the technical deficiencies identified with respect to the criminalisation of money laundering and terror financing.
- 'Substantially addressing' the technical deficiencies related to customer due diligence and other preventive measures.
- Augmenting its outreach programme to provide guidance to the financial sector on suspicious transaction-reporting obligations and engaging in extensive compliance monitoring and
- Bringing several of the Designated Non-Financial Businesses and Professions within the scope of anti-money laundering and countering terror financing measures.

In its 2013 Plenary Meeting, the FATF decided that India had reached a 'satisfactory level' of compliance with all the core and key recommendations and could be removed from the regular follow-up process. It pointed out that though India had stepped up investigation into the cases of money laundering and terror funding, yet the cases of conviction in such cases has remained low.[35] The Report said that according to the update provided in May 2013, the number of money-laundering investigations increased from

798 on December 31, 2009 to 1561 on April 30, 2013. This shows that the number of investigations conducted had increased consistently. On prosecutions, the FATF noted that they had increased from 6 on December 31, 2009 to 36 on March 31, 2011. However, there was only a marginal increase from November 30, 2011 (37) to 42 on November 30, 2012. The number of persons convicted for terror financing had remained low—namely, five in total between 2006 and March 2013.[36]

In its report on 'Terrorist Financing,' the FATF Report to the G20 leaders, released in November 2015, the FATF revealed that India had seized assets worth 3 lakh euros (over 2.12 crore INR) of 37 entities, till August 2015.[37] Thus, India's compliance with global standards in countering money laundering and terror funding is on the right track. However, the gaps need to be addressed and worked upon.

Demonetisation and Its Effects on Terror Financing

The recent demonetisation move by the Government of India (November 8, 2016) is expected to make a major dent in terror financing. Terror financing in India is mostly done thorough hawala, couriers and counterfeit currency. In all these channels, cash is used. And, 86 per cent of India's cash was in the denominations of INR 500 and INR 1000, which have been demonetised.

The Indian Statistical Institute, Kolkata, undertook a study on the behalf of the National Investigation Agency, which says that INR 70 crore fake notes had been pumped into the economy every year. 90 per cent of the fake notes were routed into India through Bangladesh (Nepal *and even Sri Lanka*). They were sent from Pakistan by sea and air routes. The security features of INR 500 and INR 1000 were compromised. The suppliers of raw currency, ink, silver thread are the same for India and Pakistan. India has tried to convince these suppliers based in UK, Germany and US to stop the sales to Pakistan but was unable to do so. With demonetisation, there will be a major dent on counterfeit currency. However, it may be so for some time, i.e. until Pakistan is able to create the duplicate copies of the new notes. Though it is being claimed that the new notes have better security features, but still, in this game, nothing can be 100 per cent-immune. In order to sustain the efforts, enhanced detection measures must be put in place in public sector banks and forensic expertise to understand the technology in faking currency.

The demonetisation move will have its impact on starving the terrorists of their funding sources, but the impact must not be exaggerated. The financing of small-scale terrorist operations will not be affected that much as such operations do not require large amounts of money. The recent attacks in Uri, Pathankot and Nagrota signal a shift in the strategy. Now, the terrorists have resorted to sending small fidayeen groups for quick and lethal attacks on military installations. Such attacks are precise and have an element of surprise. They do not require huge funding. For such attacks requiring small sums of money, the terrorists might resort to formal financial channels like banks and MSBs after the demonetisation.

Operational financing of terrorism will be hurt where financing requires huge sums of money to run the terrorist organisations like Hizbul in Kashmir. It includes funds for logistics, spread of ideology and other structural costs like payments to the cadres and other facilitators including the 'retainer ship' money to the separatist leaders. For these, 'donation' funds were collected in Pakistan and sent to India through the hawala networks, which mostly relied on the old 500 and 1000 INR notes. After demonetisation, those notes are nothing but just a piece of paper and therefore, funding public unrest, students' protests and Intifada stone throwers in Kashmir, are already witnessing a drastic reduction in incidents of protests and unrests, which might not be a coincidence in a strict statistical sense. Further, one can also witness that the terrorists starved of funds, are resorting to new strategies like looting banks, etc.

Large amounts of terror funds are temporarily parked in property, gems and jewellery. Hence, these areas need to be tackled. After demonetisation, the terrorists may resort more to the use of formal channels like banking, digital economy and international trade for financing and the movement of funds. Hence, in the long run, a multipronged strategy is needed but, at least in the short run, demonetisation has dealt a major blow to terror financing and Naxalite funding.

Recommendations Specific to India

Identifying Suspicious Transactions: In a majority of the countries, the current legislative framework for preventing the use of the financial system for terrorist activities is based on the OECD's 48 recommendations. The current CTF regime is modelled on anti-money laundering measures. Though there is a lot of overlapping between the terror financing and money-laundering activities, there are some fundamental differences which must be taken into account. In money laundering, criminal elements need to deposit large amounts of money into the financial system whereas, in financial transactions related to terrorism, the amount of money used is considerably less and is usually consistent with the client's declared profile, which makes it almost impossible to detect.

The financial sector uses several IT programs to detect suspicious transactions of the customers. Each client is given a specific profile that describes 'expected usual practice' of the said client which includes the number of transactions and the amounts involved that are expected to take place over a certain period with a reasonable margin of deviation from the norm. When the client's transactions cross the said margin, the IT program issues an alert. But on closer scrutiny, many of such transactions are found to be 'false positives.' Submitting a large number of 'false positives' for further investigation takes up time and money. Hence to avoid such a situation, it is recommended to maintain the current profile of the clients, consider adequate tolerance ratios for each type of transaction, establish an adequate frequency for review in accordance with the risk presented and the context of conditions of the time and the market must be factored in as it may affect the operations being carried out.

1) India must develop a Terrorist Financing Tracking Program (TFTP) like the US's arrangement with the Belgium-based company, SWIFT (Society for World Wide Inter-Bank Financial Telecommunication). It operates a worldwide messaging system used to transmit financial transaction information—seeking information on suspected international terrorists or their networks. It helps in a better coordination of the CTF efforts at the global level. However, while developing such tracking systems, due care must be given to respect and protect the privacy of the customers.
2) India must also work towards developing a set of indicators for identifying terror funding. Currently, most of the STR filings are the cases of general money laundering crimes. These are filed on the basis of KYC practices. Better implementation and strict compliance of the KYC practices is desired.
3) The financial intelligence units get such data in bulk and no follow-up action is taken. At this stage, it is necessary to have a nuanced

approach towards terrorism and develop a set of indicators which have a clear focus on terrorism-related cases. Finance professionals may not have a very strong understanding of terrorism issues. Therefore, when such indicators are developed, people specialising in terrorism in general and terror finance in particular, must be roped in. To equip the finance professionals with skills and understanding to detect terrorism-related cases, capacity-building initiatives like training programmes, seminars and interactive sessions with terror finance experts must be organised for financial institutions and finance professionals.

4) The Financial Intelligence Units are generally manned with people from revenue/customs services or administrative services. Terror finance is an altogether different and specialised field. Unless one has a strong background in geopolitics/international relations, terrorism issues and terror financing, one cannot detect such cases of terrorism. Therefore, people with an intelligence, diplomatic and security background or a sound understanding of special traits of flow of terror funds, must be hired. With this background as the base, they must have a strong expertise in finance in general and terror finance in particular.

   In India, one can witness the fast spread of some fundamentalist schools like the Deobandis even in the remotest parts of the country. In our interactions with inhabitants of the remote and inaccessible tribal villages of southern Rajasthan like Karawada, Peeth, etc. (Dungarpur, Rajasthan), we came across the spread of Deobandi doctrines which preach more orthodox and puritanical versions which are quite contrary to what people have been following traditionally. As a result of this missionary activity and religious awareness, there is a huge increase in zakat donations. One can see lavish mosques being built with unknown and undocumented sources of funding. There are lots of preachers and *Tajheez* coordinators working among the populace. The state intelligence bodies like CID and local IB units have neither the trained and skilled intelligence professionals nor the technical know-how and facilities to track and infiltrate such networks. We had interactions with district police officials and administrative officers. Most of them did not possess the elementary knowledge of concepts like zakat, Deobandis, Barelvis, *Tajheez*, etc.

5) Hence, the authorities need to take special steps to build the capacity of state intelligence bodies and law enforcement agencies because to

track such activities in a country like India, HUMINT plays a quintessential role. First and foremost, the IPS and state-level police officers and administrative officers must be imparted with some conceptual training in terrorism-related issues like terror financing, zakat and *Tajheez* donations, grass-roots level jihadi networks and the ideology which works underneath. Further, they must also be made aware of the UN resolutions against terrorism, the global AML/CTF regime and the sanctions list of Security Council. Then they must keep track of such religious activities like the visits of religious leaders, zakat collections, preaching, etc., by building good relations and networks with the community leaders at the local level.

6) In India, with schemes like the Jan Dhan, a breakthrough has been achieved in the area of financial inclusion. However, there is a risk of Jan Dhan-like banking schemes or other development schemes involving cash transfers being used for terror financing. The cost of individual terrorist operations is very small as discussed earlier in this paper. Hence, if several Jan Dhan accounts of people belonging to low economic strata are used for any such transfers or deposits, it will be difficult to detect.
7) Further, charities operate among the poorer sections of the minority community. There is a possibility of luring people from the lower economic strata to use their bank accounts for terrorist activities either by using several bank accounts to transfer large sums in parts or even for zakat with the covert intentions of assisting terrorist activities. Hence, to counter this, active intelligence is needed round the year at the grass-roots level where the charities operate to gather information about the *Tajheez* coordinators and the people involved.
8) Special focus must be given to immigrant communities in India. Keeping track of the missionary activity in their areas and the religious scholars and people visiting their localities, in general, is a must. The financial information leaves a trail which can be immensely helpful in preventing the terrorist incidents not just in India but all over the world. STRATFOR, a global intelligence portal, has informed that the locally based immigrant communities and the poorer sections of society can be used to help organisations like the AQ with logistics, finance and for building sleeper cells. Hence, robust intelligence and surveillance can nip horrific terrorist incidents right in the bud.
9) There is a need for developing tools to measure radicalisation. The

National Radicalization Index is one such tool that can be developed with several indicators as its components. The detailed description of the tool is beyond the scope of this paper. But such a tool will help in focusing on the areas where radicalisation is higher, as there might be greater flows of terror funds from such areas.

10) There is an urgent need to effectively curb hawala networks. For this, it is imperative to get timely intelligence and understand their style of functioning. Given the fact that they have strong roots in India's cultural and economic fabric, it is better to engage them and explore their utility in controlling terror finance. However, simultaneously, they must be regulated or brought under some kind of surveillance or formalisation through a licensing system on the pattern of US and Afghanistan.

11) Further, continuous research is needed in the field of terror finance. The diverse aspects of terror funding like the role of the unorganised *Tajheez* sector, new payment methods, use of illicit trade in high-value and low-value goods, extortion money, etc., must be thoroughly investigated and new research material and reports generated. Such knowledge creation will be immensely helpful in charting out the innovative strategy to combat terror financing, in response to the new methods and sources of terror finance adopted by the terrorist organisations. Organisations like the AQ are very strict about book-keeping and finance. Financial activity leaves a trail. Hence, the expertise in forensic accounting combined with other relevant intelligence inputs can prevent several terrorist incidents from happening.

12) Further, there must be systematic efforts to understand the evolving terrorist operating methods, strategy and their area-specific characteristics and then, intelligence-led indicators must be developed to target the cases of terror financing. There must be regular dialogue between the private and public sectors and the non-profit sector to develop a more risk-based focus and generate better cooperation from the prominent stakeholders.

13) Adequate efforts are needed to protect the charities engaged in real humanitarian work from abuse by terrorist organisations. Charities are an important link in the entire terror finance apparatus. These constitute both a source and a channel for the movement of funds. But the use of charities for terror financing can be in a very deceptive

and clandestine manner. Hence, a blanket ban on the activities of all charities or a mass closure of their accounts is not advisable because most of them are engaged in humanitarian work and in providing the necessary relief and aid. If charities face harsh repression, it prepares ground for further radicalisation. Hence a cautious approach is needed. A sustained and constructive engagement with the charities is called for to get over this problem. A dialogue between the private sector, charities, regulatory authorities, intelligence agencies and bank authorities can help in formulating a strategy to prevent the use of the charities for terrorist activities and establish a risk-based AML/ CTF regime. For this, technical expertise can be obtained from the best practices adopted by the US Treasury Department. The charities can have a presence in the small and remote towns of northern India or, in Kerala, in the form of numerous *Tajheez* coordinators, collectors or preachers, and they can also have their operations in international capitals like Riyadh, New York City, Washington DC, Madrid and London. In the light of their widespread, transnational, complicated and deceptive nature of operations, it is necessary to have a proactive approach in intelligence collection and surveillance. There must be round-the-year watch and surveillance of suspicious charities and there has to be a coordination that can help in connecting the dots while studying their operations in small remote towns and the world capitals. The information derived from such proactive and pre-emptive intelligence and surveillance activities must be shared with the private sector and other donors to such charities to dissuade the donors from making grants to such charities.

14) In our review of the literature on terror financing in India, we have come across a generalist approach characterising the research work on terror financing. However, the financial profile of every terrorist organisation is different. Groups involved in the Naga insurgency, Naxalite violence or separatism in the North-East may be very different from transnational Islamic extremist groups in their style of operations, organisational culture and financing. Hence, a nuanced and focused approach is needed which goes into the specifics of a terrorist organisation and is based on the specialisation and expertise in different strains of terrorist activity.

15) India has adopted its model of combating terror finance based on its own requirements and conditions, as indeed it should be. However,

the multiplicity of bodies dealing with the said issue at different levels, generates a degree of lack of coordination and cooperation. Currently, there are multiple bodies dealing with the issues of money laundering, both or in some cases, simply money laundering. Some of them are as follows: (a) Financial Intelligence Unit and FATF Cell (Ministry of Finance) (b) RBI (c) special cell called Combating Financing of Terrorism (CFT) Cell (Ministry of Home Affairs)—to name a few. Though it may not be possible to achieve a complete unification of all the tasks performed by all such entities under one body, it is certainly advisable to create one nodal body on the lines of the US Office of Financial Intelligence and Terror Finance, to coordinate all such activities conducted to combat terror finance. Because of different intelligence bodies and ministries dealing with the issue, unnecessary turf wars and frictions are created between the bureaucracies of different entities. There is a tendency to hide the sources of information gathered, and this makes it immensely difficult to connect the dots in the investigations. Hence for coordinated action, a nodal body with comprehensive powers and functions, and personnel with a background in forensic accounting, security affairs and intelligence affairs and police services on the lines of the proposed National Counter Terrorism Center (NCTC), should be created.

16) Similarly, in the legal domain also, there are multiple acts like the Unlawful Activities Prevention Act (UAPA 1967), the Prevention of Money Laundering Act (PMLA 2002), Foreign Contribution Regulation Act (FCRA 1976), the Narcotics Drug and Psychotropic Substances Act (NDPS 1985) and the Foreign Exchange Management Act (FEMA 1999) that come into play while dealing with the acts of terrorism including terror financing. While the specific laws have their relevance and cannot be totally annulled, as far as acts of terror, including terror financing, go, it would be desirable to merge the provisions into a single all-encompassing national law to cover all aspects of terror with an all-India applicability on the lines of the US Patriot Act, duly modified to suit the conditions and special requirements of India. It must deal with the diverse aspects of terrorism including terror financing and lay a robust legal framework for dealing with terrorism. This is not going to be easy, since evolving an across-the-board national consensus on such matters, in the given political scenario, will take time and a huge deal of effort.

17) There is also a need for improving the prosecution rates in money laundering, terror financing and drug trafficking cases. The FATF has also, in its report on India, as mentioned in the earlier part of this paper, highlighted the low prosecution rates. The State needs to create a smart and efficient cadre of prosecution lawyers in such matters. Secondly, for an efficient delivery of justice and to prevent the decay of crucial evidence, speedy trial is needed. In criminal trials, jurisprudential principles of criminology like 'burden of proof' and 'to prove guilt beyond reasonable doubt', etc., often favour the accused. But in cases involving terror financing, money laundering and crimes against the State, there should be some exceptions to the said rules and the cases of prosecution side should be examined with the presumption of faith.
18) The Emerging Terror Financing Risks (ETFRs) Report (2015) of FATF highlighted that various social media platforms are today being used by terrorists for fundraising campaigns. A regular watch of terrorist financing, recruitment and propaganda activities is a must. Further, it is advised to infiltrate networks using encrypted services. Such networks are widespread in reach, but their consequences regarding raising financing and supplying new recruits are localised, so here also, the role of HUMINT in infiltrating them at the local level is highly important.
19) Better information-sharing between the Centre and the states on the issues of terror finance, threat assessment and best practices is desirable. Special capacity-building programmes for state-level police and intelligence officers must be organised to train them in the international best practices. Similar programmes for the financial services sector must be organised to generate awareness them among them on the issues of terror finance and FATF recommendations to combat terror finance.
20) In the South Asian region, effective institutional mechanisms are missing for the purpose of well-coordinated multilateral efforts. Since SAARC members have already accepted the International Convention for the Suppression of the Financing of Terrorism of 1999 and UNSCR 1267, India must take a strong initiative in developing such multilateral mechanisms in South Asia to combat terror financing. India can initiate the regional database by using the Colombo-based dormant Terrorist Offences Monitoring Desk and integrate the

information related to terror financing, money laundering and suspicious transactions from the Financial Intelligence Units (FIUs) of the member states.[38] Further, such institutions can also be the conduit for putting a diplomatic pressure on Pakistan to stop sponsoring terrorist groups against India.

21) In order to bring transparency in receipt and use of foreign donations, random checks can be undertaken to verify the last five years' transactions of select NGOs having dubious records. Charitable organisations with links to Saudi Arabia, Pakistan and Middle Eastern countries raise funds before Eid prayers and other religious festivals. Efforts must focus on such organisations regarding prior research and the consequent strategy and action for combating terror financing. Finally, the timely monitoring and evaluation of the effectiveness of all the existing systems and of the new ones proposed or being established, on a regular basis, is not only desirable but rather, inescapable. India can no longer afford to continue to exist in a 'reactive' mode: it must, in the field of terror financing and related matters, be seen as proactive.

The Authors

C.D. Sahay is a Dean, the Centre for Neighbourhood Studies and Internal Security Studies, at the Vivekananda International Foundation, New Delhi. He is a Former Secretary (Research and Analysis Wing), Cabinet Secretariat.

Abhinav Pandya, PhD, is a public relations, economics and policy consultant. He is also a freelance journalist.

*

END NOTES

1. Ramanand Garge, 'Combating Financing of Terrorism; An Indian Perspective', Vivekananda Foundation, Oct. 2015.
2. Personal interactions of the authors with the intelligence officials and residents.
3. Juan Miguel Cid del Gomez, 'A Financial Profile of Al-Qaeda and its Affiliates, *Perspectives on Terrorism*, p. 9.
4. 'Drug Seizures in West Africa prompt Fears of Terrorist Links', *The Observer*, 29/11/2009.
5. Nikos Passas, 'Informal Value Transfer Systems, Terrorism and Money Laundering', a report to the *National Institute of Justice*, 2003, p. 30.
6. John Roth, Douglas Greenburg and Serena Wille, 'National Commission on Terrorist Attacks upon the United States: Monograph on Terrorist Financing', p. 26 and p. 134.
7. Jacob Shapiro, 'Bureaucratic Terrorists: Al-Qaida in Iraq's Management and Finances', in

Bomber, Bank Accounts, & Bleedout, Brian Fishman (ed.), Combating Terrorism Center at West Point, p. 73.

8. Matteo Vaccani, 'Alternative Remittance Systems and Terrorism Financing', *World Bank Working Paper*, No. 180, 2010, p. 7.
9. Michael Freeman and Moyara Ruehsen, 'Terrorism Financing Methods: An Overview', *Perspectives on Terrorism.*
10. 'U.S. Money Laundering Threat Assessment', p. 7.
11. "San Diego Jury convicts Four Somali Immigrants of providing Support to Foreign Terrorists: Defendants sent Money to Al-Shabaab in Somalia', Office of the United States Attorney, Southern District of California (22 February 2013).
12. Freeman and Ruehsen, op. cit.
13. Ibid.
14. "U.S. Money Laundering Threat Assessment," p. 1.
15. Freeman and Ruehsen, op. cit.
16. Mitchell Prothero, 'Beirut Bombshell', *Fortune* (4 May 2006).
17. Moyara Ruehsen, 'Diamonds are a Terrorist's Best Friend', www.moneylaundering.com, 2005.
18. See FATF, 'Trade Based Money Maunder in. Paris', 2006.
19. Freeman and Ruehsen, op. cit., p. 21.
20. Fishman, Brian (ed.), *Bombers, Bank Accounts, and Bleedout*, Harmony Project (New York: CTC West Point).
21. White House, 'Fact Sheet on Terrorism', 2001.
22. IMF, 'Anti-Money Laundering and Combating the Finance of Terrorism - Report on the Review of Effectiveness Program', 2011.
23. Aimen Dean, Edwina Thompson and Tom Keatinge, 'Draining the Ocean to Catch one Type of Fish: Evaluating the Effectiveness of the Global Counter-Terrorism Financing Regime'.
24. Ibid.
25. Ibid.
26. Ibid.
27. Ibid.
28. Ibid.
29. FATF, 'Anti-Money Laundering and Terrorist-Financing Measures and Financial Inclusion', 2013.
30. World Bank, 'Three Quarters of the World's Poor are "Unbanked"', 2012.
31. Richard Falkenrath, '9/11 Commission: A Review of Second Act', 2005.
32. Aimen Dean et al., op.cit.
33. Garge,op. cit.
34. http://www.icwa.in/pdfs/IB/2014/FinancialActionTaskForceIB09082016.pdf
35. 8th Follow-Up Report Mutual Evaluation of India, FATF, June 2013, http://www.fatfgafi.org/media/fatf/documents/reports/mer/India_FUR8_2013.pdf accessed July 20, 2016
36. http://www.icwa.in/pdfs/IB/2014/FinancialActionTaskForceIB09082016.pdf
37. Ibid.
38. Garge, op. cit.

5

Taxation and Extortion: A Major Source of Militant Economy in North-East India

Brigadier Sushil Kumar Sharma

In India's North-East, most of the "UGs" or underground militant groups employ a taxation system that is at times not just unfair but even spurious, for they give nothing in return in terms of basic services like water, electricity or roads, except for ensuring that the person paying or his family is not harmed or targeted by any militant group. There is no guarantee of that either. A 'tax' structure instituted by the undergrounds, particularly in Nagaland, Manipur, Assam, Tripura and parts of Meghalaya, has existed for decades. In Manipur, officials are expected to pay up to 25 per cent of their annual income and have no option but to oblige. There is a not-so-subtle irony here; the "tribal" states like Nagaland, Mizoram and Meghalaya as well as the hills of Manipur, which is the focus of this study, are not taxed by the Government of India; however, they pay heavier taxes to the illegal set-up devised by the armed groups.[1] The parallel state of economy thus created is a leading cause of worry, both for the Government and the populace. This study is aimed at presenting the methodology of 'extortion' by the insurgent groups in Manipur, its impact and recommends measures to combat the menace.

Empirical Findings

Taxation and extortion are the two major source of fund generation by the Underground Groups in the insurgency-affected areas. Rakhee Bhattacharya, Associate Professor of North East Studies at JNU, New Delhi, observes in her study on the taxation strategy of the militants in the North-Eastern states that "the modus operandi of the militants to collect funds is by sending demand notes of the amount of money followed by request notes to the targeted persons, specifying the time and place of collection". For those who refuse, the threats are clear: pay or die. The United Liberation Front of Asom (ULFA) has, over the years, collected vast amounts of money from tea gardens. Shopkeepers too are required to pay to several insurgent groups. Similarly, all truck and bus drivers whose vehicles ply on any road, be it a state's remote roads or the main highways, have to pay illegal road taxes. In Manipur, more than a dozen rebel groups are active, each claiming to represent the interests of one ethnic group or another. In several states, smuggling across the Myanmar border is rampant and the illicit cross-border trade is duly taxed by the insurgents. To illustrate how well-organised these practices are, Bhattacharya reproduces a printed and numbered receipt from the "Revenue and Tax Department" of the "Government of Twipra Kingdom"—the insurgents' name for the state of Tripura that borders Bangladesh. The income from all these activities is used to pay for arms and other necessities for the rebel armies—and to support the leaders' lavish lifestyles.

In 2007–2008, the National Socialist Council of Nagalim's Isak–Muivah faction (NSCN-IM), a militant group fighting for Naga independence, collected 630 million rupees, or US$ 14.6 million, in "taxes" and other "revenues", according to Bhattacharya's research. To sustain armed insurgencies, especially those that do not receive support from foreign governments, is expensive. Rebels in southern Thailand are known to collect money from the 200,000–300,000 strong migrant work force of southern Thai Muslims across the border in northern Malaysia. Resources allocated by the government directly or indirectly, fund the insurgent groups 'through a regime of collusion, extortion and intimidation', thus facilitating a sponsoring of the uprising. According to Bhattacharya, the insurgent economy accounted for 22.3 per cent of the region's GDP in 2004. The funding methods are as follows: donations, foreign aids, extortion/tax, kidnapping/looting and siphoning off of the government development funds.[2]

The "rebel groups have enforced their own 'Land Revenue and Trading Act,' 'Household Tax' and around 17 different kinds of taxes. The rebels tax those who deal in forest produce and bamboos, they tax shops and businesses, they impose taxes on houses, farms and transport plying through the highways". Two techniques adopted by the rebel groups for fund-raising, according to Bhaumik, are taxing households and families systematically on the basis of their incomes and endowments and asking for huge one-time lump-sum payments. Some rebel groups, like the ones in Tripura, have mostly negotiated ransoms after abductions, rather than to abduct someone for not paying up. Among the industries most hit by such rebel 'taxation' are the tea-producing companies. "Some tea companies have even indicated the payments made to the rebel groups in their annual balance sheets". Also, road blocks on highways, such as the one connecting Nagaland and Manipur to the rest of the country, are used for 'ruthless and systematic' extortion of money from trucks travelling into the two states. It has also been found that the ULFA raised funds by subverting the public distribution system in Assam. "The bulk of the essential commodities meant for the poorer sections of the population found their way to the black market through dealers who had close links with the ULFA, generating up to Rs. 600 million a month, much of which found its way into the ULFA's coffers."[3]

Nagaland Home Minister Imkong Imchen observed that the business community was bearing the brunt of such illegal collections and ultimately the consumers became the victims as the prices of essential goods and construction materials spiralled in the town from where the goods were supplied to other parts of the state.[4] Although a ceasefire has been in force in the state of Nagaland since August 1997, there has been no end to extortions. The Mokokchung incident, where the people resisted against illegal taxation, could have definitely sent a message to all underground factions and perhaps they would realise that it is time to review their relationship with the public.[5]

Drugs are a major source for terrorist funding. This has been exploited in the Indian context as a result of porous borders with states like Nepal, Myanmar and Bangladesh. There are also linkages between criminal gangs, terrorist groups and state intelligence agencies to exploit the vulnerabilities on the borders for drug trafficking. The NSCN has the best-organised and elaborate tax collection system. The taxes are collected in Naga-inhabited areas, irrespective of state boundaries on behalf of the self-styled 'Government of People's Republic of Nagalim' (GPRN). The collection is executed by the armed wing at the 'rate of Rs 100 per individual per annum as ration tax'; the GPRN itself levies 24 per cent of an individual's annual income as royalty tax and Rs 10 as house tax.

The UNLF is the oldest Meitei insurgent group formed in 1964 and is active in Manipur. An analysis revealed that the largest percentage of funds is generated by the group from extortion or taxation. This accounted for Rs 10,113,967 for the year 2008. Extortion is also carried out under the head of 'business centre' which includes a number of businesses being run in the area. These include brick kilns (called brick farms), stone-crushing businesses, retailers, Fast Moving Consumer Good (FMCG) distributors, motor companies, hotels, petrol pumps, hospitals and clinics. A number of government departments have also been paying taxes. The rate of extortion for these departments varies from 2–10 per cent. This includes a large number of government departments like horticulture, agriculture, Zila Parishads (State Finance Commission) and the forest department. Members of the State Legislative Assembly have also made a contribution, with shares ranging from 5–10 per cent. The transport sector, given the reliance of the state of Manipur on surface movement, is also a large contributor. All the bus services being run in the states, including school buses, have contributed Rs 500 to Rs 5,000 per month.[6]

A suggestion made by the eminent North-East expert, Sanghita Das, for not allowing the local press to operate was that if those press/media houses do not publish all extortion-related activities or statements of the militant groups, then it may not be practical.[7] An effort by the Assam Rifles to enforce a similar ban in Nagaland has met with large-scale press protests as an effort to suppress the freedom of the media.[8]

Contextualising the Argument

After understanding the empirical findings of various scholars on Taxation and Extortion, there is a need to examine the methodologies and measures to overcome this menace. The existing literature on the subject has furnished the details of Taxation and Extortion in a generic manner covering the various sources of funding of the militant organisations, the financial amounts involved and overall effect on the region. However the current methodology and remedial measures have not been touched upon. Peace in Manipur is no doubt elusive; however, it needs to be addressed with a special reference to the aspirations of the people of the region in all aspects including social, economic and cultural factors. A concerted effort has been made to study the latest extortion and taxation methods in understanding the system in depth so as to evolve an effective solution. The primary objective is to find a means to end this conflict in the minds of the locals. Manipur, being one of the most conflict-ridden states of India, has been chosen for the study.

The Objectives

This study, while bringing out the genesis of the ills of taxation and extortion in Manipur, also aims to bring out the local perspective on the issue and provide a strategy for combating the menace. The objectives of the study are as mentioned below:

- To understand the dynamics of extortion/taxation and its linkage with the prevailing insurgency in the state of Manipur.
- To bring forth the methodology of illegal taxation and extortion by the underground organisations (UGs).
- To analyse the methodology of taxation/extortion and suggest a way forward for countering the same.

Data Sources, Methodology and Scope

The study is primarily based on the writer's own experience as a serving combatant in the state of Manipur. A review of the existing literature on the subject was carried out to obtain a current perspective on the subject. A field survey has been carried out in order to obtain the viewpoints of the people, right from the grass-root level to the intellectuals who contribute on a regular basis in the media, nationally and internationally. The perceptions received from wide-ranging strata of society were studied, analysed and incorporated while authoring the study. Besides, an exercise was also undertaken to solicit the opinion of experts from various domains in order to carry out a holistic analysis on the issue in the light of the views obtained from the common people. Coupled with the writer's own perception and knowledge gained over the years of intensive interaction and study, this detailed analysis has formed the basis of arriving at the strategy for preventing illegal taxation and extortion in Manipur and addressing the ill-effects associated with the menace.

Understanding Extortion and Taxation

The dictionary defines extortion as "the crime of getting money from someone by the use of force or threats". Under the Common Law, extortion is a misdemeanour consisting of an unlawful taking of money by a government official. Many statutes also provide that any threat to harm another person in his or her career or reputation is extortion. Finally, extortion may be committed by an officer's taking a fee for a service that is not performed. The service refrained from must be one within the official capacity of the officer in order to constitute extortion. These are various connotations of extortion from the angle of establishing guilt/offence/punishability[9].

Taxation vs. Extortion

The insurgents have devised a number of means to generate revenue, primarily from within their areas of operation. They regularly levy 'revolutionary taxes' on the people based on their economic status. In the process, the officials of the state, businessmen, and contractors are the most sought after. The various government departments are also accused of paying a fixed percentage of their revenue to the armed groups. The line that divides a tax from extortion is that the former is rationalised, while the latter is not. The logic in the case of underground taxes is that these are levied to fight a people's war. The legitimacy of these 'taxes' (?) remains as long as an insurgency remains a people's war.[10]

Extortion and Taxation in North-East India

Extortion is a feature common to all insurgency movements—whether it is a demand for an independent country, like by the NSCN, the ULFA, the People's Liberation Army (PLA) etc., a separate state, e.g. by the Garo National Liberation Army (GNLA), the National Democratic Front of Bodoland (NDFB) or additional autonomy/facilities like by the Zeliangrong United Front (ZUF), KLNLF, etc. Different groups call it by different names like tax collection, donation, voluntary contribution or facilitating commission and so on. However, the variety of names doesn't take away the fact that the practice of demanding money from individuals/groups/firms is in return for favours. These "favours" may be freedom from an explicit/implicit threat of violence or protection from rival groups. The reasons for these groups resorting to extortion are not difficult to fathom. Every group needs funds to meet the organisational expenses. Owing to a dwindling ideological support base of these groups, voluntary contributions are increasingly failing to meet the requirements. The insurgents in North-East India have over a period of time, perfected this system of extortion.[11]

A Major Source of Funds for the Underground Groups

Taxation and extortion are a major source of funds for the UGs. These UG take away a major chunk of funds meant for development and have devised a systematic methodology for siphoning off the government money. The local saying goes on to say that "today all underground groups are Government contractors and all Contractors are underground groups". Sources reveal the NSCN (IM) had a budget of Rs 120 crore for the year 2013, which was a 10 per cent increase from its previous year's budget.[12] Since its formation in 1979, the ULFA has been relying on extortion from business groups—oil majors and tea firms. But with the big money drying up due to global recession, it started collecting money in small doses to maintain an annual budget of Rs 30–35 crore.[13]

One of the questions asked in a survey, which was carried out in Manipur, was: "*What is the primary source of funding for the insurgent outfits?*" Not surprisingly, a majority of the respondents (over 81%) answered that taxation and extortion are the most common sources of funds for the insurgent outfits. It can be concluded that money is collected routinely and in an organised manner from individuals, transporters, small and large business houses, by instilling fear and in certain cases by killing those who resist the insurgents' demands. A further analysis to understand the views of all tribes and categories highlights that irrespective of tribal affiliations, a majority of the people of Manipur feel that taxation and extortion are the prime sources of funding which is sustaining the insurgency in Manipur.

Taxation and Extortion in Manipur

Manipur is one of the leading conflict-ridden states of India. The state has witnessed an emergence of revolutionary groups based on ethnic affinity vowing to fight for the aspirations and rights of the Nagas, Kukis, Meiteis, Muslims (Panghals) or even Nepalis, who have been residing in the state and sharing common resources since ages. The erstwhile ideological struggles have mostly degenerated into an economic opportunity for the young and impressionable youth struggling to seek suitable job opportunities which are far and few to find. Illegal taxation and extortion by underground outfits in Manipur has therefore established its space firmly in the society and has almost gained acceptance among the masses as an inevitable evil. These groups have devised a number of means for generating revenue, primarily from within their areas of operation. They regularly levy 'revolutionary taxes' on the people based on their economic status. This system of extortion has been, over the years, refined to such an extent that based on the payment of commissions by contractors, these groups influence the award of government contracts for developmental projects.

Institutionalised Extortion

The extortion network of the various insurgent groups operating in the state is spread over all the nine districts, including four in the Valley and five in the Hill areas and is well institutionalised. Places of worship, educational institutions, health centres, commercial establishments and the civilian population are all under the net of extortion spread out by the insurgents. There have been incidents of closure of educational institutions and private hospitals due to the extortion demands of the insurgents.[14] While the NSCN (IM), whose General Secretary hails from the Ukhrul district in Manipur, allegedly collects between Rs 20 to 30 crore from Manipur, all other groups also heavily depend upon extortion to run their organisations. Conservative estimates put the total sum drained away through extortions at about Rs 100 crore per year.[15]

Key Players and Their Role in Extortion

It is a known fact that the militant organisations are virtually running a parallel government in many districts in the state and even influence the decisions of the state government in awarding contracts, supply orders and enrolment in the government services. In Manipur, everybody is paying extortion money to one or more of the terrorist groups for their safety including politicians, police personnel and families of the serving and retired service personnel. The worst hit in the extortion rackets run by the insurgency groups are the commercial establishments like chemist shops, grocery stores, cement traders, salaried classes, government employees, public sector undertakings, road, railway construction companies, etc. The armed groups issue "decrees" to government institutions and place posters on signboards of shops, offices and hand over demand notes through couriers demanding donations to their cause. Kidnappings are also resorted to in order to demand huge ransoms.

Ceasefire/Suspension of Operations Groups (SOO)

Despite being in Suspension of Operations (SOO) and Ceasefire with the State and Central Government in Delhi, these surrendered or ceasefire groups have gained greater freedom and indulge in widespread taxation and extortion activities. The security forces are constrained from taking strong action against the groups, while the cadres move around freely without weapons and extort money by virtue of their influence and coercive capabilities. The groups under ceasefire/SOO arrangements have been consistently violating the ground rules with the resultant dividends in terms of revenue being proportionally substantial.

Youth and Women's Organisations

The lack of adequate employment opportunities within the state has forced the youth to fall prey to the influence of terrorist groups. The lure of easy money is seen as a motivating factor which draws the youth into extortion-related activities. A large number of youth, especially girls in the age group of 18–24, are victims of the nefarious designs of the terrorist groups, as seen from the pattern of arrests in extortion-related incidents in the state. The increasing involvement of young women in insurgency-related activities has come to light in the recent past, which is a disturbing trend. This has been evident from the arrests made in the recent past of many women over ground workers involved in extortion activities by acting as couriers. It also brings to fore the reliance of terrorist groups on women over ground workers, exploiting their apparently clean image, in furthering their nefarious designs.

Over Ground Workers

Over Ground Workers (OGWs) are the eyes and ears of the terrorist groups. They are the intermediaries in all extortion-related activities, beginning from placing demands to the collection of extortion money. These people can be categorised into two types: those having a militant background or sympathisers and those who involve themselves for the lure of easy money; the latter being more prevalent. The over ground worker community has no discrimination of age, sex or ethnicity. At most of the times, extortion is carried out by over ground workers or unarmed cadres. Even if caught red-handed, the evidence is not enough to book them for long durations. This also reduces the motivation of the security forces to apprehend the extortionists and gives the group some amount of deniability. There have also been instances wherein the local youth have impersonated militants and demanded extortion money.

The State Administration and Militant Nexus

There is sufficient evidence to indicate that the state administration including politicians in Manipur have linkages with the insurgent groups. For the last couple of years, the Valley and Hill militant groups have penetrated the state and central administration and carved out specific areas of influence. Previously, when the monthly salaries were disbursed, a percentage used to be deducted and paid to the militant groups. The state tried to circumvent this by introducing a payment of salary through net banking wherein the money is credited directly into the staff account. In fact, Manipur among the NE states, has taken the lead in becoming net-banking-friendly. However, the issue has not died down as militant organisations resorted to collecting their percentage at the source itself before the salaries got credited/deposited to the bank accounts. The militant groups have also subverted the government's public distribution system in Manipur through the local politicians.[16]

Outsourcing of Tax Collection and Extortion

It has come to light that almost all the insurgent groups operating in Manipur are outsourcing their tax collection by giving out contracts on a yearly basis. These contractors carry extortion slips of the respective groups and are located in Dimapur and Silchar. Commercial vehicles moving on NH2 and NH37 make the payment and collect the receipt. These receipts are then shown to the over ground workers before the vehicles are allowed to move further on these highways. Unemployed youth are recruited to carry out the extortion on the highways with the receipt of the organisation's name. the loyalty of the persons is maintained by paying them well.

Terrorist Groups and their Dynamics

The prominent Naga groups, namely the NSCN (IM), the National Socialist Council of Nagaland (Khaplang) (NSCN-K) and the newly formed group ZUF, have been actively involved in extortion and tax collection in the entire state. They have established a streamlined and a well-established extortion racket. Their influence along the NH37 (Imphal–Jiribam) and NH2

(Dimapur–Imphal) for collection of road tax is well known. The frontal Naga organisations in Manipur such as the Zelingrong Students Union of Manipur (ZSUM) and the All Naga Students Union Manipur (ANSUM) have also been involved in extortion activities for the Naga groups. In a recent statement the NSCN (IM)'s Cease-Fire Monitoring Cell (CFMC) office reiterated that the NSCN, as the "de-facto Government", has the "legitimate right to levy tax in Nagalim (which includes the Naga-inhabited areas of Manipur)".[17]

Kuki Groups

The Kuki groups are also under Suspension of Operations Groups (SOO) with the state government as part of their respective umbrella organisations—the United People's Front (UPF) and the Kuki National Organization (KNO). However, they too have been carrying out extortion and tax collection in Senapati and Churachandpur districts, where they are dominant.

Meitei Groups

The Meitei groups which are dominant in the Valley districts of Manipur, have been resorting to extortion in their areas of influence from various agencies. A Coordinating Committee (Corcom) has been formed which is a congregation of seven militant organisations which includes the UNLF, PLA, PREPAK (3 factions), KYKL and KCP. The maximum extortion in Manipur is carried out by them; either given voluntarily by the people or taken by force. All the major public departments pay 1 to 2 per cent of their revenue to the CORCOM and the minor departments pay separately to these organisations.

Targets of Extortion

Each insurgent group in the state promises to protect its ethnic population from actual/perceived injustices or violence by other ethnicities. In return, they get shelter, popular support and "tax" for the sustenance of the group. The individual amounts are usually small, but with a large population base, it adds up to substantial sums. It is generally voluntary and does not have a fixed limit. The Senapati district of Manipur is a good example having a population base of various ethnicities (Naga, Kuki, Nepali, Meitei, etc.) with a long history of ethnic clashes. The district has witnessed the presence of underground groups of different ethnicities, ostensibly for the protection of their tribal villages and bastions. The cadres of most of these groups do not carry out any overt activities (including carrying weapons), but provide their tribe a sense of security by their presence, in return for which the group gets tribute/tax.

Businessmen and Contractors

The major contributors of finance for the terrorist groups are the businessmen and contractors. The Free Trade Agreement between Myanmar and India has provided a fertile environment for trade and commerce to flourish. The huge returns in terms of profit have provided a very good platform for the militant groups to slake their financial thirst. The contractors pay a fixed amount generally ranging from 10 per cent to as high as 25 per cent of the contract amount to the underground groups in the area of influence of the group. For smaller contractors, who are involved in construction work, a sum of Rs 2000 per trip is imposed. The tax is collected from their respective location, in case of a regular contract; in case of a temporary contract, it is collected at different places along the highways.

The Civil Administration and Political Leaders

The civil administration officials and political leaders involved with controlling and spending huge funds pumped into the North-Eastern states for development purposes, also, naturally, become the targets for extortion. This is true even in Manipur as the civil administration officials and political leaders are targeted by the militant groups for extortion. The extortion from the salaried class is done by forcing it to withdraw a sum of money as per a fixed percentage of the respective salary. The government social sector schemes like the MGNREGA and other development activities have become an easy target for the UGs.

Commercial Vehicles

As stated earlier, commercial vehicles moving along the national highways and load-carrying or passenger vehicles are also subjected to taxation by the UGs. The payment of tax allows the entry and unhindered movement of the vehicles along that particular stretch of the highway under the influence of that particular UG.

Illegal Business

Illegal businesses which include timber trade, wildlife, narcotics and human Trafficking are additional sources of income to these militant groups. The syndicates involved in this illegal trade pay a hefty amount to the groups to carry out their activities in the region.

Periodic/Annual Tax Collection

Over a period of time, most groups have established a well-oiled network for extortion or "tax collection". There are well laid-down rates and a periodicity of collection. Locals, especially from the same ethnicity, take it as an integral part of life and there are rarely any complaints or official reports against this low-level extortion. The amounts in question are usually small, ranging from Rs 120 per family "tax" levied by the NSCN (IM) in the Naga villages of "Nagalim" to Rs 10,000 per month paid by many truck operators having regular services. Usually, the tax collection is carried out annually; however, special demand notes are also served upon individuals, transporters or business houses from time to time.

A particular village could be under the area of influence of more than one UG. For example, in Tamenglong, three groups i.e. NSCN (IM), NSCN (K) and ZUF are active. In such situations, villagers and business establishments have to pay taxes to more than one UG. The village chairman collects the tax on behalf of the militant groups from the villagers and hands it over to the UG. The tax is deposited by the village chairman at a predefined location or even in a bank account.

Methods of Extortion from the Local Business

The latest extortion racket run by the insurgent groups consists of a series of stages with couriers and use of mobile phones. It does not involve any direct contact between the hierarchies of the group with the people being targeted and makes use of civil intermediaries. There are thus various mid-level operatives who form the complete chain of the extortion racket. To understand the modus operandi of the fund flow an analysis of the VBIGs (Valley Based Insurgent Groups) was carried out. The study revealed as follows:

- **Stage 1.** The quantum of money to be demanded is decided by the District Commanders (self-styled Captain/Lieutenant) of the terrorist groups in consultation with the finance head of the group depending on the financial status of the target or the size of contract which is due to be executed through the government. This is done through a text message or a call on the mobile of the individual or by sending a note to the residence or office.

- **Stage 2.** Once the demand figure is finalised, the district commanders contact the project officers (self-styled Sergeants), primarily terrorist, for progressing the extortion activity. The communication between the two is through mobile phones and use of codes.
- **Stage 3.** On receipt of the demand notes/extortion note, the project officer contacts the over ground workers and delivers the extortion notes to the over ground workers through a woman courier.
- **Stage 4.** On receipt of the demand note, the over ground worker first contacts the target through an intermediary and places the demand discreetly. If the target has a mobile phone then the target is threatened with dire consequences and a demand placed. The demand note which is placed in writing (on the letterhead of the terrorist group) specifies the cause of the group for its struggle/agenda and the need for the target to pay a specified sum for the 'cause' before a specified date. The consequences for not adhering to the diktat are left vague, probably to intimidate the target.
- **Stage 5.** On receipt of the demand note, which usually bears a mobile number, the target is made responsible for communication with regard to his readiness to pay. Throughout this period, the target does not usually receive any call from the over ground worker. However, the target does receive a call, a day prior to the deadline. Failing to pay up on the specified date does not result in an immediate retribution by the terrorist group, but depending on the target value, as an indication of their disappointment, the terrorist groups use scare tactics on the target by giving him threatening calls and at times resorting to lobbing a grenade in the target's house or in the vicinity. The targets are also intimidated by placing a bullet or a grenade in the house. In some cases, the target or some officials related to the target's organisation are kidnapped and a ransom demanded.
- **Stage 6.** On negotiating the amount to be paid, the target makes a confirmation on the mobile number. The meeting point for collection is fixed and usually changed at the last moment to obviate any chances of the police/security forces being involved. The over ground workers under normal circumstances dispatch a lady confidante to reconnoitre

the meeting point and on confirmation of the area being "safe", usually another lady would meet the victim and the money would be collected. The courier would then hand over the money almost immediately on vacating the area to a third person who would turn over the money to the over ground workers.

- **Stage 7.** Once the money reaches the over ground worker, he communicates to the project officer about the collection detail and the project officer thereafter dispatches a courier to collect the money. On receipt of the money the project officer contacts the district commander and waits for a courier to pick up the money.
- **Stage 8.** On receipt of the money the district commanders deposit the money in a fictitious account (at times as high as 10–12 accounts) and the money is then siphoned off by the higher echelons of the terrorist groups.

Extortion from Commercial Vehicles

Commercial vehicles which move along the national highways, load-carrying or passenger vehicles are also subjected to taxation by the underground groups. Truck owners have to pay an annual tax to the groups which is dictated/determined by the number of trucks and the value of the goods being transported. Sometimes, the collection of this money is outsourced to a civil contractor who in turn pays the UGs in bulk at the beginning of the financial year.

Types of Extortion

The two types of extortion techniques presently in vogue are:

- **Latent Extortion**. In this type of extortion, the money is generally collected on a monthly basis. The so called "Road/Vehicles/Goods Tax" is collected from commercial vehicles registered either in Manipur (Imphal) or Nagaland (Dimapur). Since most of these vehicles form part of various unions like Truck Unions or Taxi Unions, the extortion money to the tune of Rs 1,000 to Rs 25,000 depending on the tonnage and type of vehicle, is paid to the concerned UGs by the unions.
- **Active Extortion**. This kind of extortion is directed against commercial vehicles which are not registered with the unions in Imphal or Dimapur. The "tax rates" generally range from Rs 1,000 upwards per trip. However, private cars are not taxed.

Quantum of Taxation and Extortion

A field survey was carried out to find out the amount of taxation and extortion being carried out by the UGs in Manipur. The updated and broad classifications of 'taxes' are:

- **Income Tax.** Every government employee is required to pay an amount equivalent to 25 per cent of his/her one month's salary as 'income tax' which is collected annually. The demanded amount is directly deducted by the Drawing and Disbursing Officers (DDO) from the salary of all employees and handed over to the representative of the militant group at a designated date, time and place.
- **House Tax.** The house tax is one of the oldest and most reliable sources of revenue for the militant outfits in this region. The present tax collection is carried out between March and May of each year. The rates are Rs 75 to Rs 200 per house, out of which Rs 10 per house is given to the village representative collecting the money on behalf of the outfit.

Commercial Tax

This 'tax' is levied on commercial enterprises and is very broad-based, in order to enable maximum collection. The 'tax' amount varies according to the estimated annual income of a businessman. The latest taxes consist of:

- **Tax on Commercial Assets.** It is an annual tax levied on the owners of local carrying agencies and buses who are required to pay Rs 5,000 per year for each truck/bus as a "road permit' to ply in Manipur and Nagaland (the permit is valid for one year and is required to be renewed during March).
- **Shops.** All shopkeepers are required to pay an 'annual tax' which ranges from Rs 500 to 2000 per annum.
- **Toll Tax.** This is levied on truck owners for each load-carrying trip made by the vehicles and is in addition to the road permit. The current rate per truck per trip varies from item to item being transported and is as follows:[18]
  - Iron Rods - Rs 7,000
  - Cement - Rs 3,000
  - Timber - Rs 1,000
  - Firewood - Rs 300

    - Charcoal - Rs 5 per bag
    - Sand/Aggregate - Rs 300
- **Contract and Additional Tax**. All contractors, builders and businessmen are required to pay 15 to 20 per cent of their annual income.

Transporters

The two national highways are the lifeline of the state of Manipur. The collection of taxes from commercial vehicles has become a major source of revenue for the UGs. The current details of collections being carried out by these groups are given below:

- Rs 100 to Rs 200 per trip from light vehicles (taxis) and Rs 500 to Rs 1000 from buses.
- Truck 10 wheeled National permit - Rs 10,000 to Rs 15,000.
- Trucks Interstate or highways - Rs 5,000 to Rs 8,000. The money is recovered at the entry point itself.
- Trucks local - Rs 3,000 to Rs 5,000.
- Buses – Tourists/Interstate Rs 8,000 to Rs 10,000.
- Bus local - Rs 500 to Rs 800.
- Bulldozers/JCBs – Rs 10,000 to Rs 25,000.
- Lorries carrying bamboos pay Rs 1.5 per bamboo beside a permit tax of Rs 200 to Rs 500 per trip.
- Lorries carrying timber pay Rs 1000 per trip.

Government Undertaking Schemes/Development Projects

NREGS/MGNREGA. This has become an easy and wholesome source of revenue for the militants. Around 25-30 per cent of the MGNREGA funds are collected by the UGs. The lack of adequate banking facilities and proper accountability due to weak governance as also the presence of linkmen/over ground workers in the civil administration, further facilitates such extortion activities.

North-Eastern Frontier Railway Project. The private companies involved in the project have paid huge amounts to these groups. An astronomical sum amounting to crores of rupees has been given to the villages as compensation and a significant portion of this has found its way into the UGs' coffers.

Tax from Government Departments

UGs are reportedly siphoning off revenue from government departments by pressurising the civil administration. The latest rates of monthly collection from the government departments are as under:

- Public Health Engineering Department (PHED) - Rs 7,000
- Education - Rs 1,20,000
- Public Works Department - Rs 1,80,000
- Petrol/Oil/Lubricants - Rs 60,000
- Electricity - Rs 60,000
- Forest - Rs 72,000

Revenue from Surrogate Groups

The NSCN factions have found a novel way of generating revenue from smaller UGs, termed as surrogate groups, operating in the North-Eastern states. Important groups are the Dima Halam Daoga (DHD) in Assam, the Hmar Peoples Convention in Mizoram, the Kanglie Yawol Kamba Lup (KYKL) the and Kuki Revolutionary Army (KRA) in Manipur.

Effects of Extortion

Development Activities. The illegal revenue generated through extortion has had wide-ranging ramifications on the state as it impedes its developmental projects. This adversely impacts the investment climate in the state and has a cascading effect upon the overall economic activity of the state, especially related to employment generation. One of the questions asked in the survey was: '**Has Extortion and Taxation affected development activities in the region?**' 85 per cent of the respondents answered that taxation and extortion are affecting the development activities in the region.

Rise in Prices. The 'parallel' system is burgeoning into a problem of enormous proportions. The illegal 'taxes' levied on trucks is being borne by the common people.

Social Sectors

Employment Generation. The lack of safe and congenial business environment and other opportunities are leading to large-scale unemployment in the society which further fuels the insurgency, thus completing the vicious circle.

Healthcare and Education. The fear of insurgent violence has affected all the social sectors like health and education in Manipur. The government-run institutes are largely defunct, especially in the remote areas.

Increase in Levels of Corruption. The insurgents, over a period of time, have infused a sense of 'acceptable unaccountability' in the government departments. The corruption in the government departments has consequently increased unabated.

Sustaining Insurgency

Taxation and extortion have become a major source of fund generation for the UGs in sustaining the insurgency. One of the questions asked in the survey was: "whether the people are paying taxes due to fear?" The respondents were to respond with a 'Yes', 'No' or 'Can't say'. Not surprisingly, almost 82 per cent of the respondents answered in 'Yes', implying that a majority of the people are paying taxes to the insurgent organisations under coercion and threat of life. People are aware of the ill-effects of the taxations and extortions. Most of them hate to pay tax.

The Impact of the Naga Peace Accord on the Taxation Activities

While the recent Framework Agreement for Peace was signed between the GOI and NSCN (IM), the impact of this agreement is to be analysed as regards the taxation and extortion activities by the group. It is a well-known fact that the funding for all insurgent groups basically stems from taxation and extortion activities with the other contributors being foreign funding, contraband trade and host of other illegal activities. Over a period of time, the ideological leanings have been shunned by these groups in favour of making the quick buck, especially at the lower level of activists who find the extortion and taxation activities an easy source of livelihood. Even if an early settlement of the vexed Naga problem is reached, the group may continue with its taxation activities till such time the financial autonomy package fructifies and a majority of the cadres are comprehensively rehabilitated. In the interim, it needs to fund its day-to-day activities including maintaining and sustaining its cadre strength. Thus, there may not be a visible dip in the taxation activities till a final settlement is reached and the cadres are rehabilitated.

The Findings of the Survey

A detailed survey was carried out to critically analyse the views of the people on illegal taxation and extortion by the Militants in Manipur. The survey used two comprehensively designed questionnaires (one for Field Survey and another for Interviews) and the response of a wide cross–section of the population of Manipur comprising common people, professionals, intellectuals, scholars, government officials and even militants, was collated. A detailed analysis of the collated response has been carried out and the views factored into the recommendations.

Do you think that the people are paying taxes to militants willingly and it is justified?

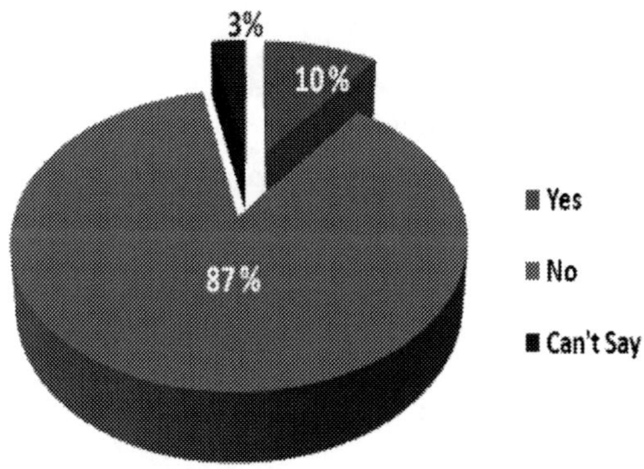

People are Paying Taxes to Militants Out of Fear

One of the questions asked in the survey was: "Do you think that the people are paying taxes to militants willingly and is it justified?" Not surprisingly, a large majority of them (over 87 per cent of the respondents) felt that paying taxes to the militants was not justified and that they were not paying taxes willingly. During the field survey and interactions with the locals/population of Manipur, it emerged that the people are paying taxes to militants only due to fear of losing their lives. On the flip side, the militants perceive taxation as a voluntary contribution for their revolutionary cause in order to provide security to their people where the government has failed.

Extortion is affecting the Development Process in Manipur

Another question which was asked in the survey was: "Do you think extortion by militants is affecting the development process in Manipur?" Around 81 per cent of the respondents felt that extortion by militants is directly affecting the development process in Manipur. The local population of Manipur is not supporting the militants and is also not willingly donating money to their organisations.

Do you think extortion by militants is affecting the development process in Manipur?

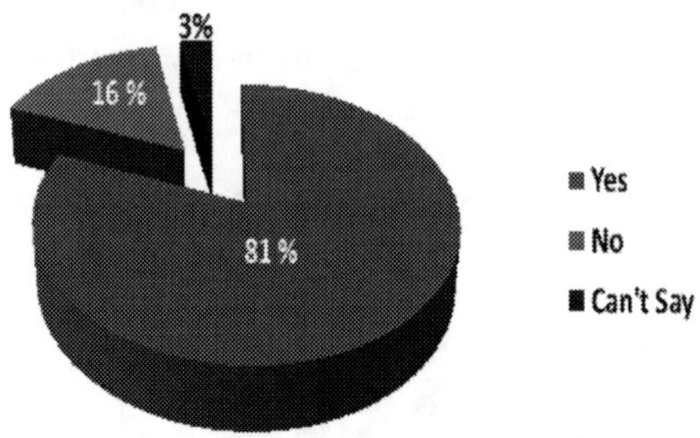

The people in Manipur feel that the taxation and extortion money is being demanded under threat or at gunpoint. They feel that the lack of development of the state, especially in the interior areas, is due to the siphoning off of their legitimate earnings, be it salary or wages, by the militant groups under the garb of taxation. The common man is being harassed time and again and the money parted is being used by the militant groups for their own profitable ends. The insurgency in the North-East has become a business, which adversely affects the developments projects and discourages the business activities in the State. The people of Manipur are against extortion and taxation and feel that it is affecting development.

The Way Forward to Check Extortion

The ideal solution against extortion is resistance from the people affected by it. 'People should resist extortion' is like saying that the 'victim must fight back the rapist'. Cases where the victims fought back have been there and in such cases the aggressor becomes the victim.

Need for Focused Perception Management/Psychological Initiatives

The challenge in Manipur lies in shaping the perception of the several communities and tribes residing in the state against extortion and taxation.

Carefully planned psychological initiatives to bring out the ills of extortion will help in effectively addressing this menace. The following are some of the suggested themes for changing and influencing the attitude of the common man:

Poster campaigns against extortion:

- Use of audio/visual media to expose the ills of extortion. Shorts films, documentaries and public commercials in the visual media, use of FM channels and other state-run media to highlight the plight of the people due to extortion can work well;
- Highlighting the lack of progress in the state due to the siphoning of funds by the terrorist groups and influencing the minds of the target audience by repeatedly condemning extortion through the vernacular print media;
- Garnering support of the NGOs to organise roadshows on anti-extortion themes;
- Engaging the youth and fertile minds against extortion;
- Including the facets of extortion and its evil aspects in the curriculum of the education system;
- Organising debates at school levels to influence the minds and attitudes of the youth at a tender age without overplaying the theme.

Effective and Good Governance

An absence of governance in the remote areas encourages the UGs to run a parallel government and indulge in taxation and extortion. Effective and good governance are keys to development and will curb the menace of extortion. Following measures are recommended:

- MGNREGA money should not be routed through village chiefs and be directly credited to the people employed for the project. The Pradhan Mantri Jan Dhan Yojana (PMJDY) started on August 28, 2014 is a great step forward for the enforcement of this system.
- The Lokpal and Lokayuta mechanisms should to be implemented in letter and spirit to make all the officials and politicians accountable for their actions. The Manipur Lokayukta Bill, 2011, which was passed on February 27, 2014, is a right step forward in this direction.
- An effective use of the RTI Act could help ensure transparency and effectively check all illegal financial transactions and dealings carried out by the public servants out of public funds.

- The government agencies should make all-out efforts to avoid a leakage of information regarding the government development plans including the allotment of funds and contractors.

Effective Civil Administration

The role of state/central government in curbing extortion is most important and crucial because this problem can only be resolved through strong political will. Certain measures that can be proposed are:

- The state and district administration must ensure that the development projects are distributed in a scientific and transparent manner according to the requirement of the area and not under the influence of any UG;
- The establishment of an Anti-Extortion Cell at the Centre/State/District level, linked to the affected police station.
- A 24x7 Anti-Extortion Helpline needs to be established either in conjunction with the police or independently along with dedicated Quick Response Teams.
- The civil administration must provide security to important officials so that they can work without any fear of the UGs and their extortion demands.

Use of Technology

Technology should be effectively exploited to monitor and curb extortion activities. Some suggested measures are as follows:

- A more effective use of interception and monitoring equipment to monitor the UG conversations using both wireless and commercial mobile phones with a view to detecting and neutralising the attempted extortions.
- A-24 hour helpline needs to be established for taking extortion complaints. These helplines must maintain absolute anonymity to ensure the security of the people.
- Economical GPS (Global Positioning System) or RFID (Radio Frequency Identification)-based monitoring chips could be installed on goods carriers to curb waylaying in connection with the extortion demands by the UGs.

E-Transactions to Reduce Taxation and Extortion

Presently, the various funds allotted for developmental and other works in the state fail to achieve the desired results due to a siphoning off of the funds before they reach their destination. This has been compounded by the lack of robust financial mechanisms like banks or ATMs in the rural areas, which are very far and few between. Hence the local populace is at a disadvantage, having to physically carry huge amounts of money in conducting their transactions. They thus become vulnerable to the menace of extortion and taxation. A more widespread availability of banking services and financial solutions to the far-flung areas, promoting e-transactions for various government projects, will go a long way in solving the vexed issue.

Legal Aspects

From the legal point of view, extortion still remains a bailable offence. Even after being caught red-handed, the individual is released on bail within a couple of days. This leaves him/her free to continue the activities and compounds the frustration of the security forces. A stringent law on the lines of the Money Laundering Bill needs to be enacted to prevent and punish activities related to extortion. Not reporting extortion threats should also be treated as connivance to an offence. Rewards to informants must be institutionalised to encourage people to openly oppose the extortion or illegal 'tax' collection by the UGs.

Role of Police/Central Armed Police Forces

The common man heeds to the extortionist's demand due to fear of retribution. Efforts to create a congenial security environment by the security and paramilitary forces could go a long way in checking the ever-growing menace of extortion. The strengthening of the police force, especially at the beat constable level, could be one important measure. Despite having the highest police-to-population ratio of 627 per 1,00,000, the Manipur Police is still short of approximately 7,000 policemen which must be immediately addressed. Priority should be given to fill vacancies both in terms of men and weapons, particularly in the remote areas.

Special training needs to be imparted to the police, especially including the explanation of technology (related to interception), in order to enable them to check extortion and illegal tax collection in their area of responsibility.

Cash rewards akin to seizure of drugs and contrabands can be announced for the busting of an extortion racket.

Role of Army/Assam Rifles

The Army/Assam Rifles are mandated to carry out counter-insurgency operations in the state except in the de-notified areas. In the course of its operations, the Army/Assam Rifles do apprehend persons carrying out extortion activities. At times, weapon, drug and money consignments are also busted. However, handling of cases involving taxation/extortion falls under the purview of the civil police forces. They need to work in cohesion with the state police, the central police, the paramilitary forces and various intelligence agencies in order to ferret out organisations and people involved in extortion and ensure that strict action is taken against them as per the law of the land.

The Army/Assam Rifles, being the only visible face of administration in remote areas, can educate the masses in the remote corners of the state on the ill-effects of extortion and its evils through various audio-visual aids. They could also organise excursions or tours by a select group of youth to other states and cities in order to expose them to the benefits of development and how the people/youth in these remote areas can also contribute to the development of their areas and move ahead to join the mainstream life. The Army also needs to take recruitment rallies into the remote areas to wean away the youth from the influence of illegal groups by providing them a chance to join the Army and earn a livelihood for their families. This would also add to the security of that region as also provide a wider intelligence base.

Development Activities

Major business powerhouses should be encouraged to establish their centres in the region by giving them tax incentives and other benefits. An amendment may be passed to the Company Act providing for the opening of a certain percentage of the company's production centres or outlets in these regions.

Security for Infrastructural/Developmental Projects

In Manipur, the ongoing railway construction project is pegged to be worth approximately Rs 6000 crore which is to be completed over a ten-year period. Even if we apply an illegal taxation template of 5 per cent, the amount being siphoned off by the insurgent groups is very high. With Phase–I of the project between Jiribam and Tupul nearing completion and the majority of tunnels nearly ready, the next step would be providing security for the plying of trains on these routes. Similarly, the security-troop density on the national highways in the hinterland needs to be increased to safeguard the interests of the vehicles plying on these roads and to prevent them from being exploited by the insurgent groups. The raising of National Highways/Railway Protection Force comprising of local youth or rehabilitated cadres will address the twin needs of provisioning security to these projects and the elimination of taxation/ extortion activities.

The state must provide comprehensive security to contractors involved in infrastructure development like the Trans-Asian Railway Line, Asian Highways, etc., to facilitate a timely completion of these projects and to deter the UGs from extortion. The following measures are recommended to make these development projects less vulnerable to extortion:

- The antecedents of the contractors and subcontractors must be verified in advance to avoid the projects going into the hands of UGs/ their supporters.
- Financial payments for the projects to be linked to the physical progress, quality of work, duly authenticated by an independent authority.
- Institutionalising an independent audit of the development projects.
- The local social bodies should be incorporated in the development projects to generate employment as well as to ensure that the people become stakeholders in these developmental projects.

Role of Frontal Organisations/NGOs

Non-Governmental and Social Organisations play a major role in Manipur. However in the absence of stringent checks, these organisations have transformed into frontal organisations for the UGs. Therefore, the following issues must be addressed:

- A strict scrutiny of funding and transparency of financial transactions; their annual financial and social audits, etc., should be mandatory for their continuance.
- These organisations must be effectively utilised for mobilising the masses to shun violence, resist extortion activities and concentrate

on development issues instead. The Action Committee against Unabated Taxation (ACAUT) comprising of civil society, frontal organisations, student and youth organisations and the business community in Nagaland is a positive example.

Role of Socio-Political Organisations

There are innumerable socio-political organisations in the North-East which champion the cause of their tribes and ethnicity. They command huge influence over their respective communities. If they are rightly taken aboard, they can influence the youth to give up their erring ways and bring about a change in society. It is often seen that some socio-political organisations take the easy way out whenever confronted, by citing their inability to curb the illegal taxation/extortion activities. Such groups need to be channellised with a sustained involvement by the stakeholders.

Anti-Extortion Cell "Special Task Force"

There is a need to set up a central task force with the members of the bureaucracy, enforcement agencies and civil society and with a built-in transparency to prevent the corrupt practices in the state. Special police units specifically tasked for fighting extortion must be trained in skills to gather information on extortion networks and zero-in on the persons involved in these networks.

Strict Actions against Government Officials abetting Such Activities

There is a need to impose a certain degree of accountability amongst the government officials who are responsible for handling the government funds in such areas. Often, they cite various reasons misgivings and accept the situation as a fait accompli. Over the years, a lack of accountability and non-supervision by the higher-ups and a general acceptance of the situation have resulted in rampant extortion and taxation activities by the insurgent groups. There is an urgent need to fix accountability, and strict actions need to be implemented against the defaulters to deter them from getting away with their callous attitude in handling the government funds. Developmental programmes must be taken up in mission mode as a programme and budgeted as such so as to reduce pilferage and enhance transparency in fund utilisation/expenditure.

Strict Enforcement of SOO/Cease Fire Ground Rules (CFGRs)

Surrender/Ceasefire Agreements need to be reviewed with an inclusion of clauses for strong action (e.g. stoppage of stipend, long jail terms, etc.) or non-applicability of terms of agreement for cadres found indulging in extortion. Repeated instances of extortion by a group can be exploited by the government authorities to put additional pressure on the group leaders during negotiations.

Rehabilitation of Surrender/Ceasefire/SOO Cadres

In the absence of a clear road map for a comprehensive rehabilitation of the surrendered/ceasefire/SOO cadres, and an avoidable delay in the implementation of the rehabilitation policy beyond creating camps for the cadres, has forced them to restart their illegal activities. These delay tactics are detrimental to peace not only in Manipur but also in other parts of North-East India. The Kuki groups which are in SOO with the Government of Manipur are affected by such activities. These cadres are disillusioned and actively involved in extortion and taxation. A comprehensive rehabilitation programme of these cadres is a must for having a lasting peace and prosperity in the region.

Role of Religious Organisations and Educational Institutes

There is a dire need to revitalise the moral and ethical education system in these affected areas, highlighting the ill-effects of taxation and extortion. This can be best brought out by the Church communities and educational institutes in the North-East. In Manipur, the Church has a major influence on the community for inculcating moral and ethical education among the youth and wean them away from the lure of easy earnings out of extortion and insurgent activities. It can best be done during the Church services through sermons, and teachings by important personalities. The same needs to be reinforced by the educational institutions in their respective curricula. The Church as a powerful institution can respond and initiate possible solutions and influence the opinion of the masses. Even in Mizoram, the Church acts as a strong restraint against the perceived administrative excesses.

Employment Generation

The menace of taxation and extortion activities can be curbed if the youth, the chunk of the manpower involved in these activities, are given an alternative. Sustained jobs and regular pay have a deep impact on the psyche of any youth. In the North-East, the affluent are able to send their wards to the best of educational institutions across the country to keep them away from the ill-effects of the insurgency. However, the poor, especially the rural ones, find their wards sucked into the insurgency affecting their area in no time. Poor educational infrastructures in such areas, lack of job opportunities and misplaced ideologies make a heady cocktail for the insurgent groups to target youth by employing them in the taxation and extortion industry. Hence, there is a definite need to address the issue and look out for practical ways to ensure quality education and employment opportunities to such youth. Increased vacancies for recruitment in government jobs, armed and police forces would augur well for such youth. In this regard, the following measures may be undertaken:

- Focus on skill development among the youth.
- Education affects the actions of the youth. The regular bandh culture and lack of schools and quality education is affecting the youth. Focus should be on the development of schools and colleges in all parts of the state.
- Promotion of handicrafts which are unique to the state, thus offering avenues for the youth adept in these crafts.
- New ways of employment generation will weed away the youth from anti-national activities.
- Central government schemes to be exploited to the maximum for employment creation.

Miscellaneous Measures

- The timber trade should be legalised, generating a legitimate revenue for the state. Local artisans should be encouraged to constitute cooperatives for showcasing local furniture and woodcraft, thus churning the local economy. Illegal extortion from timber smugglers will be checked to a large extent. The opening of furniture showrooms and provision of transport facilities will facilitate their recognition at the national level as well.

- Empower and enhance the number of Forest Conservation Guards through focused qualitative and quantitative means at the government level.
- Effective and comprehensive rehabilitation of surrendered militants is an important aspect from the point of view of encouraging more to follow suit. In addition, ensuring that the surrendered cadre do not fall victim to the insurgent groups again, remains critical to the success of any such policy.

Conclusion

In the recent years, among the insurgent groups, there has been a gradual but visible substitution of ideology by sheer greed. Tax collection must remain a monopoly of the legitimate government running the administration and not lie in the hands of any underground groups proclaiming themselves to be the representatives of the people. Such parallel taxation structures are financially sustaining insurgencies in North-East India. Therefore, to create a tangible impact on the prevailing CI environment, it is imperative that this lifeline be effectively choked. Ideological insurgent groups are becoming "extortion funded insurgent groups". These extortion networks are now well established, and have been evading detection by suitably adapting to the latest technology. It is therefore imperative that all stakeholders in the state's future must show a resolute determination to stamp out the menace of extortion. The people, government machinery and the security forces have to work in consonance. No single arm of the government can tackle the issue alone. Most importantly, the people of North-East India have to realise the ills of extortion and say 'no' to it in order to make a beginning. There is an imperative need to instill practical and effective measures to curb this menace of extortion that is bleeding the fragile economy of the North-East and is an insurmountable impediment to the peace, progress and development of the region.

The Author

Brigadier Sushil Kumar Sharma has been the Deputy General Officer Commanding of a Mountain Division in Assam. He has been awarded a PhD from IGNOU for his study on North-East India, and is presently posted as DIGP, CRPF, in the North-East Region.

*

END NOTES

1. Sanjoy Hazarika, 'Insurgents are a Taxing Burden on the Northeast', *The Sunday Guardian*, December 5. 2013, available at http://www.sunday-guardian.com/analysis/insurgents-are-a-taxing-burden-on-the-northeast, Accessed on September 23, 2015
2. Rakhee Bhattacharya, 'War and Taxes', in *Development Disparities in Northeast India*. New Delhi: Foundation Books, Cambridge University Press India, 2011. Accessed on September 23, 2015
3. Subir Bhaumik, *Troubled Periphery: Crisis of India's North East*, SAGE Publications.
4. 'Nagaland Govt to crack Whip on Illegal Collection', *Zee News*, May 30, 2012, available at http://zeenews.india.com/news/north-east/nagaland-govt-to-crack-whip-on-illegal-collection_778579.html Accessed on December 24, 2014
5. Nitin A. Gokhale, 'No New Taxes, Bro', *Outlook*, September 22, 2003, available at http://www.outlookindia. com/article/No-New-Taxes-Bro/221495 Accessed on January, 23, 2015
6. Vivek Chadha, 'Terrorism Finance Sources and Trends in India', *Journal of Defence Studies*, Institute for Defence Studies and Analyses, July 2014, available at *http://www.idsa.in/jds/8_3_2014_TerrorismFinance.html* Accessed on Februry 23, 2014
7. Sanghita Das, *Manipur and The Paradox of Security*, New Delhi: Anmol Publications.
8. '5 Naga Papers publish Blank Edit in Protest', *The Tribune*, November 18, 2015, available at http://epaper.tribuneindia.com/642271/The-Tribune/TT_18_November_2015, Accessed on February, 25, 2014
9. http://www.merriam-webster.com/dictionary/extortion, Accessed on February, 25, 2014
10. R.S. Jassal, 'Mutual Accountability and Ill Effects Of Extortion on Our Society', January, 23, 2011, available at http://manipuronline.com/features/mutual-accountability-ill-effects-extortion-society/ Accessed on December 25, 2014
11. Arunav Goswami, 'Insurgency in Northeast India: Changing Times, Changing Tactics', Centre For Development and Peace Studies, October 21, 2010, available at http://cdpsindia.org/point-of-view53.asp, Accessed on February, 25, 2014
12. *ANI*, 'Govt. to act Tough against Outfits involved in Extortion in Northeast', *Business Standard*, July 12, 2013, available at http://www.business-standard.com/article/news-ani/govt-to-act-tough-against-outfits-involved-in-extortion-in-northeast-113071200686_1.html, Accessed on February, 28, 2014
13. Rahul Karmakar, 'NE Rebels demand Extortion 'In Kind'", *Hindustan Times* Guwahati, April 08, 2013, available at http://paper.hindustantimes.com/epaper/viewer.aspx, Accessed on March, 28, 2014
14. Arunav Goswami, op. cit., 11.
15. Samudra Gupta Kashyap, 'Northeast's Worst-Kept Secret: Extortion Rackets', *Indian Express* Guwahati, Wed Dec 01 2010, available at http://archive.indianexpress.com/news /northeast-s-worstkept-secret-extortion-rackets/718390/, Accessed on April 19, 2014
16. Sanjibarua, 'Gulliver's Trouble: State and Militants in Northeast India', *Economic and Political Weekly*, October 12, 2012, available at www.epw.in/.../gullivers-troubles-state-and-militants-north-east-india.ht...Accessed on July 06, 2014
17. *Nagaland Post*, 'NSCN IM has Legitimate Right to Levy Taxes', July 17, 2014, available at http://manipurupdate.com/nscn-i-m-has-legitimate-right-to-levy-tax-says-cfmc/ Accessed on July, 10, 2014
18. Phanjoubam Tarapot, *Bleeding Manipur*, Har Anand Publications, 2003.

6

ANTI-TERROR LAWS IN INDIA AND PAKISTAN: A COMPARATIVE STUDY

Navroz Singh

> *"Terrorism must be outlawed by all civilized nations-not explained or rationalized, but fought and eradicated. Nothing can, nothing will justify the murder of innocent people and helpless children".* —**Elie Wiesel**

There is little doubting the fact that if there is one word which, quite ominously, has acquired the distinction of being a cult term in contemporary times, it is terrorism. A perverted, distorted, even depraved, agenda of snuffing life out of the innocent population in an attempt to avenge a capriciously defined rationale is the only explanation that can be given for an act as inhumane and diabolical as terrorism. Indeed, measures seeking to deal with and defeat the objectives of such a dastardly act which poses an onerous challenge to humankind must receive an unequivocal sanction. Or else, Dante's premonitive quote does stare one in the eye and quite justifiably so, for, "the darkest places in Hell are reserved for those who maintain their neutrality in times of a moral crisis".

The Necessity of Extraordinary Anti-Terror Laws

Terrorism and India share a rather unfortunate relationship. India's geostrategic coordinates force it to battle rather difficult circumstances. Externally fuelled insurgencies and cross-border terrorism impose a major threat to the Indians even now. Beginning with Pakistan organising a terrorist invasion into the Kashmir Valley in October 1947, such 'war by other means' has assumed every contortionist form it could, ultimately degenerating into a sponsorship of or collusion with savage, endemic, unabated terrorism under a nuclear cloud. Every opportunity to destabilise the Indian state was sought to be exploited by its ill-wishing western neighbour: be it the 1980s Sikh militancy movement or the beginning of the rebellion in Kashmir in the late 1980s. East Punjab presented an interesting case for Pakistan. The emergence of the crisis coincided roughly with the rise of the Pakistan-controlled and coordinated jihad against the Soviets in Afghanistan, creating an endless supply chain of modern weapons and what came to be prominently identified as the 'Kalashnikov Culture'. It is a well accepted argument that Pakistan's Inter-Services Intelligence (ISI) experimented with its tricks in the Afghan laboratory and sought to replicate these in Punjab and subsequently in Kashmir, trying out the strategy of 'bleeding by a thousand cuts' on India.

The situation in Kashmir and Pakistan's unabashed training, logistical, doctrinal and financial support to the Kashmiri insurgents doesn't require much explanation given its global acknowledgement. The US State Department in a report on 'Patterns of Global Terrorism' (April 2001) specifically identified Islamabad as the chief sponsor of the militant groups fighting in the region. A similar conclusion was endorsed by a report by the National Commission on Terrorism, reflecting thus the current thinking in most US and Western policymaking and intelligence circles, which supports the claim India has consistently been making against Pakistan. Sponsoring militancy in Kashmir was seen by Pakistan as an effective way to offset the existing power asymmetries, maintaining a so-called 'balance of power' in the region against an economically, militarily and demographically superior India, while creating a palisade of unrest and instability along the country's strategically significant northern and north-western borders.

The net result of these circumstances was the essentiality for India to graduate from the Criminal Procedure Code and the Indian Penal Code inherited from the Raj, towards something more substantial, which met the imperatives of the dynamic and increasingly threatening situation.Thus, the necessity of stringent laws to combat those who harm the sovereignty and integrity of India cannot, therefore, be overstated. When confronted with armed militancy, democracies face what is often known as the 'democratic dilemma'. For liberal democracies like India, the decision to put into place a set of extraordinary laws to curb activities which affect the stability and safety of its citizens, is indeed, exceptionally difficult. Even a cursory glance through the Constituent Assembly debates is enough to acquaint the reader of the priority given by the founding fathers of the Constitution in India to the protection of individual rights and accord the citizens' freedom and liberty to lead their lives in an environment of peace and stability. Republicanism and national sovereignty need to, and can, coexist.

The Constitution is indeed the supreme law and the fundamental rights granted thereunder to the citizens as enshrined in Part III are inalienable. But, parallel to the sanctity accorded to individual rights is the priority which must be accorded to the security of the state. Extraordinary situations demand extraordinary laws which empower the law-enforcing agencies and the courts to bring the perpetrators of terrorism to justice. The United States, for instance, has a great tradition of enforcing civil liberties. Numerous judicial pronouncements have upheld fundamental human rights. A State which proudly wears its badge of democracy and leaves no stone unturned to flaunt it, when faced with the threat of terrorism post-9/11, did not bat an eyelid in enacting the PATRIOT Act, which though draconian, received bi-partisan support. Despite intense criticism by the international community, the Guantanamo Bay continues to exist and 'enhanced investigation techniques' (a euphemism for torture) such as water boarding and electric-shock interrogation continue to be administered by a State which declares itself as the upholder of democratic values and human rights. Similar was the reaction of President Hollande post the Paris attacks in November 2015, evident through the official declaration of 'Emergency Procedures'.

In India too, the threat level has undisputedly risen. Mumbai, Delhi, Gurdaspur, Pathankot, Jaipur, Ahmedabad—the list of terror targets in the country is menacingly long. The spectre of the abomination called the Islamic State looms large. Indeed, these are difficult, even desperate, times. However ironical it may seem, laws granting extraordinary powers to the security forces in the face of such extreme threats are necessary evils for the protection of rights that a democracy like India guarantees its citizens. The parliamentary debates post-26/11 attacks put on record the rather fascinating and indeed compelling justification for the reason why India desperately needed to enact an anti-terror law which gave teeth to its law enforcement and security agencies in dealing with the pandemic threat of terrorism. The debate records an eminent member of the then opposition stating categorically that while it was true that the battle against terrorism cannot be fought in the courts of law, requiring an enhanced degree of coordination between the police force, the armed forces, the intelligence agencies, the executive, legislature and the judicial system, it can still not be denied that a system to equip the investigative agencies to use all justifiable means, with adequate safeguards, to book the culprits is unapologetically put into place. This mechanism is necessary to ensure the imposition of a psychological deterrence against those who nurture nefarious objectives against the Indian state. To quote, "the preventive impact of this law (the debate was with reference to the Unlawful Activities (Prevention) Act) is that it reflects the determination of the Government and the Indian State in fighting terrorism, and the Indian State is then adequately equipped in terms of law, to investigate the crime and expeditiously punish those who are responsible for that crime". Hence, the use of special/security laws is justified on the grounds that the existing criminal laws are not adequate to deal with the militancy that is "well-armed, far more dangerous and modernized". Radicalisation through modern means of communication across the globe poses a potent threat which the international community is struggling to combat. In this context, what is at stake is not just law and order, but the very existence of state and society. There is therefore, a need to have special laws with a far higher deterrence value.

India has a long tradition of special/security laws dating back to its pre-independence years. These laws have been enacted, repealed and re-enacted periodically, since independence. Such special laws fall under four categories, as follows:

1. Exclusive laws against terrorism, like POTA.
2. Security forces' empowerment laws that give immunity and additional special powers to the security forces like the Armed Forces Special Powers Act.
3. Laws of proscription that criminalise terrorist groups and a range of undesirable activities like the Unlawful Activities Prevention Act (UAPA).
4. Exclusive laws on control of finances, money laundering, drug-trafficking, cyber warfare, and so on.

Pakistan's Perspective

Pakistan has never shied from accusing the Indian security establishment of gross human rights abuses against the civilian population, particularly in the state of Jammu and Kashmir under the garb of its anti-terror laws, most notably AFSPA. While the voices which call for the revocation of this law have become louder over decades, the Indian Army has repeatedly expressed the necessity of such a law given the strategically sensitive location of the state. The Pakistani rhetoric against India is clearly malicious, self-serving, and most of all, hypocritical.

In line with the 'feeding snakes in your backyard and expecting them to not bite you' theory, Pakistan, most certainly, has never been, nor shall ever be, immune to the disastrous impact of terror. Extraordinary laws granting leverage to the security agencies in that State have traditionally been formulated keeping in view the threat Pakistan faces from its own 'non state actors'. Most recently, the Protection of Pakistan Act has reignited the debate surrounding the 'necessity' of such laws, both within Pakistan and in the international community. This law, like most others, has been described by its defenders as essential for 'granting necessary powers to investigating agencies to meet exceptional circumstances faced by Pakistan and to make necessary improvements in the legal system so that proper evidence is presented in courts'.

Pakistan: Protection of Pakistan Act, 2014

The Protection of Pakistan Act, 2014 (POPA) has been justified by Pakistan on the grounds of national security and the need for a stricter law to counter terrorism across the country. The law, however, has received scathing criticism for its provisions which violate all known norms and standards of civil liberties. The POPA raises serious questions about the propaganda attack Pakistan launches against Indian anti-terror laws.

To begin with, Article 2 of the law, Clause (d) subclauses (a) and (b) define "enemy alien" as a militant "whose identity is unascertainable as a Pakistani, in a locality where he claims to be residing, whether by documentary or oral evidence; or has been deprived of his citizenship, under the Pakistani Citizenship Act, 1951 (II of 1951), acquired by naturalization". The definition of a militant, apart from the rhetoric of an individual found guilty of waging a war or insurrection, or raising arms or taking up, advocating or encouraging or aiding or abetting the raising of arms, or waging a war or a violent struggle against Pakistan, its citizens, the armed forces or civil armed forces, contains a rather unsettling clause. Article 2, Clause (f) subclause (d) declares anyone who may 'threaten' or 'attempt' to act in a manner prejudicial to the security, integrity or defence of Pakistan to be a militant and subclause (e) subclause (ii) takes this further to include any person against whom there is 'reasonable ground' that he acts under the directions or in concert or conspiracy with or in furtherance of the designs of an enemy alien. Clearly, terms like 'threaten' or 'attempt' or 'reasonable ground' in the absence of further qualifications come across as vague, hollow and designed to suit the possibly nefarious objectives of the State as it may deem fit given the evolving circumstances. Clause 3 continues this trend. Under subclause 1, the use of armed and civil armed forces is justified even under 'reasonable apprehension' of a scheduled offence. Same Article, Clause 3, subclause (ii) under the explanation part allows causing death or grievous hurt on the "prior information but *without any clear identification* of individual(s) who may have been *or are going to be involved* in the planning, commission or financing of a scheduled offense... (sic)". The code of Investigation under Clause 5 continues to reveal similar frightening provisions such that it mentions, "all scheduled offences shall be cognizable and non-bailable", unlike the Indian laws where provisions for bail exist but with caveats.

Clause 6 takes up the hugely controversial provision of preventive detention. Numerous independent analysts have highlighted the horrors allowed by the presence of this clause in legal enforcement and labelled its existence as being contrary to the very essence of a democratic state. Article 10 of the Constitution of Pakistan provides safeguards against arbitrary arrest and detention. The ninth clause of the Article however explicitly states that "nothing in this article shall apply to any person who for the time being is an enemy alien". And subclause (1) of the preventive detention clause in the POPA 2014 mentions an enemy alien shall "be detained by the Government to prevent him from acting as aforesaid for such period as maybe determined by it from time to time in accordance with Article 10 of the Constitution". Clearly, the provisions of the right to be informed of the grounds of arrest, or the right to be produced before a magistrate within a period of twenty-four hours of such arrest and similar such clauses do not apply to those declared as enemy aliens by the state, thus granting a clear ground for exploitation to the state and those appointed by it. Clauses (2) and (4) of Article 6 of the Act bring in another hugely contested issue of "internment camps" where the requisitioned force may detain any enemy alien or militant after a notification of that act. The period of detention is clearly indefinite and reports of gross human rights violations abound.

This paper in the concluding paragraphs makes a mention of a 'shroud of secrecy' gradually enveloping the Pakistani society. The justification of this statement is provided through the ninth Article of the Act, Clause (2) subclauses (a) which allows for withholding information regarding the location of the detainee or accused or internee or internment centre established or information with respect to any detainee or accused or internee or his whereabouts and (b) which even allows the Government to not declare the 'grounds for detention' of a detainee, accused or internee who is an enemy alien or militant. The 'exclusion of public from proceedings of Special Courts' (Clause 10) further contributes to this environment of secrecy used in favour of the enforcement agencies. Clause 15 denies the presumption of innocence until proven guilty which turns on its head the basic principle of the justice system as it exists in Pakistan.

Numerous reports thus suggest how the law enables the Pakistani security establishment to engage in grave human rights violations, including enforced disappearances, torture and extrajudicial killings. Among its many provisions, the law, which, some say, empowers the security establishment to convert Pakistan into a replica of the Guantanamo Bay, also allows the security forces to detain a terrorism suspect for 90 days without presenting him before a court, and calls for treating terrorists "as enemy aliens" to be dealt with "strictly without any compunction". This law stands in complete violation of the International Covenant on Civil and Political Rights which Pakistan ratified in 2010. Quoting Article 20 of the law, "No member of the police, armed forces or the civilian armed forces acting in aid of civil authority, Prosecutor General, a prosecutor, Special Judicial Magistrates or the judge of a Special Court shall be liable to any action for the acts done in good faith during the performances of their duties". It therefore grants Pakistan's security forces and judicial officers acting under the law effective immunity 'for the acts done in good faith during the performance of their duties'. This violates not only Article 2(3) of the international covenant, which requires governments to ensure that anyone whose rights or freedoms are violated 'shall have an effective remedy, notwithstanding that the violation has been committed by persons acting in an official capacity', but also the very Constitution of Pakistan. Such immunity from prosecution to state agencies has been notably responsible for the 'missing person phenomenon' in Baluchistan, particularly, and elsewhere in the country. Peaceful political protesters and critics of government policies are particularly vulnerable to abuses under the new law because of a dangerous ambiguity in its definition of terrorist acts. Besides 'killing, kidnapping, extortion', the law classifies vague acts, including 'Internet offenses and other offenses related to information technology' as prosecutable crimes without providing specific definitions for these offenses. The terms are so ambiguous that a non-violent online political protest could be considered 'threatening the security of Pakistan'.

In addition, the law expands the powers of arrest without warrant for the police, members of the armed forces and 'civil armed forces'. Under the new law, forces are provided the complete and absolute discretion to 'enter and search without warrant any premises to make any arrest or to take possession of any firearm, explosive, weapon, vehicle, instrument, or article used or likely to be used in the commission of any scheduled offense'. The law permits them to do so without sufficient judicial control in violation of the guarantees against arbitrary arrest and the privacy and the security of the home under the ICCPR. The law also includes members of the armed forces in the process of investigation and grants powers to the law enforcement agencies to "shoot at sight". Cases of forced and non-voluntary confessions abound which could then be treated as valid evidence in courts of law.

The whole idea of 'the right to be presumed innocent until proved guilty according to law' is totally abandoned. Instead, the law removes the burden of proof of criminal conduct from government prosecutors and requires the criminal suspects to prove their innocence. It goes on to state that those arrested for suspected terrorism offenses 'shall be presumed to be engaged in waging war or insurrection against Pakistan unless he establishes his non-involvement in the offense'.

Pakistan: Actions (in Aid of Civil Power) Regulations, 2011

Another draconian law that has been passed in Pakistan is the Actions (in Aid of Civil Power) Regulations. Internment remains a contentious and deeply contested issue under the provisions of this Act as well. Also, what continues through this law is the language of apprehension which lacks precision in identifying the crime. Chapter 5 (dealing with Internment) Article 9 Clause 1 justifies the internment of an individual who has committed or is "likely to commit an offence" under this regulation. Who determines or investigates the likelihood or probability of such an occurrence and by what standards of judgment, is a question demanding expatiation—sadly, not provided in the text of the law. Continuing further to Clause 11 dealing with the 'Duration of Internment': "the Power to intern shall be valid from the day when this regulation deemed to have come into force, or the date the order of the interment is issued, whichever is earlier, *till the continuation of action in aid of civil power*". This clearly provides the interning authority with unquestioned authority to detain the internees for an indefinite, unspecified period in a blatant violation of the international human rights conventions which Pakistan is a part of. Worse, it is aimed to legitimise the unlawful detention of hundreds of people who were in the custody of the security forces.

Chapter 7 dealing with Offences and Punishments also requires a closer examination. Clause 16 subclause 1 states: "Whoever *challenges or is suspected of an act of challenging the authority and writ of the Federal or Provincial Government* or to attempt to assert unlawful control over any part of the territory of Pakistan *or resorts to the acts of waging war against the State*, shall be deemed to have committed an offence under this regulation". This clause opens the possibility of the right to question the existing dispensation through the constitutionally provided and protected Freedom of Expression being termed as challenging the authority of those in power and thus be recognised as an offence under the regulation. Subclause 3, "spreading literature, delivering speeches electronically or otherwise thus inciting the people in commissioning any offence under any law shall be deemed to have committed offence under this regulation", is subject to the same criticism that is made of the POPA. The concern is regarding the uncertainty and ambiguity of the nature of the offences and the 'mode of incitement'—therefore, in declaring an individual as a criminal under the law. There is an inherent subjectivity in the interpretation of the clause itself which most certainly, can be used, after being carefully twisted by the government to serve its objectives.

After the enactment of the Actions (in Aid of Civil Power) Regulations 2011, Pakistan faced an international condemnation for its practice of indefinite detention, which was arbitrary and without charges. The Amnesty International released a report in which it pointed out towards widespread torture and abuse in Pakistan's tribal areas in which the prisoners were being held by the military and intelligence agencies without charges. To quote from the report,

> "Amnesty International research shows that, rather than seeking to apply and strengthen the human rights safeguards of Pakistan's ordinary criminal justice system in the Tribal Areas, the Pakistani authorities are applying old and new security laws that authorize prolonged, arbitrary, preventive detention by the Armed Forces, and breach international Human Rights law. The AACPR in particular, along with the century old Frontier Crimes Regulation 1901, provide a framework for widespread human rights violations to occur with impunity."

Pakistan's Attorney General Irfan Qadir had at that time admitted that the State was holding over 700 suspected militants 'without charge' under a law that has come under fire for its barbaric nature and loosely structured regulations which were open to manipulation and abuse to suit the interests of those who wield power. For long, the entire law was not even made public, and only those parts of the legislation which favoured the government were released selectively. Latif Afridi, a senior lawyer in Pakistan's Khyber-Pakhtunkhwa province, in reference to AACPR, stated how the law had failed in helping Islamabad's struggle against the Taliban.

Years after the law was enacted in the Khyber-Pakhtunkhwa province and the adjoining tribal areas, the Taliban remain active and unleash new terror campaigns. The law is also considered as an attempt by the Pakistani state to engage in systematic abuses to crush a separatist insurgency in the south-western province of Baluchistan. Not just that, the law, by its very nature, violates Pakistan's supreme law—the Constitution binds the security forces to produce a detainee before a court within 24 hours of their arrest, a provision which the AACPR doesn't seem too keen on honouring.

The 21st Amendment to the Constitution of Pakistan

Not satisfied with the extremely draconian POPA and AACPR, the Pakistani establishment went a step further by passing the 21st Amendment to the Constitution of Pakistan. This amendment, which contains a two-year sunset clause—January 2015 to January 2017—was enacted post-2014 Peshawar Army Public School massacre. Its statement of objects and reasons explains,

> "an extraordinary situation and circumstances exist which demand special measures for speedy trial of offences relating to terrorism, waging of war or insurrection against Pakistan and prevention of acts threatening the security of Pakistan. There exists grave and

> unprecedented threat to the territorial integrity of Pakistan by miscreants, terrorists and foreign funded elements. Since there is an extraordinary situation as stated above it is expedient that an appropriate amendment is made in the Constitution".

This amendment has been viewed critically for its provision of 'speedy trial Military Courts' which have recently been empowered to even pass death sentences on civilians. Critics point out that this shall lead to the strengthening of the grip of the military on a state that was ruled by military dictators for close to four decades and even today, is struggling to chart its course on the democratic path. Hassan Javid writes for *The Nation*:

> "In a context where the dominant narrative in Pakistan is increasingly revolving around an uncritical acceptance of, and endorsement for, the actions of the military, it must be recognized that by voluntarily agreeing to establish these courts, Parliament is essentially institutionalizing yet more military control over politics in Pakistan, rolling back much of the progress that had been made since the ouster of General Musharraf in 2008.

All the proposed checks and balances trumpeted by the government—the idea that the courts will only operate for two years, or that they will not be involved in non-terrorism related cases—do not change the fact that a democratic government has chosen to relinquish a considerable amount of space to the military. Given the history of civil-military relations in Pakistan, this is a dangerous precedent to set...rather than strengthening Pakistan's courts and police force, or propagating a counter-narrative aimed at delegitimizing the pernicious discourse of extremism propagated by the country's millenarian zealots, the political establishment, including the military, have been content to choose the path of expediency, preferring to tolerate any and all atrocities in the name of 'strategic depth'."

Indeed, Javid hits the nail in the following statement: "you cannot bomb poverty out of existence (although you can bomb the poor), and all the military trials in the world will not undo the damage done by decades of state-sponsored ideological indoctrination". Pakistan has much to learn.

Pakistani lawyer Saroop Ijaz, writing for the *Human Rights Watch*, was of the view:

> "The Pakistani government's decision to use military courts to prosecute terrorist suspects was a de-facto admission that the country's civilian

> criminal justice system is broken. Authorities have sought to justify military courts as necessary for the "speedy trial" of terrorist suspects and to circumvent perceived "loopholes" of the civilian justice system. Such criticism is not without basis. Pakistan's civilian courts have a well-earned reputation for prosecutions undermined by both corruption and a glacial pace".

Frightening, indeed!

It has been more than a year since the military courts came into existence in Pakistan. Had they been successful, even to a limited extent, the terrorist attacks in Pakistan should have declined. Rather, they have increased. From a total of seventeen terror strikes in 2014, the number went up to twenty in 2015. Sure, a 17.64 per cent increase may be marginal in empirical terms, but fortunately, humanity doesn't operate on mathematics. An 18 per cent increase also implies a corresponding rise in the number of people who fell prey to the brutal objectives of terror. Hardly three months into 2016, and the list of terror strikes was already seven. The death count? Quoting official figures—at least a hundred and fifty three!

The predominant fear among the civil society groups is that the life of the military courts might be extended beyond the current two years. But at the same time, Pakistan's civilian courts, including its Supreme Court, had been powerless in getting the executive government to enforce their judgements. Now, the entire process is controlled by the military and carried out in complete secrecy, beginning with the appointment of military judges to the trial itself. The mode of operation is maintained as secretive as possible: no official case files or evidence as record, no sharing of proceedings with the apex court—even death sentences are confirmed or commuted by the Chief of Army Staff, who moves with alacrity. These courts are thus nothing more than kangaroo courts.

The Indian Perspective

The Armed Forces Special Powers Act (AFSPA)

It requires to be stated at the outset that the AFSPA is not an anti-terror law in the conventional sense of the term, but a law and order provision which seeks to aid the operations of the military in the areas declared as 'disturbed' through appropriate constitutional measures. Based on a colonial-era law enacted to face down the Quit India movement in 1942, its immediate precedents were similar acts of 1947 implemented to control the Partition-related riots in Punjab and Bengal. The AFSPA in its present form was promulgated under constitutional provisions in September 1958 to control the Naga insurgency that had broken out in the mid-fifties and since then, has been invoked to contain volatile and dynamic situations in the prescribed 'disturbed areas' upon the ineffectiveness and consequent failure of the prevalent law and order machinery to perform its designated tasks.

The AFSPA exists in support of a foundational structure which necessitated its implementation in the regions the government so decided. This is also the reason why despite repeated attempts and demands from diverse sections within civil society, the Act stays. The Act provides a legal basis and legal cover to the Army's operation in internal security duties. Without AFSPA, the Army has no power of entry, arrest or justified and necessary offensive action as demanded by the dynamic situation that both terrorism and militancy impose. Unlike a normal law and order situation in which the army operates in aid of civil authority and has to get express permission of the civil authority to take offensive action, such debilitating constraints are not practicable in a terrorism setting.

The AFSPA has come under bitter criticism from within India and outside. What needs to be understood, however, is the nature of the soldier and the reason for his deployment in the designated disturbed area before criticising the provision of the law. Deployment of a soldier for national security assignments cannot be equated with other law enforcement agencies in general and the police forces in particular. The soldier being a custodian of national security is called upon when all other means of security maintenance fail or there is a grave threat to the national security and integrity from external or internal demands. The training given to the soldier to use weapons depending on the nature of the threat is a constitutional provision which he is endowed with across the world. However, this training is through a special provision of the law and the constitution which the respective states make. This constitutional provision not only accords the necessary powers to the soldier to defend his deployment, but is equally important to sustain his motivation and morale against extreme threats under adverse circumstances. Protecting the military role of the soldier is thus the reason why special provisions like the AFSPA have gained legal legitimacy given the exceptional context of their invocation.

Coming to the law itself, the AFSPA can come into force only in areas designated as 'disturbed areas' through a due process of law and not by the arbitrary will of those in power as clearly defined under Article 2. In such areas, where law and order have failed completely, the deployment of security forces becomes essential. Since failure is not an option for the forces once they are called upon to defend the country's integrity, there is a need to make exceptional provisions that assist them to discharge their responsibilities. The principal articles of the Act, namely 4(a), 4(b), 4(c) and 4(d) empower the armed forces to undertake counter-insurgent operations at the tactical level.

The most important segment of the Act is its fourth clause:

> "Any commissioned officer, warrant officer, non-commissioned officer or any other person of equivalent rank in the Armed Forces may, in a disturbed area:
>
> (a) If he is of opinion that it is necessary so to do for the maintenance of public order, after giving such due warning as he may consider necessary, fire upon or otherwise use force, even to the causing of death, against any person who is acting in contravention of any law or order for the time being in force in the disturbed area prohibiting the assembly of five or more persons or carrying of weapons or of things capable of being used as weapons or of fire-arms, ammunition or explosive substances;
>
> (b) If he is of opinion that it is necessary so to do, destroy any arms dump, prepared or fortified position or shelter from which armed attacks are made or are likely to be made or are attempted to be made, or any structure used as a training camp for armed volunteers or utilized as a hide-out by armed gangs or absconders wanted for any offence;
>
> (c) Arrest, without warrant, any person who has committed a cognizable offence or against whom a reasonable suspicion exists that he has committed or is about to commit a cognizable offence and may use such force as may be necessary to effect the arrest;
>
> (d) Enter and search without warrant any premises to make any such arrest as aforesaid or to recover any person believed to be wrongfully restrained or any arms, ammunition or explosive substances believed to be unlawfully kept in such premises and may for that purpose use such force as may be necessary".

Thus, Article 4(a) authorises any officer, commissioned and non-commissioned, to use force for the maintenance of public order. Article 4(b) empowers the forces to destroy a fortified position, cache or an arms dump. Article 4(c) empowers the arrest, without warrant, of a person who has committed a cognisable offence; and Article 4(d) permits search, without warrant, of a suspected premises to recover arms, ammunition and explosive substances. Obviously, the absence of these four legal provisions would render the security forces incapable of fulfilling their assigned role. Also, as previously stated, the AFSPA comes into operation only after an area has been declared 'disturbed'. In such a situation, its non-availability would imply that a soldier cannot fire upon a terrorist, take necessary action to destroy a hideout, arrest a suspect when in doubt, and lastly search any premises to recover arms and ammunition. The law also explicitly states under Article 5, "Any person arrested and taken into custody under this Act shall be made over to the officer-in-charge of the nearest police station with the least possible delay, together with a report of the circumstances occasioning the arrest". A constitutional provision against potential right violations is clearly guaranteed. Thus, as Brig. Harinder Singh mentions, it is not at all surprising that while several activists often raise their voice against the law, the affected states are hesitant in recommending the annulment of the Act. They realise the consequences of dilution in governance in the absence of an effective law and order enforcement capacity.

Despite the geographical and tactical sensitivity of the regions of its implementation, nowhere is any reference found for the possibility of indefinite detention or internment of offenders under the Act as is a norm with the Pakistani laws. Rather, there is a clear provision of a person arrested under the act to be handed over to the officer-in-charge of the nearest police station with the least possible delay (Article 5). As compared to the Pakistani special laws, therefore, AFSPA, with its built-in safeguards, stands very low on the measuring scale of a law being draconian.

It would be fair to investigate the UAPA from the Indian perspective before going ahead with a comparative analysis of the Indian framework against the Pakistani provisions.

India: The Unlawful Activities Prevention Act (UAPA) [with Amendments]

The decades after independence, particularly the 1980s, witnessed a number of legislations being enacted to tackle specific contingencies: Jammu and

Kashmir Public Safety Act (1978); Assam Preventive Detention Act (1980); National Security Act (1980, amended 1984 and 1987); Anti-Hijacking Act (1982); Armed Forces (Punjab and Chandigarh) Special Powers Act (1983); Punjab Disturbed Areas Act (1983); Chandigarh Disturbed Areas Act (1983); Suppression of Unlawful Acts Against Safety of Civil Aviation Act (1982); Terrorist Affected Areas (Special Courts) Act (1984); National Security (Second Amendment) Ordinance (1984); Terrorist and Disruptive Activities (Prevention) Act (1985, amended 1987); National Security Guard Act (1986); Criminal Courts and Security Guard Courts Rules (1987) and the Special Protection Group Act (1988).

However, it needs to be noted that while such laws were enacted to tackle specific, largely isolated instances, a severe lack was felt of a legislation which sought to deal with the menace of terrorism as a whole. Distinguishing 'terrorism' from 'ordinary crime', the Supreme Court of India in the "Hitendra Vishnu v/s State of Maharashtra" case noted that:

> "'Terrorism' has not been defined under Terrorist and Disruptive Activities (Prevention) Act (TADA) nor is it possible to give a precise definition of 'terrorism' or lay down what constitutes 'terrorism'. It may be possible to describe it as use of violence when it's most important result is not merely the physical and mental damage of the victim but the prolonged psychological effect it produces or has the potential of producing on the society as a whole. There may be death, injury, or destruction of property or even deprivation of individual liberty in the process but the extent and reach of the intended terrorist activity travels beyond the effect of an ordinary crime capable of being punished under the ordinary penal law of the land and its main objective is to overawe the Government or disturb harmony of the society or 'terrorise' people and the society and not only those directly assaulted, with a view to disturb even tempo, peace and tranquillity of the society and create a sense of fear and insecurity. A terrorist activity does not merely arise by causing disturbance of law and order or of public order. The fallout of the intended activity must be such that it travels beyond the capacity of the ordinary law enforcement agencies to tackle it under the ordinary penal law...What distinguishes 'terrorism' from other forms of violence therefore appears to be the deliberate and systematic use of coercive intimidation. It is therefore essential to treat such a criminal and deal with him differently than an ordinary criminal capable of being tried by the ordinary courts under the penal law of the land..."

At present, the only nationwide anti-terror law under implementation in India is the Unlawful Activities Prevention Act (UAPA). The provisions under the previously enacted laws including the Terrorist and Disruptive Activities (Prevention) Act (TADA) (1985–1995) and the Prevention of Terrorism Act (POTA) (2002–2004) have been merged under the now overarching UAPA. The UAPA Chapter I clause 2 subclause (f) defines "unlawful activity" in relation to an individual or association "as any action taken by such individual or association (whether by committing an act or by words, either spoken or written, or by signs or by visible representation or otherwise):

(a) Which is intended, or supports any claim, to bring about, on any ground whatsoever, the cession of a part of the territory of India or the secession of a part of the territory of India from the Union, or which incites any individual or group of individuals to bring about such cession or secession;
(b) Which disclaims, questions, disrupts or is intended to disrupt the sovereignty and territorial integrity of India".

Moreover, the declaration of an association as unlawful is certainly not an arbitrary decision, but the principles of democratic deliberation and opinion are allowed to exist, as expressed under the provisions of Chapter II, Clause 4:

> "Where any association has been declared unlawful by a notification issued under sub-section (1) of section 3, the Central Government shall, within thirty days from the date of the publication of the notification under the said sub-section, refer the notification to the Tribunal for the purpose of adjudicating whether or not there is sufficient cause for declaring the association unlawful. And, on receipt of such a reference under sub-section (1), the Tribunal shall call upon the association affected by notice in writing to show cause, within thirty days from the date of the service of such notice, why the association should not be declared unlawful".

The decision of the Tribunal shall be published in the official gazette thereafter, keeping a limited scope for any secrecy, apart from what is deemed essential in view of the national interest.

The amendment introduced in 2008 for the first time defined, in legal terms, what exactly constitutes a Terrorist Act. According to Section 15 of the UAPA:

"Whoever does any act with intent to threaten or likely to threaten the unity, integrity, security or sovereignty of India or with intent to strike terror or likely to strike terror in the people or any section of the people in India or in any foreign country:

(a) By using bombs, dynamite or other explosive substances or inflammable substances or firearms or other lethal weapons or poisonous or noxious gases or other chemicals or by any other substances (whether biological radioactive, nuclear or otherwise) of a hazardous nature or by any other means of whatever nature to cause or likely to cause:

   (i) death of, or injuries to, any person or persons; or

   (ii) loss of, or damage to, or destruction of, property; or

   (iii) disruption of any supplies or services essential to the life of the community in India or in any foreign country; or

   (iv) damage or destruction of any property in India or in a foreign country used or intended to be used for the defence of India or in connection with any other purposes of the Government of India, any State Government or any of their agencies; or

(b) Overawes by means of criminal force or the show of criminal force or attempts to do so or causes death of any public functionary or attempts to cause death of any public functionary; or

(c) Detains, kidnaps or abducts any person and threatens to kill or injure such person or does any other act in order to compel the Government of India, any State Government or the Government of a foreign country or any other person to do or abstain from doing any act, commits a terrorist act."

A further amendment to the UAPA in 2012 expanded this definition to include 'economic security'. Significantly, it also specifies the punishment for raising funds for terrorist activities in an attempt to curtail such crimes at the stage of inception.

Much criticism has been levelled against the Act since its inception, but what is often ignored in the process are the circumstances under which the Act and its subsequent amendments came into force. At the time when the Unlawful Activities (Prevention) Bill was moved in the Parliament, a consensus had emerged to impose reasonable restrictions on certain rights guaranteed under Part III of the Constitution to make powers available for dealing with activities directed against the integrity and sovereignty of India. The Bill was passed in both Houses of the Parliament and received the assent of the President on December 30, 1967, and was most notably amended post the withdrawal of POTA in 2004 and later after the horrific 26/11 attacks in Mumbai in 2008. The 2012 Amendment hinges primarily on the economic and commercial aspects of illegality, thus being beyond the purview of a paper focussing on the counter-terrorism dimension. It however, demands praise for making an attempt to plug in possible legal loopholes in the context of commercial crimes.

The UAPA clearly defines a list of offences and the punishments to be awarded in each case, leaving no scope for arbitrary pronouncements. This list has been expanding with changes in the nature of the crimes and the threats that India faces, as seen through the 2008 and 2012 Amendments. Under the UAPA, there is no mention of confessions to the police being accepted as evidence in court, thus allowing for the due procedure of law to be followed in pinning the guilt. Provisions for bail exist, with caveats, no doubt. Given the nature of the threat that India faces from elements which seek to destroy its unity and integrity and threaten its stability, granting such exemptions comes across as rather generous as against the content of the Pakistani laws evaluated in the preceding sections. It needs to be noted here that while laws like the National Security Act, 1980 allow provisions which can, given the nature and extent of the threat, be invoked in terrorism-related cases, the model of inbuilt safeguards and the rather cautious system of checks and balances ensures their judicious application through a well-defined legal mechanism, as opposed to an arbitrary invocation.

Comparative Analysis

When we compare the Indian anti-terror laws with those of states like Pakistan, one needs to analyse the basis, validity and liability of the basic constitutional frame of the respective nations. Pakistan, having been ruled by military regimes for more than four decades in its history of existence, has struggled in giving a democratic hue, in word and deed, to its Constitution. The military rulers have often modelled and re-modelled the framework legitimising the functioning of the state and its 'government' to fulfil their interest of retaining and sustaining power within the military–intelligence nexus. Despite the existence of elections, the reins of real power continue to be in the hands of the military. Any voice of dissent opposing the de-facto rulers in uniform has been suppressed by making special provisions which seek to protect its armed forces rather than the state. In addition, the blowback of terrorism that Pakistan has nurtured through its military establishment could have been tackled only through extreme and extraordinary laws framed and forced upon the political establishment by the military. In India, on the other hand, the due processes of democratic deliberation and eventual acceptance in Parliament have been the norm.

As compared to Pakistan where even criticising the army or its actions in the Parliament, or otherwise, is considered a serious offence under its Constitution, leave alone punishing army officials accused of human rights violations, the Indian General Officer Commanding-in-Chief (GOC-in-C) of the Northern Command, Lt Gen Sanjiv Chachra claimed that over 120 Armymen including 41 officers have been awarded exemplary punishment for committing human rights violations (in Jammu and Kashmir) during the last 20 years following an investigation into each of the allegations by an independent and autonomous body. The guilty including 41 Army officers and 83 JCOs and other ranks were expeditiously tried by army courts and awarded exemplary punishments ranging from dismissal from service without any service benefits, to imprisonment. This amply demonstrates that all cases of alleged HR violations are thoroughly investigated and the personnel found guilty, promptly punished. The Indian Army has repeatedly stated its position that it is its primary responsibility to ensure at all times that the *awaam* (people) are not put to any inconvenience or harassment due to the Army's necessary actions in a terrorism-plagued state. The Army has also strictly maintained its commitment of zero tolerance towards HR violations. In addition, an HR branch has been functional at the Army Headquarters since March 1993. Such branches exist in formations up to the Brigade and Sector level in the Indian context and even a capsule course on the importance of respect for human rights is also conducted for troops undergoing pre-induction training at various battle schools.

It is difficult to put the Indian and Pakistani anti-terror laws on a common platform of comparison. It would be an attempt to compare apples and oranges, so to speak. The Pakistani laws, as may have been evident by now, far outweigh their Indian counterparts in their extent of arbitrariness, draconian nature and lack of due process, not to mention the secrecy in which the trials are conducted. Despite facing an onerous challenge from the forces of terror which seek to destabilise the security and prosperity of India, the Indian judicial procedures have repeatedly emphasised the need to invoke safeguards which seek to uphold the basic norms and standards of civil liberties, much unlike Pakistan.

The International Commission of Jurists' Eminent Jurists Panel on Terrorism, Counterterrorism and Human Rights after its visit to Pakistan in 2007 concluded certain noteworthy observations in its report titled 'Assessing Damage, Urging Action'. The panel reported that, increasingly, a 'culture of secrecy' has shrouded the processes of investigation of terrorism cases and suspects were placed under secret and arbitrary detentions in a way that they could not avail the basic protections afforded by international human rights and humanitarian law, human rights standards and constitutional guarantees. Pakistan, thus, as a state whose own human rights abuses targeted at those 'it considers' as waging a war against itself, holds no right to point fingers at the rest given the nature of evidence and investigation which boldly stands to weaken its claims. Funnily enough, a state whose highest court empowers its already-neck-deep-in-controversy military courts to pass death sentences on civilians and rules that 'secret' military court are legal, thus ceding almost the entirety of the judicial space to its military establishment, seeks to question the democratic credentials and their implementation in the world's largest democracy!

Wait, what was that quip again, 'those who live in glass houses shouldn't throw stones at others', wasn't it?

The Author

Ms Navroz Singh is a Research Intern with the Vivekananda International Foundation, focusing on the Central Asian Republics. She is a graduate with honours in Political Science from Miranda House, University of Delhi and holds a postgraduate diploma in Conflict Transformation and Peace Building from the Aung San Suu Kyi Centre for Peace, Lady Sri Ram College, University of Delhi.

*

REFERENCES

'700 Alleged Militants held in Limbo in Pakistan', *CNS News*, 2013. Retrieved from http://www.cnsnews.com/news/article/700-alleged-militants-held-limbo-pakistan

'AFSPA 1958: Read the "Bare Act"', *Kavitajoshi.blogspot.in.*, 2006. Retrieved from http://kavitajoshi.blogspot.in/2006/10/afspa-1958-read-bare-act.html

'Arbitrary Executions', *Daily Times*, 2015. *Dailytimes.com.pk.* Retrieved from http://dailytimes.com.pk/editorial/27-Aug-15/arbitrary-executions

Armed Forces Special Powers Act: The Debate. (2012). *IDSA.* Retrieved from http://www.idsa.in/system/files/Monograph7.pdf

Ashraf, S., 'Will Military Courts help Pakistan eliminate Terrorism?". *East Asia Forum*, 2015. Retrieved from http://www.eastasiaforum.org/2015/09/01/will-military-courts-help-pakistan-eliminate-terrorism/

'Constitution (Twenty-First Amendment) Act, 2015', *Pakistani.org*, 2015. Retrieved from http://www.pakistani.org/pakistan/constitution/amendments/21amendment.html

Ijaz, S., 'Dispatches: Pakistan's Military Court's Mistake', *Human Rights Watch*, 2015. Retrieved from https://www.hrw.org/sq/node/280013

Javid, H., *'The Folly of Military Courts', The Nation*, 2015. Retrieved from http://nation.com.pk/columns/04-Jan-2015/the-folly-of-military-courts

'Justice On Speed', *The Nation*, 2015. Retrieved from http://nation.com.pk/editorials/28-Jan-2015/justice-on-speed

Katoch, D., 'Military Courts: Pakistan's Counter Terrorism Intervention', *Claws.in*, 2015. Retrieved from http://www.claws.in/1325/military-courts-pakistans-counter-terrorism-intervention-maj-gen-dhruv-c-katoch.html

Khan, A., 'Military Courts: Two Amendment Bills tabled in NA', *The Express Tribune*, 2015. *The Express Tribune*. Retrieved from http://tribune.com.pk/story/816951/military-courts-two-amendment-bills-tabled-in-na/

Kine, P., 'Pakistan's Dangerous Anti-Terrorism Law', *Human Rights Watch*, 2014. Retrieved from https://www.hrw.org/news/2014/07/21/pakistans-dangerous-anti-terrorism-law

Kine, P., *'Are Military Courts the Best Way to fight Terror?', The Express Tribune*, 2015. Retrieved from http://tribune.com.pk/story/822903/are-military-courts-the-best-way-to-fight-terror/

Manoharan, N., 'Special Laws to Counter Terrorism in India: A Reality Check', *Vifindia.org*, 2012. Retrieved from http://www.vifindia.org/print/1502

'Pakistan admits to holding 700 Militants without Charge', *Reuters*, 2013. Retrieved from http://www.reuters.com/article/us-pakistan-detainees-idUSBRE90N0HD20130124

'Pakistan: Withdraw Repressive Counterterrorism Law', *Human Rights Watch*, 2014. Retrieved from https://www.hrw.org/news/2014/07/03/pakistan-withdraw-repressive-counterterrorism-law

'Pakistan's Dangerous Anti-Terrorism Law', *Nipsa.in*, 2014. Retrieved from http://www.nipsa.in/news/pakistans-dangerous-anti-terrorism-law.html

Press, A., '700 People being held without Charges in Pakistan, Official says', *Nytimes.com*, 2013. Retrieved from http://www.nytimes.com/2013/01/25/world/asia/pakistan-700-people-being-held-without-charges-official-says.html?_r=0

Refugees, U., 'Pakistan admits to holding 700 Alleged Militants without Charges', *Refworld*, 2013. Retrieved from http://www.refworld.org/docid/5122358d22.html

Shah Azmi, A., 'New Pakistani Counterterrorism Law draws Criticism from Rights Groups', *RFE/RL*, 2014. Retrieved from http://gandhara.rferl.org/a/25245630.html

Sharma, A., 'Anyone found Guilty of Human Rights Violation in Jammu and Kashmir will face

Law: Army', *The Indian Express*, 2014. Retrieved from http://indianexpress.com/article/india/india-others/anyone-found-guilty-of-human-rights-violation-in-jammu-and-kashmir-will-face-law-army/

Singh, H., 'AFSPA: A Soldier's Perspective', *Institute for Defence Studies and Analyses. Idsa.in.*, 2010. Retrieved from http://www.idsa.in/idsacomments/AFSPAASoldiersPerspective_hsingh_060710

Soofi, A., 'Legal Face of the Enemy', *Dawn.com*, 2013. Retrieved from http://www.dawn.com/news/791771/legal-face-of-the-enemy

'The Actions (in Aid of Civil Power) Regulation, 2011', *The Institute for Social Justice (ISJ)*, 2011. *Isj.org.pk*. Retrieved from http://www.isj.org.pk/the-actions-in-aid-of-civil-power-regulation-2011/

'The Protection Of Pakistan Act', 2014. Retrieved from http://www.na.gov.pk/uploads/documents/1404714927_922.pdf

'The Unlawful Activities (Prevention) Act', 2012. Retrieved from http://mha.nic.in/hindi/sites/upload_files/mhahindi/files/pdf/UAPA-1967.pdf.

7

Rising Trend of Religious Radicalisation in Bangladesh

Ambassador Tariq Karim and Dr Madhumita Srivastava Balaji

Bangladesh, the world's third largest Muslim majority nation, has, right from its independence, cherished and followed the cardinal democratic values of freedom, equality, justice and religious tolerance. These, in a major way, also played a pivotal role in the nation's freedom struggle.

This is not to say that these principles were universally accepted by all sections of the community in the erstwhile East Pakistan that eventually became Bangladesh. As had been mentioned in one of our earlier papers 'Politics of Confrontation' (VIF July 2015), Bangladesh's tryst with democracy began a new chapter in the nation's history when the newly independent nation adopted its first Constitution in 1972 with the tenets of nationalism, democracy, socialism and secularism. The then political environment of the country was probably not conducive to fully accept these principles of democracy as it had just witnessed the vicissitudes of political assassinations followed by an extended period of 'junta rule' that lasted for nearly two decades. Nevertheless, the aspiration for democracy encouraged Bangladesh to restore a Parliamentary form of democracy in 1991.

However, in terms of acceptance of the principle of secularism, there always appeared to be some misgivings and reservations amongst those elements which were also opposed to the Liberation War then and even now. The recent cleansing process of the intellectuals in Bangladesh appears to be a part of the systematic conspiracy by a section of its political and religious leadership, possibly aided from outside, which was then vehemently opposing the principles of democracy, freedom, equality, justice and religious tolerance. As Amb. Tariq Karim puts it, "the goal is not to replace the government, or cause public mayhem, but instead to silence individuals for expression of atheism. These are assassins targeting secular minds".

The aim of this paper is to study and access the depth of penetration that the radical and Islamist-oriented ideology has managed to slowly establish since Bangladesh came into existence, followed by its recent outward manifestations through blogger killings and hacking of secular and free-minded individuals. Thereafter, the study shall attempt to examine the possible role that can be played by the educated and enlightened civil society in countering the infested Islamist-oriented Ideology and whether there is any viable solution to the present state of crisis that the country is witnessing.

Growth of the Islamist-Oriented Ideology since the Inception of Bangladesh

Though the rise of religious extremism manifested through blogger killings and silencing of liberal thinkers in Bangladesh is a relatively new phenomenon, the extreme nature of violent contest over the Islamic character of the society and the state is grounded deeply in a prolonged history of ideological disputes. As a part of undivided Pakistan (1947–71) the ethnic Bengalis suffered under the obdurate and archaic control of the Punjabi-dominated Urdu-speaking elite in the western half of the country. Although the Bengalis in the eastern province of undivided Pakistan constituted well over half of Pakistan's total population as aggregated in all its five provinces, they were subjected to extreme racial and cultural subjugation and economic exploitation and deprivation. The long simmering resentment of the Bengali community finally acquired political traction when it was politically disenfranchised following the only free national elections held in December 1970 that resulted in the Bengalis winning the majority in the National Assembly, but being prevented from forming the national government. The chain of events following this eventually vented explicitly in the Declaration of Independence in 1971. During the Liberation War, the Bengalis were subject to grisly and inhuman torture. Bangladesh's War of Independence has been the genesis of this

Secular–Islamic divide that still impacts the country's politics. The secular and democratic politics of the Awami League were fiercely opposed by the Jamaat-e-Islami, the foremost religious political movement that favoured a unified and undivided Islamic Pakistan.

Bangladesh's tryst with democracy and secular principles established a new chapter in the nation's history when the newly independent nation adopted its first constitution in 1972. But these principles never found a favourable ground and acceptance with the other existing political and Islamist-oriented Parties. The opposition to the liberal and progressive ideology of the Awami League coming from the Bangladesh Nationalist Party (BNP) and other fundamentalist parties led by the Jama'at, have largely been responsible for the growing radicalisation within Bangladesh since a long time. The genesis of the deep-rooted ideological conflict between the Awami League, the BNP and the fanatic Islamist parties can well be traced back to the divisive policies pursued by the British when they were contemplating the division of the Indian subcontinent, to an extent that this tussle between the two warring ideologies significantly contributed to the eventual emergence of the Awami League and the Bangladesh Nationalist Party as the two principal political entities in the country. Pakistan too left no stones unturned to stir up the clash between the regional identities vis-à-vis the religious identity.[1] the Bengali identity was deeply entrenched in the cultural ethos of Bangladesh whereas the concept of religious identity was the game-plan of the Pakistani elite, the Islamist-oriented parties and their supporters. To accentuate their identity, they purposely pursued policies which ended up in an exploitation of the resources of East Pakistan. As a result, Bangladesh became effectively a prisoner of transition from 'one colonial rule to another'.

A sustained economic discrimination further contributed significantly to an early consciousness of a separate and secular identity in the then East Pakistan. Further on, Jinnah's Declaration in Dhaka of Urdu being the only state language of Pakistan made matters worse for the regionally active Bengalis of this region.[2] It was against this backdrop that the Awami League under the towering leadership of Sheikh Mujibur-Rahman became the only probable platform for pursuing the national aspirations of the Bengalis of East Pakistan.

Even though with the birth of Bangladesh, the ideology of secular nationalism triumphed over that espoused by the fanatic 'Islam-pasand' parties backed by Pakistan, Islamic resurgence as is being witnessed today in

Bangladesh, was never given up as a long-term strategy of all the fanatic parties of West Pakistan and also the Pakistan Army which could not come to terms with the creation of a separate nation founded on the tenets of secularism and Bengali nationalism.

The developments in Bangladesh, post-creation, presented an ideal ground where the Islamist parties could work underhandedly to spread the growth of an "Islamist-oriented" ideology. Moreover, the overly complacent attitude of the 'natives', that their nation was presumably immune to all kinds of Islamist militancy, eased the surreptitious infiltration of radical Islamism into the Bangladeshi polity. The natives failed to detect or check the growing menace of Islamic orthodoxy which aimed at destroying the fabric of their flourishing democracy. To make matters worse, the alliance between the non-Bengali residents of East Pakistan and members of the Jama'at (Jama'at-i-Islami) took away the secular sheen the country once proudly possessed.[3]

Thereafter within a short duration, two military coups took place, wherein the system of parliamentary democracy was replaced by presidential ones that came in the form of military dictatorships. As a result, the middle class and the urban elite now stood completely alienated. The military action that overthrew the first elected government of the newly independent nation set the foundation for military and quasi-military rule and the growth of Islamist-oriented parties dominant in the country, where once the principles of freedom of speech, secular thought and righteous democracy had prevailed.

Thereafter, fundamental changes were brought into the Constitution which could be seen as a departure from the secular thought process. General Zia-ur-Rahman removed the reference to "secularism" as a fundamental principle of Bangladeshi nationhood from the Preamble of the Bangladeshi Constitution and replaced it with a new clause asserting that "absolute trust and faith in the Almighty Allah" should be "the basis of all actions". Hence, secularism was dropped, and even the pillar of socialism was redefined. The Islamic Preamble now acknowledged the primacy of Islam, thereby emphasising the Muslim identity over the cultural Bengali identity. Now the identity of the nationals as Bangladeshis rather than Bangalis which was earlier favoured by the Awami League was being encouraged in the country. A war-footing-style effort was also launched by the newly formed BNP in collusion with the Islamist parties to negate the role of the Awami League during the War of Liberation. The Jama'at and other Islamist-oriented parties officially gained a very significant role during Zia's reign. From earlier having been universally viewed as colluding and active partners with the Pakistani military in the assault on Bengalis of erstwhile East Pakistan, they were rehabilitated now and allowed once again officially to function as a political party in Bangladesh.[4]

An increased role of Islam in Bangladesh's culture and politics was further carried on from 1982–1990 through another military takeover by General Ershad. He permitted the rise of other splinter Islamic parties to counter the growth of Jama'at. The highlight of General Ershad's rule was the amendment to the Constitution that declared Islam as the state religion. Radicalisation was thus being sown sequentially on the Bangladeshi soil.

In the current context of growing Islamisation, the BNP remains deeply committed to conservatism, nationalism and anti-communism. It seeks to represent the Islamic conscience of Bangladesh. The Awami League's ideology stems from its commitment to secularism and staunch belief in Bengali nationalism and pluralist democracy. The ideological fault lines, questions of secularism, Bengali nationalism and above all the role of Islam, are the underlying causes for the persistent growth of radical ideas in the country.

Causes of Radicalisation in Bangladesh

The major causes for the growth of radicalisation in Bangladeshi society were in the form of absence of good governance, lack of social justice, absence of rule of law, antagonistic relations between leading political parties bordering on extreme hostility, politically engineered violence and politics of vendetta. The current wave of global pan-Islamic resurgence has also influenced a significant section of Bangladeshi Muslims as manifested in the widening network of deeply radicalised religious entities well beyond the existing Jama'at-e-Islami network that it inherited at the time of independence. The propaganda and political platform of these institutions are primarily faith-driven, exploiting the religious sentiments of the poor and deprived masses. Ideological conviction is the most predominant feature of radicalisation and extremism where the radicals exploit the people's religious sentiments. The madrassas owing allegiance to Wahhabi and Salaafi schools of thought, played an important, rather critical, role in their primary strategic agenda of moulding the young minds towards radical Islam. Women also formed an important component of their campaign as a crucial motivator within the families and local societies. It may also be relevant to mention here the direct and indirect impact of the Pak-supported and Saudi-backed Afghan Jihad in influencing the growth of radical Islamic philosophy in Bangladeshi society. It is well known that a significant number of Bangladeshi Muslims volunteered or were recruited for participating in the Afghan Jihad through Pakistani and Saudi-backed local Islamic bodies in Bangladesh. The returnees from the Jihad built or strengthened new or existing units that continued to spread the message of radicalisation. Also, the influential Tablighi Jamat network of Pakistan played an important role in spreading the message of radicalisation in a significant manner. Lately, online methods of spreading radicalisation among the educated youth have come to acquire a key role, even in Bangladesh.

Another interesting aspect of radicalisation in the country is the popular perception among the common people that the radicals and extremists elements have been utilising the civil society network for spreading their radical activities. A large number of survey respondents think that the NGOs and the community section of the civil society are widely involved in and are being used by the radicals and the extremists followed by professional groups, social workers and media. Some CSOs and NGOs are directly founded and funded by the radical organisations. Fund collections from the expatriate communities in the name of religion are a common practice. The veracity of this perception and the extent of its influence if true, need to be investigated and conclusively established through empirical studies.

Security Manifestations of Radicalisation

The two recent major terrorist attacks in Dhaka (July 1–2, 2016) and the Eid congregation 90 km north of Dhaka (July 7, 2016) focused national, regional and international attention on the extent and depth of radical Islamists in the country. Briefly, in the July 1 incident, a highly motivated group of 6 'home-grown' radical youth attacked an upmarket restaurant in Dhaka's posh suburb and brutally killed 24 patrons and two policemen before being neutralised by the security forces. One terrorist was captured alive. According to media reports, the group of highly radicalised youth owed allegiance to the ISIS but the government sources strongly maintain that they belonged to a local terror group. In the later incident of July 7 close to the venue of Eid prayers near Dhaka, the same message came out. The truth perhaps lies somewhere in between. While it is true that the ISIS/ISIL, if imagined as a corporate entity, does not have a corporate branch office in Bangladesh, local militants, whether remnants of older Islamist groupings (particularly the JMB) or its neo-avatar, the new JMB, have most likely established indirect links via several degrees of separation as well as over the electronic media. If the end-goal of ISIS is to establish one (its own) exclusive brand of Islam then its ambition would also seek to portray followers (soldiers) throughout the present-day Muslim world. In a world transformed by the 21st century globalisation that has rendered time and space irrelevant, the ISIS need not establish physically located branch offices located far away from its present epicentre; virtually located surrogates are good enough to try and establish beach-heads for its vaulting ambitions.

Since Bangladesh has traditionally been an inclusive, secular and tolerant society, the country had therefore, generally not experienced any major or frequent political upheavals, and historically, only Islamist-oriented people were attracted to any violent extremist ideology. This was despite Bangladesh's problems of widespread poverty, limited land and areas of poor governance. However, today Bangladesh is caught at the crossroads between two parallel, violently opposed ideologies and the irreconcilable strains have split the political and social instincts of the country into two distinct parts.

Violent extremism first captured attention in Bangladesh with a string of increasingly spectacular attacks throughout the early and mid-2000s.[5] Bangladesh has come a long way since August 2005 when the Jamaat-ul-Mujahideen Bangladesh (JMB), an indigenous extremist Islamist-oriented organisation carried out a string of 500 homemade bomb attacks which happened within a time frame of 30 minutes in 63 of Bangladesh's 64 districts. Though the perfectly synchronised explosions killed only two, the JMB's dramatic display of religious militancy captured global attention within no time. Bangladesh was now on the international map as the hotbed for radicalisation. The then BNP-led government banned the militant outfits of JMB and HUJI-B in 2005, but that was merely in letter and not seriously implemented on ground.

Bangladesh is presently witnessing a resurgence of radical Islam. The rapid expansion of home-grown and jihadi-affiliated militant groups have raised fears of a deep radical Islamisation of the pluralistic Bangladeshi society. Ever since the ISIS declared the establishment of the 'Caliphate' in June 2014, Bangladesh has witnessed the emergence of pro-ISIS outfits, which pledge allegiance to ISIS and support their recruitment drives both online and on the ground.

The kind of violence which is being perpetrated by the radical Islamist groups today is in a way linked to what is happening generally in the Islamic World. The al-Qaeda and the ISIS are targeting the Asian subcontinent in a major way and Bangladesh is fast emerging as a fertile hunting ground by both these terrorist outfits. The two have set up their own modules which are largely active in the indoctrination of youth and their recruitment for participation in the West Asian battlegrounds. The location of Bangladesh makes it a critically important geo-location for the ISIS's end-goals. With a burgeoning population of over 165 million, on the eastern flank of Bangladesh are located Indonesia, Malaysia, Thailand and the Philippines; while on its western flank is the huge Muslim population in India, rivalling in numbers Pakistan's Muslim population. In ISIS's strategic calculation, if Bangladesh could be induced to fall, its shock waves would travel both to its east and west. One should not lose sight of one important factor here: while the possession of territory to form an Islamic State may be important, in today's virtually connected world, it is no longer a *sine qua non*. Spreading the ideology is perhaps far more important at this point of time.

Initially, the Bangladeshi government in 2005 had banned five militant groups namely Hizb-ul-Tahrir,[6] Jamait-ul-Mujahideen Bangladesh, Harkat-ul-Jihad Bangladesh, Jagrata Muslim Janata of Bangladesh and Shahadat-e-Al-Hikma in 2003. The Ansarullah Bangla Team (ABT) has been the latest one to be banned in 2012. A newly emerged group called the Jund-al-Tawheed wal Khilafah (JTK) has reportedly started openly seeking recruits from Bangladesh. Authorities suspect that the JTK is the key platform for recruiting Bangladeshi militants bound for the Syrian battlefield.[7]

Presently, 14 radical Islamist-oriented groups are under the radar of the Bangladeshi government. The ABT's growing activities are alarming as it aims at the establishment of a Sharia state in Bangladesh. The al-Qaeda Chief Ayman-ul-Zawahiri's video released in September 2014 heavily influenced the Bangladeshi youth. The dreaded international outfit launched its wings called[8] Al Qaeda in Indian Sub-Continent (AQIS) to wage Jihad in South Asia. The Ansar-ul-Islam that projects itself as a part of the AQIS, claimed responsibility for killing three bloggers. The larger objective of this militant outfit is to join the AQIS after the al-Qaeda's adequate expansion in

Bangladesh. Between the various terrorist outfits, al-Qaeda's extensive and long standing regional network across South Asia has helped it gain an edge over the ISIS which is a relatively new starter. Unlike the ISIS which focuses on holding and expanding territories in Syria and Iraq and recruiting fighters for these theatres, the al-Qaeda has a long history of alleged engagements in South Asia dating back to the 1980s when it and South Asian militants fought together in Afghanistan. The AQIS takes keen interest in exploiting local grievances in India, Bangladesh and Myanmar. The authorities in Bangladesh have arrested a significant number of militants from groups linked to the al-Qaeda. These include militants from JMB, ABT and Harakatul-Jihad-al-Islami Bangladesh (HUJI-B). The latest outfit to enter into the militant scenario is Ansar-ul-Islam Bangladesh which is believed to be the new AQIS affiliated outfit in Bangladesh. The law enforcement agencies are also deeply worried about what they refer to as the "New (or neo) JMB", another militant group whose nefarious designs to attack the country's personalities and major infrastructural facilities is immensely disturbing.

The Manifestation of Radicalisation through Blogger Killings

The cold-blooded murder of Xulhaz Mannan and his colleague Rabbi Tonoy by Ansar-ul-Islam in Dhaka on April 25, 2016, demonstrates a pattern of organised killings, targeting the secular bloggers, religious heads, academicians, foreign aid workers and minorities. It is alleged that the renewal of extremism which is represented in the blogger killings, is linked indirectly to the 'secular authoritarianism' of the Awami League. The boycott of the BNP and Jama'at of the 2014 elections which gave the Awami League a landslide victory, was amid widespread violence.[9] This move stirred up afresh the secular vs. Islamic tension and bred radicalisation. The rise of this extreme form of violent Islam is occurring at the time when Bangladesh's politics has become deeply polarised and is creating a governance vacuum. A list of major violent incidents beginning from 2014 is attached.

These attacks and killings have opened up a new chapter of conflict between the values of a syncretic, secular and humanist Bangladesh on the one hand and on the other, a rigid and extremely fanatic world view where there is no space for other religious sentiments. Given Bangladesh's economic growth and modernisation, these killings have been a cause of concern as they might adversely impact the growing economy of the country and of course, its tolerant secular values.

The successive governments of Bangladesh have focused intensely on tackling internal terror and terror-prone propaganda. Even the earlier BNP–Jama'at government had banned militant organisations like the HUJI and JMB in 2005, preceded by the Jagrata Muslim BD and Shahadat al-Hikma in 2003. It may be apt to study here the following three developments tackled by the governments of Bangladesh.

The emergence and activities of the Hefazat-e-Islam in 2013 raised severe concern. Though the group was formed in 2010, it gained momentum only after it staged a march from Chittagong to Dhaka in 2013 as counter-dissent to a largely secular youth protest movement seeking the death penalty for the convicts of war crimes. The Hefazat-e-Islam released a set of thirteen demands which included a blasphemy law with a death penalty provision for all who insulted Islam. This declaration struck counter to Bangladesh's age-long culture of modernisation and that of a gloriously inclusive civilisation. Although the Hefazat-e-Islam may not have been a declared terrorist group yet, it may not be far from becoming one.

The second area of concern relates to the displaced and dependent Rohingyas. India and Bangladesh have been vocal about their grave concern over the radicalisation of these migrants by the LeT's two front organisations, Jamaat-ud-Dawa and Fala-i-Insaniyat foundation which are active among the Rohingya youth. Further on, a formation of partnership between the Rohingya Students' Organization and the HUJI-B has been a cause of concern for the authorities.

The third area of concern is the dramatic spread of the self-proclaimed Islamic State into Afghanistan and Ayman-al-Zawahiri's announcement last year of a new Indian subcontinent-specific AQIS, which captured substantial attention.[10]

It has almost been three years, since the first atheist blogger was hacked to death in 2013. The assaults on other free-minded bloggers and thinkers have shaken the country and captured international headlines. In 2013, the isolated murder of Rajib Haider caused alarm but it did not appear at that time to indicate towards blogger killings and the radicalisation of Bangladesh. The subsequent murder of Avijit Roy was prematurely presumed as a one-off radical lone-wolf action. But, when the third attack happened, the clear outline of a definite pattern behind these systematic and targeted killings became a more compelling evidence of the linkages for all to see. The tragedy of this manifestation of intolerance and bigotry has been receiving global attention since 2013–14. The 'publication' of a hit list of 84 bloggers to be hacked if they continued to write 'anything objectionable' against the tenets of Islam, sent alarm bells ringing in the hitherto placid social order and amongst the law enforcers in Bangladesh. More than 20 people have been killed in the hate crimes since 2013. It is unfortunate that but for the murderer of blogger Rajib Haider in 2013, no one else had been convicted or punished for any subsequent attacks, though it must be mentioned that in recent times the enforcement of the law to bring the perpetrators of such dastardly acts, has been receiving much more serious attention what with regular arrests and prosecution.

As far as the reaction towards the killing of the bloggers is concerned, the ruling Awami League reacted intensely for the first time, after the hacking of Niladri Chakraborty on August 7, 2015. The reaction to such ghastly crimes from the government machinery, many felt, should have come earlier. In spite of the government's stated policy of 'zero tolerance' to terror or hate crimes, the security issues assumed serious proportions among the country's liberal thinkers and civil society which became severely concerned over the growing jihadi activities of the extreme radical groups. Presently, the government is reeling under a severe criticism for its failure to reign in the radical Islamic forces, especially after the killing of four secular-minded bloggers and now the incidents like the Dhaka Bakery attack. Containing Islamic terrorism has always remained a key issue in the governance of any nation. The Awami League's zero-tolerance policy towards terrorism has been appreciated globally. Sheikh Hasina's promise that she will not allow her country to be used for any kind of extremist agenda deserve kudos and the civil society and the liberal thinkers would be closely watching the government's ability to deliver on its promises. To this end, the government has to initiate comprehensive measures to arrest the perpetrators of such crimes and firmly stem the rising tide of the Islamist-oriented ideology and thereafter, reinstate the secular fabric of its Constitution.

The nation requires a change in the thought process of governance and the active involvement of the educated urban intelligentsia in bringing about the required systemic changes. Mere periodic and cyclic transfer of power from one party to another will not usher in the aspired changes. There has to be no betrayal of the secular traditions or thought process. '*Mukto Mona*' (free mind) has to be cultivated and encouraged.[11]

There is another spectrum of the resurgence of religious fundamentalism which may require closer attention here. The desire to keep the nation together should take the desired precedence in the warring minds of the "Two Begums". Democracy anywhere and everywhere, will always be "work in progress"—inevitably so, for human societies that establish democracy are dynamic with perceptions of the values and social mores changing, imperceptibly but inevitably, with the passing of generations, fuelled by new ideas and inventions. Inevitably, this dynamic nature of society that establishes institutions for democratic governance move ahead of the institutions set before their times by their forbears. In this sense, every democracy today, anywhere, is in different points of imperfection striving to attain perfection. Bangladesh, in this context, is no exception to this dynamic. Since Bangladesh is, viewed through this lens, also an imperfect democracy (!), radicalisation and terrorism are directly linked to the corruption and mistrust in the political process. The Hasina government can help this process by focusing on developing a sense of oneness and unity based on a consensus on major national issues, as indeed her illustrious father, the Founding Father of the Nation, Bangabandhu Sheikh Mujibur Rahman had done over four decades ago, placing the nation and state at the top. The second requirement would be that of transparency that would foster accountability and put a restraint on corrupt practices. Thereafter, transitioning to a more predictable and a plausible transparent relationship with its citizens is primary for establishing good governance.

The country suffers from a critical vacuum in the law and order system. The secular liberal democrats mistrust their legal system. The evolution of the Bangladeshi democracy into a reliable system based on consistent laws and accountability remains a major challenge. Therefore, Bangladesh should strengthen and streamline its judicial system to check the growth of extremism. Bangladesh now needs to recognise the importance of addressing radicalisation as being much more than a merely criminal issue. In spite of all the measures taken, organisations like the JMB and the Jamaat may well continue to exist and evolve because the international situation has unleashed forces beyond any one nation-state's control.

The government should also look into developing a reintegration programme for the migrant workers returning from abroad. Here, insistence on the validity of Bengali Islam can counter the destructive impulse of reductionist Islamist ideas, the seeds of which can be unconsciously imbibed by Bangladeshi labourers during their prolonged stay particularly in the Gulf and countries like Singapore, where recently four Bangladeshis have been found guilty of financing or recruiting terror.

The country has established a good reputation of having mainstreamed and empowered women; in fact, this single achievement has acted as a force multiplier that has served Bangladesh admirably well in the sphere of achieving commendable human development indices. It needs now to further build on these notable achievements and impart an intrinsic resilience to its long-cherished culture of secularism, pluralism and tolerance, and to progressively expand further the space for women in terms of freedom and choice in both public and private spheres. Confronting Islamism should focus on capitalising and building further on the empowerment of women as drivers of societal change and the moulding of mores.

The Role of Education and Civil Society in Countering Radicalisation

Traditionally, responses to terrorism in Bangladesh (as indeed in other countries), have been dominated by hard-power approaches of the government and the law enforcement agencies. But in the recent security discourses, the role of a well-educated civil society has come up in a major way in countering radicalisation.[12] It must be borne in mind that the State alone does not possess all the necessary resources and skills to counter radicalisation and deal with violent extremism. Co-opting the educated civil society enhances mutual trust, offers transparency and thereby strengthens social cohesion. Like many nations in the "Muslim World", Bangladesh too seems to be struggling to precisely define the role of Islam and Islamic tenets in society and governance.

The civil society participates alongside the state in shaping and implementing public policies designed to resolve collective problems and promote public good. Counter-radicalisation should be viewed as a package of social, political, legal, educational and ecological programmes designed to offer a viable attractive alternative to the frustrated youth hovering on the brink and weaning them back into re-merging with the larger consensually productive societal fabric, as well as to deter the already radicalised individuals from becoming terrorists.[13]

Unfortunately, very few measures have been taken so far by the civil society organisations in countering radicalisation, though it is a work in progress. In a sense, as one of the authors of this paper has argued for long, a pervasive sense of complacency that the Bangladeshis' deep-rooted culture of inclusiveness and tolerance could never be breached by extremist ideologies perhaps enabled the very same radical ideologies to be successful in their creeping annexation of political and societal space. The lack of strategic communication between the civil society and the government was additionally a major deficiency in effectively countering the onslaught of extremist ideas on Bangladeshi society. This was perhaps inevitable when the civil society and authoritarian or military-backed governments were pitted against one another; in fact, radical Islam's encroachments were actively encouraged by those authoritarian quasi-military governments. It is ironic therefore that when the same civil society made a major role in wresting back democracy for the people, the democratically elected governments are viewed by not a few as being perceived as pitted against that very same civil society, preventing it from playing a more effective role in countering radicalisation than its potential holds. This has been exacerbated not a little by the apparent fragmentation among the CSOs followed by their reluctance in addressing the causes of radicalisation. Such a fragmentation results in undervaluing the strength of the civil society as a partner in coordinating its working in tandem with the State in effectively challenging the irredentist forces of radicalism throughout the country.

Any State, particularly those in developing countries, has to effectively deal, and equally importantly be perceived to be dealing, with the underlying socio-economic and political drivers of radicalisation—aptly deemed to be hunger, poverty, unemployment, underemployment, lack of value-based education, politico-democratic unrest and corruption—by mobilising and awakening the people. The civil society groups are required to help the State to create awareness, establish methods of checks and balances and to support the democratic institutions. Further, they can influence the State to adhere to neutral, humanitarian and welfare-based orientations. The civil society has an enormous role in preparing and disseminating counter-narratives by providing to the masses the actual and correct interpretation of religion. In other words, the CSOs can play a positive role in countering the ideological aspects of the radical narratives within the democratic polity of Bangladesh. Advocacy works in partnership with the state to create the public space for an enlightened and informed debate which could be an important area of joint cooperation between the government and the civil society. The commitment against radicalisation has to come from both the sides. Dhaka has to take the required symbolic shift in its governing patterns. Equally important is the sustainability of such efforts. The maintenance of sustainability of implementation can be a major challenge faced by the civil society in countering radicalisation.

The civil society can be influential in following ways:[14]

- It has to be vigilant regarding the role exercised by the media.
- It has to cast a positive impact on the role of education in shaping the youth perceptions against terrorist ideologues.
- Assisting the government and the agencies in choking off the terrorist financing.
- Assessing the impact of Bangladesh's diasporas on Islamic radicalisation.
- Building up of counter-narratives that are essential for addressing the conditions conducive to the spread of radicalisation in Bangladesh.
- Stemming the radicalisation process in itself.

Prime Minister Sheikh Hasina and her government has taken cognitive steps to stem Islamic extremism in Bangladesh by cracking down on radical groups and emphasising the democratic principles of the country's founding. Therefore, the Bangladesh Supreme Court's recent rejection of the last and final plea against the death sentence and the subsequent hanging of Matiur Rahman Nizami for his alleged role in the war crimes during the 1971 War of Liberation, meets a substantial demand of the largely pro-liberation-minded societal forces and has the steadfast approval of the Awami League. Her current government has demonstrated its firm determination to deal firmly with the extremist Islamist groups and to roll back the Islamic trends within the country's politics. The execution has come at a time when the nation is suffering a surge of killings of bloggers, atheists, foreign aid workers and secular thinkers, and serves to drive home the message that a culture of impunity will not be tolerated, that the perpetrators of criminal activities will be held to account and crimes will be punished.

The return to democracy is a welcome development but the country continues to reel under the radical Islamist elements which violently oppose the State which continues still to be wracked by multiple layers of identity-contestations: between its Bengali (cultural) and Islamic (faith-based) identity; by questions of what sort of Muslims constitute the State—whether of the

Sufi-leaning or Wahhabi-Salafi-Deobandi inclined—and whether it will abide by its legacy of secular, pluralist democracy or morph into an intolerant, Sharia-based autocracy.[15] Without concerted efforts by the State along with an even more vigilant civil society, the political centre of gravity in Bangladesh could shift towards Islamism and its fanatic tenets. Since mid-1975, Islamic ideas were permitted the space to progressively become more prevalent in the country's political discourse. It became so, having been allowed by the ruling dispensation at that point of the country's history to re-establish itself in the socio-political fabric and was spurred by the phenomenally rising fortunes of the Jamaat-e-Islami (JI)—a powerful political and economic actor.

Impact on India–Bangladesh Relations

Bangladesh's efforts to check acts of terrorism and the growing radicalisation have been, in many ways, exemplary. Its bilateral relations with India turned a critically important corner following the game-changing visit to India of Prime Minister Sheikh Hasina in January 2010, following her landslide victory giving her a massive mandate in the elections of December 2008. In order to stem the growth of radical ideas, both the countries have denied transit shelters and sanctuaries to international terrorist groups in the past. The country condemns all acts of terrorism in the name of Islam and cooperates proactively with the International Community to eliminate terrorism. The Awami League government has played a very critical and vigilant role in the sphere of de-radicalisation. With the efforts of the Sheikh Hasina government, the investigation into the acts of terror committed in the past, have been launched afresh and have yielded positive results. The handing over of the Indian North-East insurgent leader Anup Chetia in 2015 to the Indian authorities by the present Awami League government, is a pointer in the said direction. Previously, the ULFA Chairman Arabinda Rajkhowa and Deputy Commander-in-Chief of ULFA, Rajiv Barua, were also handed over to India sending a firm message of the Bangladesh government's commitment in this direction. Thereafter, on January 28, 2013, India and Bangladesh signed an extradition treaty to curb networking among the terrorist organisations of South Asia. A coordinated Border Management Plan was agreed upon to keep a vigil along the long porous border.

The two nations have a symbiotic interest in continuing to collaborate in combating terrorism. India will have to consolidate its governing hold over the North-East by providing the region with economic connectivity, development activity, moral and socio-cultural bonding with the rest of the nation and an enhanced integration with the BBIN nations which has been envisioned by the respective countries for working together collaboratively as the best means for fulfilling their ambitious development goals. The instability in the India–Bangladesh relations can undermine not only their investments for the desired development activities currently underway but also detract from other future development. The Indian government's doctrine of "together we grow" underpins Modi's five pillars of diplomacy—namely, *sammaan, samriddhi, suraksha, sanskriti* and *samvaad*.[16]

PM Narendra Modi has called for the United Nations to speedily adopt the Comprehensive Convention on International Terrorism. This gives us a clear picture as to whom India regards as a terrorist; religion and terrorism have to be delinked. It may be borne in mind that issues related to terrorism and radicalisation are no longer purely a law and order situation of the individual countries since, on this issue, geography is irrelevant. All nations today should have a zero-tolerance policy on terror and radicalised faith-based ideology.

Fighting radicalisation and its ideology must be not only an ongoing and continuing law enforcement exercise, requiring concerted and efficiently coordinated collaboration between different agencies within one country but also demanding equally concerted and coordinated collaboration in sharing information and data with all countries, whether in the immediate neighbouring regions or located far away, wherever there surfaces evidence of terrorist suspects having set footprint there. New Delhi and Dhaka have to, not only together, work collaboratively together to thwart acts of terror, prosecute the terrorists, enact suitable laws to effectively fight radicalism and choke terror financing; if the situation or evidence so warrants, they must also establish similar collaborative networking with other countries used by terrorists as transit or "safe-haven" places. Dhaka and New Delhi have to encourage the participation of all mainstream political sections of society to marginalise, if not wipe out, any harbouring of a feeling of political alienation. The task to educate all citizens stands as a preeminent priority. A collective bonding of global standards in order to stem radicalisation is called for. The commitment to fight radicalisation has be to full, imaginative and holistic. All the necessary resources should be pooled to fight the scourge of radicalism.

New Delhi and Dhaka cannot afford any kind of ongoing conflicts, instability and schisms within their countries to come in the way of progress towards strengthening the roots and fundamental institutions of a robust, vibrant democracy free from any sort of radicalised ideology.

The Authors

Ambassador Tariq Karim is the former High Commissioner of Bangladesh to India with the rank and status of a Minister of State. He has served as Ambassador of Bangladesh to the United States, High Commissioner to South Africa, Ambassador to Iran and Deputy Chief of Mission in Beijing as Additional Foreign Secretary at the Ministry of Foreign Affairs of Bangladesh with responsibility for the South Asian region (1995–97); he advocated bold and innovative approaches to normalising troubled relations with India and resolving long outstanding problems relating to water sharing, cross-border insurgency and boundary demarcation. He was entrusted with a critically important role in finalising the negotiations that resulted in the signing in December 1996 of the landmark 30-year Ganges Water Sharing Treaty with India.

State fragility, civil society, democratic transition, human rights and rule of law, governance issues in South Asia and political Islam and globalisation issues are among his primary areas of academic interest. Thus opting for early retirement from the Foreign Service, Ambassador Karim joined as a senior faculty at the University of Maryland in 1999 and was associated also with the George Washington and the Virginia International Universities.

Currently a Distinguished Fellow at the Vivekananda International Foundation in New Delhi, Ambassador Tariq Karim is concurrently also Advisor to the World Bank on its South Asian Regional Economic Integration Programme since 2014.

Dr Madhumita Srivastava Balaji, a student of Political Science, is an alumna of the Benaras Hindu University, Varanasi, India. She holds a PhD in Political Science and the subject of her dissertation was the 'International Dimensions of Ethnic Conflicts: A Case Study of Kashmir and Northern Ireland', reviewed by the Indian Council of Social Sciences Research, New Delhi and published under the publication grant of ICSSR in 1999–2000. Having taught in colleges of the Delhi University, the author is presently a Senior Research Associate with the Vivekananda International Foundation, New Delhi.

*

END NOTES

1. Amb. Tariq Karim, *Quo Vadis, Bangladesh?*
2. Ibid.
3. Ibid.
4. Ibid.
5. Geoffrey Macdonald, 'Preventing Violent Extremism through Inclusive Politics in Bangladesh'.
6. Although the Hizbut Tahrir was banned, it did not disappear. It simply went underground and continued its activities in the shadows. Its ideology is the precursor for the IS's professed ideology, and some of the people identified with the attacks in Bangladesh in July appear to have been members, whether active or dormant, of the HT.
7. Rupak Bhattacharjee.
8. Iftekharul Bashar, 'Islamic Militancy on the Rise in Bangladesh'.
9. With hindsight, the BNP perhaps realises now that its decision to boycott and continue clinging to alliance with the Jamaat-e-Islami was a strategic blunder on two counts. Its decision to boycott at a time when had it participated, even under the changed system of electoral governance which was legally valid and when it stood a fair chance of winning sufficiently large numbers of seats, essentially vacated political space that was promptly occupied by the AL. Its continuing dependence on the JI to demonstrate street power through unabashed violence also served to alienate the population increasingly angered by mindless violence.
10. Alyssa Ayres, 'Political Polarization & Religious Extremism in Bangladesh'.
11. Mukto Mona: Blog founded by the slain blogger Avijit Roy.
12. Bangladesh Enterprise Institute, 'The Role of Civil society in countering Radicalization in Bangladesh'.
13. Ibid.
14. Ibid.
15. Ambassador Tariq Karim, op. cit.
16. Delhi Declaration, 'India-Bangladesh Relation: Bilateralism and Beyond'. Bangladesh-India Friendship Dialogue, Sixth Round, 22-23 May 2015.

ANNEXURE

Incidents of Attacks by Islamic Extremists from 2013 Onwards

April 9, 2013: Student Arif Raihan Dwip was badly injured and later succumbed to the injuries.

December 21, 2013: Self-proclaimed Saint Rahman Farok and five others were slaughtered at his Gopibagh House.

August 1, 2014: Blogger Ashraful Alam hacked to death.

August, 27, 2014: Islamic front leader Nurul Islam Farooqi died after an attack on him.

November, 15, 2014: Professor A.K.M. Shafiul Islam was hacked to death.

February 15, 2013: Blogger Ahmed Rajib Haider is hacked to death in Dhaka.

February 26, 2015: Secular writer and blogger Avijit Roy killed in Dhaka.

April 13, 2015: Online activist Oyasikur Rahman Babu hacked to death near his home in Tejgaon.

May 12, 2015: Secular blogger Ananta Bijoy Das killed in a very similar manner.

August 7, 2015: Niladri Chatterjee Niloy was hacked to death inside his home at East Gorhan.

September 4, 2015: A self-proclaimed fakir and his attendant are killed inside his sanctum in Chittagong.

September 28, 2015: Italian aid worker Cesare Tavella is shot dead in Dhaka's Gulshan area.

October 3, 2015: A Japanese national Kunio Hoshi is gunned down in Rangpur's Kaunia.

October, 5, 2015: An attempt to kill the saint fails in Pabna's Church.

October 22, 2015: An Assistant Sub Inspector of police is stabbed to death at a check point in Dhaka.

October 22, 2015: A bomb attack on a gathering of Shias before an annual procession in old Dhaka leaves over 2 dead and over 100 wounded.

October 31, 2015: Two publishing houses that printed Avijit Roy's books came under attack.

October 31, 2015: Faisal Arefin Dipan of Jagriti Prokashoni is hacked to death in Shahbag.

November 4, 2015: Motorcycle-borne attackers hack a police constable to death in Savar's Ashulia.

November 8, 2015: A Bahai community leader is killed in Rangpur.

November 18, 2015: Italian priest Piero Parolari is shot dead in Dinajpur.

November 26, 2015: A Muezzin is killed in a Shia mosque in Bogra.

December 4, 2015: A bomb attack is made on Dinajpur's Kantajev Temple during the Rash festival that leaves 9 injured.

December 10, 2015: A bomb explodes in the ISKCON Temple, leaving two injured.

December 18, 2015: An explosion inside Bangladesh Navy's ISSA Khan base in Chittagong leaves six injured.

December 25, 2015: A suicide bombing at an Ahmediya mosque in Rajshahi kills one and injures ten.

February 21, 2016: Jogeshwar Roy beheaded in north Bangladesh; ISIS claims the responsibility behind this attack.

April 8, 2016: Sylhet's Ganajagaran Mancha activist and Jagannath University student Nazimuddin Samad, who was vocal online against religious extremism, hacked to death in Dhaka.

April 23, 2016: Prof. Siddiquee hacked to death near his house in Rajshahi.

April 23, 2016: A.F.M. Rezaul Karim Siddique, a Professor from the University of Rajshahi hacked to death; ISIL later claims responsibility.

April 30, 2016: Nikhil Joarder, a Hindu tailor, hacked in central Bangladesh. The killing was later on claimed by ISIS.

May 7, 2016: Mohammad Shahidullah hacked to death.

May 25, 2016: Debesh Chandra Pramanik attacked and killed. ISIL claims responsibility; their second attack in Bangladesh in less than a week.

June 7, 2016, Ananda Gopal Ganguly had his throat slit by suspected Islamist militants.

June 10, 2016: Niranjan Pande hacked by a suspected Islamist militant.

June 15, 2016: Ripon Chakravarti, a Hindu teacher in the Madaripur district, attacked with machete knives.

July 1, 2016: Shayamanand Das, a Hindu temple worker, hacked to death in Jhenaidah.

July 2, 2016: Mong Shwe Lung Marma, a Buddhist farmer and the Vice President of Ward Seven of the Awami League, hacked to death in Bandarban.

All these killings paved way for the July 1, 2016 attack at the Holey Artisan Bakery where 28 people including 5 terrorists, one security personnel and17 foreign nationals were killed.

Action by the Security Forces

March 2, 2013: The Bangladesh Detective Bureau arrested five members of the extremist organisation Ansarullah Bangla Team for the murder of Ahmed Rajib Haider. The five, all students of North South University, confessed to the crime in front of a magistrate.

March 2, 2015: A Rapid Action Battalion arrested Farabi Shafiur Rahman, a radical Islamist and suspected murderer of Avijit Roy. It was suspected by the police that Farabi had exchanged Roy's location, identity and family's photographs with various people. Farabi had threatened Roy several times through blogs and social media sites including Facebook. He said on different posts and comments that Roy would be killed upon his arrival in Dhaka.

August 14, 2015: The Bangladesh police said that it had arrested two men, suspected to be members of the Ansarullah Bangla Team, in connection with the murder of Niloy Neel.

August 18, 2015: Three members of the Ansarullah Bangla Team, including a British citizen named Touhidur Rahman whom the police described as "the main planner of the attacks on Avijit Roy and Ananta Bijoy Das", were arrested in connection with the two murders.

December 30, 2015: Two members of Ansarullah Bangla Team, Mohd. Faisal Bin Nayem and Redwanul Azad Rana were found guilty of murder and sentenced to death for Rajib Haider's murder. It may be recalled that Ahmed Rajib Haider's murder case was handled by a "fast-track trial court". Faisal, the court said, was the one who attacked Haider with a meat cleaver. Rana is absconding and was sentenced in absentia. Another member of the outlawed group, Maksudul Hasan, was also guilty of murder and given a life sentence. Five other members of the ABT, including firebrand leader Mufti Jasim Uddin Rahmani, received jail terms of five to ten years. One person had a term of three years.

June and July, 2016: The security forces of Bangladesh carried out extensive raids and arrested over 8,000 criminals, drug peddlers and members of banned organisations after the Holey Artisan Bakery attack.

8

The ISIS and Radicalisation in the Central Asian Republics

Navroz Singh

A Threat Expanding

The expanding threat of the self-proclaimed Islamic State (IS) looms large even as most states choose to remain in a state of denial over the presence of the extremist outfit on their soil. While countries in the Western 'heartlands' may be prime targets for attacks orchestrated and directed by the group, regions geographically closer to the outfit's so-called Caliphate are the most suited for direct recruitment into its organisational rank and structure. The erstwhile Soviet Republics of Central Asia, given their geostrategic proximity to the IS and domestic instability, are emerging as the most favoured recruitment grounds to serve the terror group's objectives which seeks to spread violence and instability in its immediate and extended neighbourhood.

An oft-quoted argument is that the collapse of the Soviet Union in 1991 allowed for the revival of radicalised strands within Islam in the Central Asian states of Uzbekistan, Kyrgyzstan, Kazakhstan, Turkmenistan and Tajikistan after nearly seven decades of severe religious repression under the communists. It is believed that despite intense efforts by the communist regime to exterminate religious identity across the empire, the Central Asian populations held on to their deeply Islamic culture systems and beliefs that had been handed down and nurtured over the centuries. Immediately after the collapse of the Soviet Union, the Central Asian leadership invested heavily in the building and restoration of mosques and other symbols of Islam as the means of proclaiming their identity as being different from that of the Soviet system and enhancing their legitimacy in the eyes of the local populations.

These strategies however reflected no genuine intent on part of the leadership to revive Islam in its traditional form in the region, and were, more often than not, tools to gain legitimacy and attain certain carefully calculated political goals. Officially, the republics maintained the policy of crushing with a heavy hand, the growth of destabilising elements which sought to destroy the famed stability and secularism of these states. And, a host of concurrent factors became the reason for the growth of radical elements within the society to the detriment of the syncretic, tolerant historical cultures of the region.

Despite the best intentions, the Hanafi school of Islam, the main conventional school of religious and legal interpretation in Central Asia, greatly favoured for its rational approach, strong traditions of dialogue and incorporation of local customs and traditions, came to be replaced, in certain pockets, with a highly intolerant, violent, exclusionary version adopted by the likes of the IS. Now, with the radicalisation on an upward swing, official figures cite the number of 'conservative' elements in society to be somewhere around a few hundred. However, at least 2,000 Central Asians are *believed* to have joined the Islamic State and the actual figure, writes Deirdre Tynan of the International Crisis Group, could be as high as 4,000.[1] Increasingly marked by poverty and radicalisation, the region has become a growing source of foreign fighters.

While the risks may still be in their relative infancy, brushing aside the potentiality of violence may exacerbate the threat to a point of no return. The recent appearance of the Islamic State of Iraq and Syria (ISIS) in the region, which started with the emergence of the black flag of the so-called Caliphate from a bridge in Tashkent,[2] is gradually acquiring unprecedented proportions. A short while after this incident, al-Baghdadi appointed a Tajik jihadi to be the 'Amir' of the Raqqa province in Syria. Towards the end of September 2014, the leader of the Waziristan-based Islamic Movement of Uzbekistan (IMU), Usmon Ghazi, declared his group's allegiance to the IS. In one of the most significant events till date, the chief of Tajikistan's Special Forces, Gulmorod Khalimov,[3] was seen in an ISIS propaganda video, dressed in black and holding a gun, and declaring his country's "un-Islamic" policies as the reason behind his departure to the Caliphate's heartland. Media reports also suggested that the recent disappearance of a container holding 50 kilograms of Cesium-137[4] in Kazakhstan reflects the possibility that the extremist group is on a lookout for radioactive material.

Essentially, thus, in a region that was famous for its unique version of Islam, often termed as 'Folk Islam' ... —a secular, tolerant blend of the basic tenets of the religion fused with the local cultural practices—a disturbing trend is ferociously raising its ugly head and a haunting question which persists is that, what factors have motivated such a rapid radicalisation of the region towards practices which, until much recently, had never gained forthwith or mass acceptance among the region's races, the exceptions notwithstanding. As with the rest of the world, multiple perspectives have been put forth.

"Congratulations: Your Brother has become a Martyr": The Pull and Push Factors towards Violent Jihad

Addressing this concern elicits multiple possibilities from the respondents, owing to the highly subjective nature of the phenomenon of radicalisation. It is extremely problematic to generalise a definite trend given the variations in objectives, personality profiles of potential radicalists, motivators, socio-economic circumstances and the high degree of heterogeneity in the cultural and ethnic patterns of the region. The existing research on this subject reflects sharp polarisations: a part of the scholarship is absolutely dismissive of the threat as a potent security risk and there are others who believe that the governments of these countries must be more cognisant of this threat today more than ever before, and undertake stringent measures to put up effective resistance. Further, while some believe that radicalisation in these republics is a result of the global wave of terrorism after the emergence of the 'Islamic State phenomenon', others hold the opinion that such post-Soviet models of radicalisation are myths generated to conceal domestic mismanagement and coercive repression of cultural and religious identities by the authoritarian governments at the helm of affairs since 1991–92. While some believe that religious manifestations peaked in the period immediately after the collapse of the Soviet state, others are firm believers of the fact that religion as a way of life, as a political tool or as a mobilising social force was in resurgence during the later Soviet years. Under the Soviet rule, the religious forces may have been dormant, but nowhere even close to being exterminated.

Without delving much into this argument, this paper seeks to analyse the trends, causes and repercussions of the most recent wave of radicalisation in the Central Asian republics—the one pertaining to the influence of the Islamic State.

The Trend

The International Crisis Group, in a report[5] published during the first fortnight of 2015, attempts to answer some of these questions based on a series of interviews with security experts, political analysts, state ministers, diplomats, religious leaders, politicians and would-be migrants to the ISIS territories.

Prompted in part by the appeal of an ideology which is gaining heat globally, and by a perception of political marginalisation and bleak economic prospects, Central Asia characterises a region where complex forces are at play in determining the causes of radicalisation. A deadly cocktail created by ethnic multiplicities, cultural fault lines, domestic instability, political authoritarianism, socio-economic underdevelopment and suppression of human rights has resulted in the manifestation of collective frustrations, thus placing these countries in an extremely fragile position. Reinforcing this 'fragility' has also been the grand scheme of radical elements in the region—to foster the breakdown of what they perceive as 'Western' systems of governance and secure the establishment of a "Central Asian Islamic" Caliphate, with the latter being am extremely concerning and unsettling possibility.

The following table represents the 'fragility index' for the countries in Central Asia, calculated on the basis of parameters such as 'demographic pressures', 'refugees and internally displaced people', 'group grievance', 'human flight and brain drain', 'uneven economic development', 'poverty and economic decline', 'state legitimacy', 'public services', 'security apparatus', 'factionalised elites' and 'external intervention'. As is evident, all countries save Kazakhstan are considered to be under medium to high risks of instability.

Country	Uzbekistan	Tajikistan	Turkmenistan	Kyrgyzstan	Kazakhstan
Ranking in 178 countries	60/178	57/178	83/178	64/178	113/178
Points	83.5	83.8	76	81.1	66.5
Category	High Warning	High Warning	Warning	High Warning	Low Warning

Notes: 1. Lower the ranking, higher the threat.
2. Higher the point, larger the threat

Foreign Policy Magazine: Most Fragile States Index, 2016

Source: http://foreignpolicy.com/fragile-states-index-2016-brexit-syria-refugee-europe-anti-migrant-boko-haram/

Therefore, a policy approach which protects the best interests of these states and the region, contextualised by considering the unique opportunities and threats these republics face, becomes essential.

Causes

In terms of individual motivations, 'ideological' support is the most important factor which shapes the radical perceptions in the region. Socio-economic factors do play a part, however, as secondary to the idea of a perceived 'holy struggle' to advance Islam. Sympathisers of the IS in the region, motivated by an extremist version of religious ideology, interpret the terror group's brutality and severity in the application of a narrowly defined socio-political agenda as reflective of moral strength, in the face of what they believe is the 'hypocritical secularism' of their own rulers. The aspect of 'novelty seeking' is not entirely lost in the region. However, this principle remains largely in the shadows when more persisting and potent drivers of radicalisation exist.

While some may seek to join the extremist ranks to gain combat experience, others may be pushed by bleak economic and social opportunities in their home countries as opposed to the 'glamourised' Islamic way of life portrayed by the IS propaganda. Mairambi Olimova,[6] whose daughter's family relocated to Syria as a part of the recent wave of radicalisation in their home state of Tajikistan, describes her last phone conversation with her daughter. She was informed that the family had been given US$ 30,000 for their journey to Aleppo. They had settled into a four-bedroom apartment with a television, refrigerator and carpets. All this has been granted even though her husband barely takes part in any military activities. Rather, he inspects cars for alcohol and cigarettes, which the ISIS has banned. Additionally, the family is also given US$ 35 a month in child benefits for each of their three children. Her daughter ended the conversation by declaring that she believed that *"the Caliphate will come to Tajikistan, so that Muslims will be able to live with Allah"*.

Identity stabilisation persists as a significant cause of radicalisation. During the Soviet period, vigorous efforts were made to completely wipe out religion and its identity manifestations from the public, and even the private sphere. Consequently, intellectual platforms of Islam vanished and the classic Islamic education systems based on the methodology of the Hanafi School was almost exterminated. After generations of implementing a failed communist experiment, the Muslim communities in Central Asia were at dangerously low levels of syncretic religious education. These communities, following Soviet social reengineering, came across as the most striking examples of 'post-atheistic' societies. The danger which surrounds such societies is that, religion does not erode but only lives a temporarily dormant life. In this period of dormancy and the obvious lack of enlightened perspectives which are more likely to be inclusive and tolerant, what sustains religion in pockets is aggression, humiliation and revenge. Given a suitable trigger event, the eventual manifestation is deadly, and Central Asia is learning its lessons the hard way. At the time of its independence, the Central Asian society was characterised by low levels of education in the foundational tenets of Islam, distorted traditions and a shattered identity. These factors, as many believe, created the most suitable conditions, over a period of time, for the emergence of radical and violent interpretations of Islam.

Today, an ambiguous and uncontrolled religious schooling, perceived unfulfilled desires for social and political change, social marginalisation and lack of sustainable economic opportunities, among a host of other factors, contribute towards a rapid radicalisation of the youth in the region. Contrary to their domestic struggles, forces like the IS perpetuate a notion of politics gaining legitimacy from self-styled interpretations of religion which find resonance among the disgruntled populations. The twisted possibility of leading a life of 'morality' in line with the 'true principles' of Islam, based on a thorough system of 'Islamic education', propels people who do not find acceptance of their opinions in their home states towards the pseudo-reality painted by the Caliphate. In the psychological state of cognitive dissonance, without suitable social reinforcements, individuals surrender the power of rationalisation to an ideological metanarrative, to the detriment of their selves and the social fabric. Unfortunately, before the consequences of their actions dawn upon them, escape is a farfetched reality.

An article published by *The Guardian* exemplifies this argument through the example of a Tajik man who had worked in Moscow on numerous occasions and said that if asked to, he would definitely join the ISIS. *"There's a caliphate there. You can live there as a Muslim and you don't have to fight, Allah be praised. You can go and be a part of the only state of Allah. Without homosexuals, lesbians and other filth".*

Keeping this in view, the significance of the need to generate, propagate and proliferate counter-narratives which challenge the violent and exclusionary beliefs of the likes of IS needs to be considered. The art of piecing society together through tolerant syncretism, actively impressed upon people, enables the building of a natural antidote against the nefarious objectives of such terror groups, whose highly flawed and disconcerting interpretations of religion require to be vehemently challenged and opposed through the multitude of social, political and cultural voices.

The Radicalisation of Women

A trend increasingly on the rise, and frighteningly so, is the rapid radicalisation of women in the Central Asian states.

Radicalisation is believed to be the most effective in small, close-knit networks of friends, relatives and acquaintances. This is the reason why the 'Social Movement' and 'Group Identity' principles most effectively define the causes of radicalisation in this region. Within identified 'circles', the perpetuation and acceptance of a certain way of life as supreme and ethically rewarding in 'this life and the next' is the most compelling force of radicalisation, as seen through most interviews published by the Crisis Group and other agencies. Women, whose journeys to Syria were cut short by intelligence agencies, revealed their plans to travel to the IS-controlled territories with their children, but leaving their husbands behind. For most, the prospects of a "devout life and an Islamic environment" for their children were the strongest calls. Almost no one indicated the slightest fear of death, for themselves or their children. Rather, they expressed satisfaction and joy when presented with the prospect of their children "sacrificing their lives for Islam" and transcending to the "world of eternity".

For these women, the opportunity cost of risking it all to travel to the terrorist mainlands was not an obstacle at all. Claiming to be frustrated with the living conditions in their homelands, many sought to justify their preference for risks of living and dying in an "Islamic Caliphate" which catered to their "economic and religious needs", over living among apostates who dance to the tunes of the "infidel western world". The social impact of such a trend is indeed horrifying. The percentage increase of women who are involved in extremism-related crimes has risen by a startling 22 per cent. From only 1 per cent of such crimes being committed by women about a decade ago, the number has increased to almost 23 per cent.

One of the concomitant reasons associated with such tendencies is the inability of the law enforcement agencies to undertake stringent measures against women and children, particularly through tactics involving the use of force. This explains why extremist organisations look favourably upon recruiting women—women are not checked as frequently and strictly as their male counterparts at international entry and exit check posts. Moreover, most contacts for recruitment are men in Russia or the Chechen region who often incentivise young girls to marry them before making the journey to Syria. Several young women have unfortunately fallen in the trap and are living under despicable conditions of exploitation and brutality in the regions controlled by IS; sexual crimes are a wretched reality. With no means of contacting their families back home, return seems a distant possibility, and even if some manage to return, although the prospects are extremely bleak, acceptance within the traditional family set-ups is impossible.

Geostrategic Compulsions

The strategic location of countries in Central Asia facilitates easy access to the Caliphate-controlled territories. The security infrastructure is not equipped enough to deal with recruitment which is conducted through well guarded, secretive, nuanced techniques. Recruitment, in person, often takes place in "rear markets"[7]—closed pavilions with small, poorly lit shops which are the domain of cannabis dealers and currency exchangers. Several groups of recruiters frequent these secluded back alleys, going back and forth between the spots usually frequented by migrants and prospective employers. Visiting the area usually after dark, the recruiters, in an attempt to persuade vulnerable recruits, play on their vulnerabilities (which given the obvious lack of basic necessities are often not hard to spot) and go on to explain that in ISIS, fighting was not obligatory. Instead of a slavish existence, they believed that the Islamic Caliphate "opened to them the possibility of leading a comfortable life".

Recruitment mostly occurs in Russia, and for those who can economically afford to make the journey, in the Wahhabi hotlands of Saudi Arabia or Egypt. On the journey to Central Asia, Turkey is the penultimate destination. The citizens of Kyrgyzstan, Turkmenistan, Tajikistan and Kazakhstan do not require a visa to travel to Turkey and the citizens of Uzbekistan are issued a 30-day visa upon their arrival. Having made it till here, the journey forward is not much of a trouble, given the huge influx of tourists, traders and economic migrants who enter and exit the country daily. Furthermore, lack of coordination between the law enforcement and security service agencies poses a major problem for the exchange of precise information about those headed for Syria. Beyond their homeland, ethnic divisions are reduced to a blur with the Central Asians, Russians, Chechens, Caucasians, Daghestanis, Russians and Turks coordinating themselves into similar *jamaats* (factions).

Migration

Migration in search of economic opportunities is a major propellant of radicalisation. Migrants, most of them illegal, come in contact with source recruiters mostly based out of Russia or the Arab countries, who have been trained in or have links with hardliner religious groups in Egypt, Saudi Arabia and Bangladesh. Most migrants are working under difficult economic conditions, are socially marginalised and ill-paid despite working under dangerous job restrictions, and therefore seek a sense of relief, solace and community in religious groupings. Gulnazar Keldi, the author of Tajikistan's national anthem, at a special session of the Tajik Parliament lamented, "Many of our young people are busy with difficult work, their lives are very hard and they live in a foreign country. At this very point, people appear who promise good money and heaven on earth, and they attract them into the jihad".

To quote the example of Nusrat Nazarov, the head Tajik in ISIS, from a report[8] published by *The Guardian*, his radicalisation started during the multiple trips he undertook to the Russian capital during the early 2000s. Chechens loyal to the terrorist groups frequent the mosques in Moscow and impress upon unsuspecting believers the need for them to "go live in Syria, where the caliphate is". Upon his return from Moscow, Nazarov's younger brother recollects, Nusrat became more and more religious, repeated to those around him that his eyes had been opened to 'proper Islam' and that now his only objective was to fight for achieving the "holy aim through violent jihad".

The transformation from 'identity stabilisation' through radical understandings of religion, towards 'identity glorification' by accepting the idea of waging a 'holy war' against "apostates" and "infidels" doesn't take too long. The consequences are deadly and deafening for not only the countries to which they have migrated but also for the countries of their origin. Given the lack of necessary security measures, most return to their homelands, radicalised and militarily trained in the art of waging war. The absence of socio-economic support in their homelands upholds the circle of migration to the 'promised lands' in search of 'worldly gold', which translates into 'outworldly gains' sooner than later.

Profiling a Prototype?

The dream of an 'Islamic Caliphate' appeals to a vast cross-section of people. No specific profile of a potential radical can thus be constructed.[9] Moreover, repeated appeals made by the propagandists of the Islamic State expressing their need for educated doctors, nurses, educationists, computer professionals, enhances the possibility of recruitment from a vast and varied pool of individuals. The myth of a potential terrorist being an impoverished lunatic is thus defeated. Some wish to fight on the ground; others wish to facilitate the requirements of the foot soldiers. While their objectives and the means to attain these goals may differ, the pull of the ideology is an invariable constant. Recruits may be ex-servicemen, farmers, school dropouts, university graduates, women abandoned by their families or those who have abandoned their marital homes in search of a more fulfilling 'Islamic' life in the Caliphate. Many are driven by the decisions of their states' leaders to allow Western forces, whom they perceive to be pursuing a nihilistic agenda against their 'Muslim' brothers in Afghanistan and Pakistan, to set up bases in Central Asia. Despite the heterogeneity in profiles, all are essentially driven by the belief, which has been emphatically and craftily sold to them, that a "life in a homogenous Islamic society is more fulfilling than the one they lead in the post-Soviet economic and social model".

Assessing the Actual Threat

Despite the euphoria surrounding an extremely legitimate threat, statistics indicate that the Central Asian countries may not be the world's preeminent place for recruitment into terrorism. The numbers of fighters sourced by the IS from these states are far from overwhelming when compared to the top

MENA (Middle East and North Africa) or the European countries. Quoting figures from a report published by the Polish Institute of International Affairs,[10] the figures of per capita volunteers from these states are: 1 in 14,400 Turkmen, 1 in 40,000 Tajiks, 1 in 56,000 Kyrgyz, 1 in 58,000 Uzbeks and 1 in 72,000 Kazakhs. This implies that the total number of foreign fighters in Syria and Iraq when expressed as a percentage of the total population of their respective countries stands at 0.0001 per cent for Kazakhstan, 0.007 per cent for Turkmenistan, 0.002 per cent for Kyrgyzstan, Uzbekistan and Tajikistan. The regional average is a pretty heartening 0.002 per cent. Compare this to the top five (Tunisia, Saudi Arabia, Jordan, Morocco, and Lebanon) MENA foreign fighter source countries. The regional average as a percentage of their populations taken collectively hovers between 0.08–0.011 per cent. And to pitch this against the top five European fighter source countries (France, Germany, United Kingdom, Belgium, and Bosnia and Herzegovina), the average stands at 0.07 per cent as a proportion of their populations taken together.

It would be interesting to note that these figures exist despite the populations of the Central Asian countries being predominantly (82.40%) Muslim (Sunni Muslims: 85% and Shia Muslims: 15%) as opposed to the European countries in which a meagre 12–12.5 per cent of the total population practices Islam.

One of the reasons for such trends is the inadequacy of direct connectivity between the Central Asian states and the battlefields of the Middle East. Fortunately, positive social pressure is immense. Family members of those individuals who chose to relocate to the IS-controlled territories have expressed severe regret and disappointment over the decisions of their kin and have, in most cases, disowned them for prioritising flawed individual ideological constructs and perceptions over the needs and advice of their families.

The Guardian[11] reports the interview conducted by Daniil Turovsky (of Meduza, a part of the New East Network) with Mairambi Olimova, mother-in-law of Loik Rajabov, who left for Syria with his family to serve the Islamic State. Without batting an eyelid she says, *"Most of all I want them (the Tajik authorities) to bring him (Rajabov) here, pour gasoline on his head, and set him on fire"*. Similarly, Ibrohim, the father of Bobojon Kurbonov,[12] one of the IS fighters killed in the battle for Raqqa in Syria in October 2013, is reported to have said,

"What's there to say? Why bother? I have disowned him. He never listened, did everything without permission. Then he went to Moscow in 2013. What did he go there for? How was I to know what he was doing there? I stopped talking to him after he left. When we came back, we didn't see each other. Then he left again. I don't understand how they could convince him to go (to Syria). He left his family – me, his children. He left and has dishonoured us all. I expected something like this from him. But I couldn't strangle him myself, they'd put me away for that. And now, I am suffering because of it. It would have been better just to strangle him."

Analysing the Presence of the ISIS in Central Asia: A Country-wise Study

The trends of radicalisation in Central Asia are unevenly distributed among the countries in the region. Radical tendencies are more pronounced towards the southern, south-eastern and north-eastern parts of the region, with the heartlands being relatively secure.

Kazakhstan

In *Kazakhstan*, the most developed of the five states, radicalisation was not perceived as much of a threat until recently following a series of ISIS-related incidents in the country, which have shocked the government out of its self-induced slumber. On June 6' 2016, armed assailants attacked two arms shops to seize weapons and rammed a minibus through the doors of a National Guard base in the north-western city of Aktobe.[13] President Nazarbayev termed the attackers as "foreign-trained Salafi jihadists", "politically motivated to destabilize the country" and overthrow the present regime. A month later, on the July 12, a regional court in Aktobe convicted 12 men for plotting attacks on behalf of the IS, and less than a week later, on the July 18, two armed gunmen killed two policemen and a civilian in Kazakhstan's commercial capital, Almaty.[14]

Kazakhstan has been considered the most stable and most secular amongst all the post-Soviet republics. For a society based more on clan membership and regional identity than transnational religious extremism, the recent trends are indeed alarming. The rise of radical interpretations of Islam in Kazakhstan occurred in three, almost successive, stages. The process started in 1995 when such ideas started infiltrating into Kazakhstan from the Russian republics of

Dagestan and Chechnya. During this period which continued till 2002, the republic was permeated with the ideas of *Takfir*, a radical ideology based on accusing fellow Muslims of apostasy. The second stage is associated with the name of Sheikh Abduhalil Abdujabarov, and it is during this period that the ideas of Wahhabism and *Takfir* entrenched deeper into the Kazakh society.

The third stage started in 2011 and continues till date, strengthening its violent resolve each successive year with support from the emergence of groups such as the Islamic State. Additionally, NATO's military operation against the al-Qaeda and the Taliban in Afghanistan, and the wars in the Middle East, facilitated the spread of such ideologies during this period. Most recruits claim allegiance to the Salafi school of Islam, which is relatively unpopular among the Kazakhs who largely support the Hanafi school of Islamic law. The '*Tablighi Jamaat*', a missionary extremist organisation which though is formally banned in the country, currently handles the recruitment for the ISIS from within the Kazakh territory.

Theoretically speaking, radicalisation is most prevalent in the southern districts, which border Uzbekistan and Tajikistan. But the ISIS-related activity is also on a steady increase in the northern and western parts of the country where radical *Jamias* are the most active. The northern parts witness a high degree of activity of the ISIS-related Caucasian networks from Russia. Volunteers are recruited both within the country, in mosques and *namazkhanas* and abroad, mostly in Russia.

The most recent statistics indicate that close to 300 Kazakh citizens are fighting in the ranks of the ISIS and the numbers are set to increase. With the government responding through increased repression in the name of secularism, one view predicts that the radical elements are likely to strengthen when presented with alternatives which favour their worldview.

Kyrgyzstan

Kyrgyzstan has witnessed two revolutions in the last decade. This political tumult and turmoil underlined the inherent weaknesses of the Kyrgyz state, which has been exploited to the hilt by recruiters: corruption, poverty, ethnic rivalries and clan-based tensions, lack of democratic institutions and authoritarian laws perceived by some to be anti-Islamic.

The number of Kyrgyz nationals estimated to have volunteered to join the IS varies between a hundred to almost six hundred. The route undertaken to reach the Arab warlands is largely the same: recruitment in mosques and close-knit radical units in Russia (where most of them work as migrants on construction sites), an interlude in Turkey, from where they are guided forward to their destinations in Syria.

What makes the Kyrgyz example most interesting is that the majority of the recruitments take place in the southern part of the country—a territorial landmass dominated by the Uzbek minority which is historically more religious than the ethnic Kyrgyz and has faced violent repression in the past. Again, mostly, recruitment takes place in Russia, where the majority of the Kyrgyz migrants have settled. The accession of Kyrgyzstan to the Eurasian Economic Union in May 2015 ensured that the citizens of the country no longer have to apply for work permission to seek employment in Russia. To a limited extent, social networks as Odnolklasniki, Vkontakte and Facebook also facilitate recruitment and communication.

Tajikistan

In the case of *Tajikistan,* currently there are two main radical groups in operation: the *Hizb ut-Tahrir* and the Islamic Movement of Uzbekistan. Recently, the *Jamaoati Ansorullah*, with links to Pakistani madrassas, has also indicated its presence in Tajikistan. According to Muriel Atkin, who specialises in the role of Islam and nationalism in the political conflict in Tajikistan at the Elliot School of International Affairs, George Washington University, it is Sufi Islam which flourished in Tajikistan, based on decentralised and informal traditional Islamic practices. The cultural diversity within Tajikistan is immense. Home to not only Sunnis of the Sufi tradition, but also an Ismaili minority which is localised in the Badakhshan province, ninety per cent of the Tajiks acknowledge their ideological association with the Hanafi school of Islam. In 2015, Tajikistan's Supreme Court declared that Salafi Muslims were extremists and in referring to the ISIS, Tajik President Emomali Rahmon declared the organisation as the "plague of the 21st Century".

Geographically, most recruitment into the ranks of ISIS takes place from the western and north-eastern parts of the country such as the Gissar Valley and the Ferghana Valley, where almost 90 per cent of the population is Sunni Muslim. The Gorno-Badakhshan Autonomous region, bordering Afghanistan in the Pamir mountainous region, is home to the Ismaili Shiite population which feels increasingly threatened from the threat of Taliban incursions from bordering Afghanistan. Consequently, radical elements enjoy almost no support in this region.

Highly inconsistent and fluctuating statistics have been submitted of the number of Tajiks who have currently joined ISIS. The numbers vary between 190 (International Centre for the Study of Radicalization), to almost 2000. Official estimates are yet to cross the 500 mark. Despite such variations, little contestation is put to the claim that Tajikistan is the perfect place for extremist groups: drug trafficking, easy infiltration of financial and combative military assistance, corrupt and repressive government, economic crisis, lack of social security, unemployment, inadequate security infrastructure and poverty cumulatively contribute towards the disillusionment and alienation among youth, paving the way towards radicalisation. Needless to say, it is in Russia that the recruitment into terrorist organisations mostly takes place. The hubs are mosques and prayer rooms spread across the country, are frequented by the Chechens, who work towards consolidating young migrants and providing them with a sense of security and community through religion. Online social networking plays a limited role.

Turkmenistan

Geographically, *Turkmenistan* is located the closest to the IS-infested territories and ranks the second-highest amongst the Central Asian countries with close to 360 Turkmen speculated to be fighting in the ranks of the Islamic State. However, uniquely, religious radicalisation is not a dominant cause of concern in the country, and is limited to only a section of the minority confined to the fringes. Despite Turkmenistan being a hermetic state, with not much known about its prominent social trends, it suffices to say that the Turkmen value their clan and regional identities much more than the allure of a global Islamic movement.

The Turkmen are a source of low-paid and low-skill labour in Russia, which is where the majority of the recruitment takes place. What may motivate the Turkmen to join organisations such as the ISIS are the vast socio-economic disparities—a characteristic of the decaying social structure of the state. However, what is most peculiar to Turkmenistan is the fact that many of their Shiite brethren inhabit pockets of territories in Syria and Iraq and have often been the target of attacks and killings orchestrated by the IS. Therefore, the allure of the terror group is almost defeated by its pronounced anti-Shia

Jaborov, Safovudin, 'Youth Radicalization in Tajikistan: Causes, Consequences, and Challenges to Address', Central Asia Program, *Centralasiaprogram.org*, 2013. Web. 3 Aug. 2016.

Khalid, A., *Islam after Communism* (1st ed.), Berkeley: University of California Press, 2007.

Krausen, Erik S., 'Central Asia: Can Secular Islam Survive?' *The Diplomat*, 2015. Web. 4 Aug. 2016.

Masylkanova, Aidai, 'Radicalization in Kyrgyzstan is No Myth', *The Diplomat*, 2016. Web. 30 July 2016.

Omelicheva, Mariya Y. and Lawrence Markowitz, "A Trafficking-Terrorism Nexus in Central Asia', *The Diplomat*, 2016. Web. 28 July 2016.

Orozobekova, Cholpon, 'Central Asia and the ISIS Phantom', *The Diplomat*, 2015. Web. 7 Aug. 2016.

Putz, Catherine, '5 Countries where Freedom of Religion is Threatened', *The Diplomat*, 2015. Web. 3 Aug. 2016.

Putz, Catherine, '6 Myths of Muslim Radicalization in Central Asia', *The Diplomat*, 2016. Web. 4 Aug. 2016.

Putz, Catherine, 'Central Asia has 99 Problems, but Extremism in Tajikistan isn't the Worst', *The Diplomat*, 2015. Web. 1 Aug. 2016.

Putz, Catherine, 'Did the Missing Tajik Commander just Reappear?' *The Diplomat*, 2015. Web. 1 Aug. 2016.

Putz, Catherine, 'How Fragile is the Peace in Tajikistan?' *The Diplomat*, 2015. Web. 1 Aug. 2016.

Putz, Catherine, 'Playing 'Telephone' with ISIS Central Asia Estimates', *The Diplomat*, 2015. Web. 3 Aug. 2016.

Putz, Catherine, 'How to Fight ISIS Messaging in Central Asia? Religious Freedom', *The Diplomat*, 2016. Web. 29 July 2016.

Putz, Catherine, 'Tajikistan mulls banning Islamic-Sounding Names', *The Diplomat*, 2015. Web. 2 Aug. 2016.

Putz, Catherine, 'Tajikistan to install Surveillance Cameras on Dushanbe Mosques', *The Diplomat*, 2016. Web. 30 July 2016.

'Regional Workshop on Radicalization in Central Asia', *Undp.org*, 2016. Web. 2 Aug. 2016.

'Remarks at the Rollout of the 2014 Report on International Religious Freedom', *U.S. Department of State*, 2016. Web. 6 Aug. 2016.

Ruzaliev, Odil, 'ICG warns of growing Radicalization in Central Asia', *VOA*, 2015. Web. 10 Aug. 2016.

Snow, Shawn, 'ISIS looks for Foothold in Central Asia', *The Diplomat*, 2015. Web. 1 Aug. 2016.

Solovyov, Dmitry, 'Central Asia Crackdown on Militant Islam risks Backlash', *Reuters*, 2015. Web. 7 Aug. 2016.

Sorbello, Paolo, 'Islam and Central Asia: Threat or Myth?' *The Diplomat*, 2015. Web. 4 Aug. 2016.

Stobdan, P., 'ISIS in Central Asia', Institute for Defence Studies and Analyses, *Idsa.in*, 2014. Web. 29 July 2016.

Tahir, Muhammad, 'Radical Islam takes a Front Seat in Central Asia', *The Jamestown Foundation*, 2011. Web. 6 Aug. 2016.

'Thousands from Central Asia joining 'Islamic State': Report 21.01.2015', *DW.COM*, 2016. Web. 7 Aug. 2016.

Toktonaliev, Timur, 'Does Islamic State threaten Central Asia?' Institute for War and Peace Reporting, 2015. Web. 6 Aug. 2016.

Tynan, Deirdre, 'Islamic State threatens Central Asia', *International Crisis Group*, 2015. Web. 4 Aug. 2016.

'US Congressman: Gulf States finance Radicalization in Central Asia', *Sputniknews.com*, 2016. Web. 5 Aug. 2016.

Zhussipbek, Galym, 'Religious Radicalism in Central Asia', *Rethinkinstitute.org*, 2013. Web. 30 July 2016.

Image Source:

http://georgetownsecuritystudiesreview.org

9

MAOIST REBELLION: GROUND REALITIES

Lt Gen Gautam Banerjee

Ground Situation

The end-of-year reports emanating from various Home Departments of the states affected by the Maoist rebellion indicates that the downtrend in violence, as seen during the preceding year, continues. Even if marred by the ambush at the Darba Valley on the Chhattisgarh–Odisha Border on May 25, 2013, this is a hopeful sign. After all, de-escalatory trends in acts of anti-state insurrection offer the first hint of situational de-conflagration. If handled with a sagaciously articulated strategy of hard and soft power, it paves the way for the establishment of an environment of peace and stability in which the people may seek an amelioration of their grievances, while the government may respond with due alacrity.

Signs, however, could also be misleading, particularly when these point towards what one optimistically wants to believe. Therefore, it would be wise to rely on a first-hand ground survey of the situation while strategising for the coming phase of the Counter-Maoist initiatives. This report is an attempt towards that end.

Build-Up of the State Capabilities

It was some time in the year 2010, when pitted against a vicious Maoist onslaught, that the policymakers had to turn their illusionary rhetoric into serious intent. Thus from the time the state governments came around to accede to the Union Government's counter-rebellion strategy, haltingly but inexorably, the state apparatus is being strengthened in grappling with the Maoist menace. Even if fraught with glaring slippages, leakages and inefficiency, the build-up of the states' internal security capability has been going since then.

Build-Up of the Security Infrastructure

In an enhancement of the armed capability of the police forces, the elaborate schemes for expansion, training and modernisation continue to be exasperatingly slow in coming. The seven-year-old 'Scheme for Fortified Police Stations', which was necessitated by the Maoists' frequent mass attacks and loot of weapons, and the public outcry against the massacre of their own policemen-folks, proceeds at a languid pace; the constructions inspiring confidence neither in technical nor tactical terms. Between the threats of looming attacks, the commitment to reconstruct 400 of what are but ruins of the British-era police stations seems to be waxing and waning. As a result, the project has not crossed the half-way stage; where construction has been executed, there remain parts left incomplete.

The security infrastructure is also being built up under the Union Government-aided 'Security Related Expenditure' and 'Special Infrastructure Scheme'. The first one caters to the expenditure on the enhancement of administrative wherewithal, surrender and rehabilitation of rebels, formation of Village Defence Committees, community policing, publicity and motivation and information-gathering, while the second head funds security-specific road-building, preparation of camping grounds for police details in distant areas, construction of secure policing outposts in vulnerable locations, helipads, communication facilities, etc. the progress of project implementation is however very slow, the reasons being as follows:

a) There is an average time lag of two to three years between a political statement and commencement of the scheme at the point of execution. This lag is on account of budgetary tricks which the government must resort to in funding these schemes through a re-prioritisation and re-appropriation from a budget that is already overburdened by the game of voter appeasement. Due to an intermittent release of funds, it may take another two to three years before the schemes gather moderate pace, that is, if not diverted or relegated in favour of new expediencies.

b) The government departments, besides being culturally inefficient and unscrupulously corrupt, do not even have the necessary wherewithal to execute works across isolated areas with due fiscal and technical prudence. Public projects are viewed as licence to distribute what may be described as 'percentage cuts', compromise construction specifications and enrich politicians, contractors, state functionaries and cronies; even the intended beneficiaries of the works are weaned away from complaining.

These ingrained debilitations are unlikely to go away anytime soon.

The Build-Up of Police Forces

While recruitment to fill up existing vacancies in the state police ranks goes on, new raisings of specialised counter-insurgency forces have been undertaken at the state as well as Central levels. The state governments have thus raised between two to four such specialist battalions manned by ex-servicemen, though the manner of their employment and control remains somewhat misdirected. Among the Central Armed Police Forces (CAPFs), the Central Reserve Police Force (CRPF) has raised ten specialist battalions, referred to as the 'Commando Battalion for Resolute Action' (CoBRA) and recently renamed as the 'Special Action Force'. Fit and well-trained, these units have been deployed effectively. The concept of 'India Reserve Battalions' (IRB), manned by local levies, has been extended to raise 46 units in the nine affected states. 33 of these have been raised; some of these have even been designated as 'specialist' IRBs; the renaming appears to be aimed at finding higher emoluments rather than obtaining robust counter-insurgency ability.

The overall level of training, motivation and equipment of the police forces remains little more than basic. Training establishments being limited, the training of recruits as well as serving policemen poses the biggest hurdle. Though 12 Counter-Insurgency & Counter-Terrorist Schools (CICTS) out of 15 sanctioned in the various states have been raised, actually these are just add-ons to the existing state armed police battalion lines. Obviously, the training facilities are woefully inadequate in terms of quality as well as quantity. While announcing the intended measures to control the rebellion, the realisation that it takes three years or so before a policeman may be considered to be adequately trained in a counter-insurgency role, seems to be overlooked.

Issues which require attention in this regard are as follows:

a) Recruitment drives in the states have been prone to malpractices and mired in party and cast manipulations. Thus scams, enquiries and court cases have put paid to the process.

b) Disconcertingly, it is often found that there is a dearth of recruitable candidates, either on account of poor education or opportunistic mentality. The quality of policemen that these would make, is therefore questionable.

c) The establishment of regular CICT Schools is affected due to a lack of competent trainers and hurdles, real or invented, posed against the allotment of land.

Police Modernisation

The drive for police modernisation, funded under the 'Scheme for Modernisation of State Police Forces' has started to bear fruition. Protective and communication equipment, transport, vision devices, search equipment and light weaponry of a modern variety are being procured at a brisk pace. Thus, even after diversion of these items to serve the multitude of VIPs, much of these are becoming available to the policemen deployed on ground. The quality control and in-service maintenance of these stocks, however, remains a major problem. Unless attended to with due alacrity, this deficiency would affect the forces' efficiency, besides leading to fiscal wastage.

The Execution of Civic Schemes

The Integrated Action Plan (IAP) devised by the Planning Commission to ameliorate the root causes of the people's alignment with the Maoists, is sustained by nearly a dozen schemes. These schemes are mostly funded conjointly by the states and the Centre. Thus the nation-wide schemes—the 'Mahatma Gandhi National Rural Employment Guarantee Act' (MGNREGA), the 'Pradhan Mantri Gram Sadak Yojana' (PMGSY), the 'National Rural Health Mission' (NRHM), 'Ashram Schools', the 'Sarva Shiksha Abhiyan' (SSA), the 'National Rural Drinking Water Programme' (NRDWP), the 'Rajiv Gandhi Grameen Vidyutikaran Yojana' (RGGVY), the 'Integrated Child Development Services' (ICDS) and the 'Indira Awaas Yojana' (IAY)—are being reinforced in 82 Maoist-affected districts. Meanwhile, a 'Road Requirement Plan – Part I' (RRP-I) to develop access roads to the interiors of 34 worst Maoist-affected districts is also under planning and pilot-execution stage.

Most of the above-listed schemes remain at a nascent stage of implementation. The stumbling blocks are, as discussed earlier, the weak executive mechanism and erratic schedule of funding. Yet, the mere hint of development, combined with the prospects of managing individual and group benefits, has infused a remarkable degree of enthusiasm among the people; even the rebel cadres are attracted, much to the chagrin of the Maoist ideologues. The 'Scheduled Tribes and Other Traditional Forest Dwellers (Recognition of Forest Rights) Act, 2006' has come to the point of reckoning in the local matters. The provisions of this Act, in conjunction with the food programmes for the poor which have been sponsored by almost all the states and the recently promulgated 'National Food Security Act, 2013', has caused the Maoist cause to be further marginalised. The Maoists hope that this popular distraction from their cause is but temporary and soon the failure of what they claim to be a "morally degenerated and corrupt governing system" would strengthen the rebellion with an increased vigour.

How the Maoists have been Faring?

The preceding years have not been particularly good for the Maoists. The problems they face may be summarised as follows:

a) One, they have lost many of their iconic leaders; replacements against which have been found wanting in terms of skills and competence, if not commitment to the cause.
b) Two, they have grown to the limit of their fiscal sustainability. Therefore, to strengthen and up-stage the rebellion they have to find additional sources of funds. Contrarily, with an economic slowdown and rising pitch against the ecological and social exploitation of the natural assets, of which the Maoists themselves have been the leading crusaders, their 'collections' have been compromised. The endeavour to generate more funds has suffered a setback.
c) Three, their best efforts to strengthen influence over the urban centres has failed to bear tangible fruition. Due to this failure, a wider catchment for fund generation, manipulative propaganda and escalation to higher level of insurgency has stagnated.
d) Four, vulnerable posts and armouries having been either fortified or withdrawn, and the forces better equipped, it is no more easy for the Maoists to attack police posts and loot weapons. Similarly, with the infusion of some measures to control illegal trade of weapons and explosives, the free run of the rebels has been somewhat curtailed.

e) Four, the Maoists realise that it is a matter of time before the State gears up to stand up to their intransigence. It is therefore imperative for them to build up their armed strength to be able to confront a better prepared police force, and at the same time, sabotage the government's efforts to engage with the people through civic action. This they have to do without being branded as obstructionists in the eyes of the people and thus antagonising their supportive constituency.

The aforementioned situation has caused the Maoist rebels to take a preparatory pause—barring the opportunistic strikes to keep the threat alive—and focus on building up for the imminent confrontation with the State. The thrust therefore is on looking out for collaboration with the radical groups of the North-East and the west coast and invigorating the dormant cells among North India's university students, faculties and urban societies. Interlocutors have also been trying to procure weapons and equipment through the North-Eastern conduits—with an unknown degree of success.

Meanwhile, the build-up of the 'People's Liberation Guerrilla Army' (PLGA) as well as the 'People's Militia' proceeds undisturbed in the deep jungles. The Maoists continue to 'govern' their 'liberated zones' and continue to carry on with extortion, punishment, recruitment, etc., in areas under their 'control'. Acting smart of late, they have hijacked the mantle of 'monitoring' or even remodelling the government's development schemes to suit their or their local sympathisers' preferences—diktats that the state's executives would defy at their peril. 'Safe areas', where no incidents are to be perpetrated so as to avoid the State's reaction, have been designated in eastern Uttar Pradesh, Madhya Pradesh and Maharashtra, from where the rebellion is directed.

The Political Scene

Of late, the Maoist rebellion has assumed the character of a profitable industry in which apart from the hard core rebels, there are beneficiaries of various hues. These beneficiaries range from part-time or pretending Maoist extortionists, profiteering traders, illegal miners, unlicensed transporters, shaming contractors and corrupt officials, who are in informal league with each other as they are with many of the Maoist leaders. As for the common man, he has little to lose; on the other hand, he is relieved from the clutches of the arrogant and demanding revenue and police functionaries. At the ground level, no one seems to be complaining. Politics having become a game of voter appeasement, it would therefore be interesting to touch upon the attitude displayed by the state-level political leaders with regard to the challenge of Maoist intransigence.

All the state governments, particularly those of the six most Maoist-affected states—Chhattisgarh, Jharkhand, Odisha, Bihar, West Bengal and Maharashtra—exude a confident demeanour of being competent to tackle the situation. They firmly believe that they, rather than the distant functionaries of the Central Government, understand the situation best. Alive to the socio-economic dimensions of the rebellion, they profess that the entrenched causes of the rebellion cannot really be rooted out, and that the answer lies in diluting and then subsuming the issues into the normative course of political process. Indeed, they have a strong point.

Presently, unable to exert due authority, the state governments have chosen to look the other way, if not endorse, the coalescence of a live-and-let-live arrangement among the local activists, officials, traders, contractors and industrial houses with the Maoist Area Commanders in order to maintain societal equilibrium, even if it is a skewed one. To avoid massacre and mayhem, all the states have restrained their police from becoming too active during the transitory period of the build-up. Even then, there are some contrasts in the policies adopted by the different states. The Chhattisgarh government is engaged in a balanced police and socio-economic action; Jharkhand remains inert doing practically nothing at all for or against the State, the people or the rebels; Odisha focuses on quieter areas leaving the troubled ones out; Bihar is stoic while undertaking occasional police actions when the Maoists go too far in upsetting the nexus of the 'equilibrium'; in West Bengal, political cadres have displaced the rebels so much so that it is difficult to tell them apart and Maharashtra is surely and gradually gaining the Maoists' turf.

The nation's demand for economic development cannot be delinked with the harnessing of natural resources that lie in the troubled plateau-lands. Therefore, an eventual State–insurgent showdown is only to be expected. Presently, while both sides girdle up for that inevitability, there seems to be no urge or urgency to disrupt what may be termed as an informally understood 'equilibrium of stalemate'; barring, of course, the occasional forays against the adversary to keep the business going.

Prognosis

The rebellion is sustained not by socialist ideals but by the people's disillusionment with an apathetical state, on which the fanatical Maoists feed.

The state leadership is aware that the intransigence having grown all-profitable roots, it is banal to expect it to be defeated in a short time and by force alone. The idea therefore is to deflate the rebellion by weaning away its support base of the local people. That end is sought to be achieved by addressing the people's consternation with the governing system, or when a full redress is impractical to find, then proposing the compensatory alternatives. That it will take a long time to do so, is well appreciated. However, it is expected that as signs of the State–citizen understanding emerge, it would trigger a cascading effect in a dilution of the people's grievances. A recalcitrance from the hard-core armed rebels is to be expected yet, which is to be dealt with a duly strengthened police force. Finally, having been defanged, it is expected that the Maoist remnants would either be marginalised or assimilated into the political process, as indeed it has happened in the past with many similar groups of radicals.

In contrast, the Maoist leadership's immediate aim is to prevent the State's intrusion into their 'liberated zones' and so preserve their 'rule'. They wish to 'liberate' more such areas over which they currently exercise control or influence, but to do so, armed cadres need to be strengthened. That calls for a larger fund collection, which in turn is contingent upon the spread of tentacles over financial and political hubs. The focus of the Maoists is therefore on fund collection and procurement of weapons. They realise that they have no more than two to three years to achieve that end before the police forces are sufficiently strengthened to deal with them while the State-sponsored socio-economic measures start divesting them of the people's solidarity.

In the coming two years or so, barring disruption of development schemes for the purposes of extortion, and occasional confrontation between police forces and the rebels to keep the threat alive, the State as well as the Maoist rebels are likely to focus on their respective 'build up'.

The current phase of relative quietude is but in preparation for an eventual escalation in armed confrontation.

*

10

India's New Pre-Emptive Action and Equivalent Retaliation (PAER) Strategy

Ashish Sirsikar

Most people see India's recent surgical strikes as a retaliation and avenging of the Uri terror attack. While there is some truth in this, it is not the complete truth. India has been suffering acts of terror for two-and-a-half decades on account of Pakistan's strategy of bleeding India by 'a thousand cuts'. During the said period, while the Kashmir Valley has always been kept on boil with regular incidents of terror being principally aimed at the security forces, other parts of India have also borne the brunt of terror in the form of the Mumbai and Parliament attacks, besides others.

While Pakistan has been single-mindedly following its strategy of bleeding India to a supposed death, India has been suffering silently without undertaking any strategy of note. Hence, for Rawalpindi (Islamabad does not factor into any Pak strategy of note), Uri was supposed to be just another one of the thousand cuts which would throw India into another round of endless debates, threats, coercion but result in nothing that would hurt Pakistan (read the Pakistan Army).

What happened in India post-Uri was unexpected and hence Uri should be considered as a watershed moment in both, India's reaction to Pak-sponsored terror and Pak's cavalier approach to sponsoring terror without any fear of retribution. The attack and Pakistan's continued denial despite being provided with conclusive proof regarding its hand in the Uri terror attack, left India with no option but to jettison its so-called strategy of strategic restraint which was invariably being read in Pakistan as a sign of weakness and an incapability of taking strong effective action. In all probability, the result appears to be the emergence of India's new strategy of 'Pre-emptive Action and Equivalent Retaliation' (PAER). This strategy stems from an understanding that

a) As concerns terrorism emanating from Pakistan, those conducting it on Pakistan's behalf cannot be said to be 'Non State Actors' but instead these are 'Deep State-Sponsored Actors';
b) A purely diplomatic strategy involving only coercions and threats would not work—it would have to be supported by tangible effective actions in the military domain;
c) Elimination of terrorists would not solve the problem but the credibility of the 'Deep State' would have to be undermined.

With such an understanding, this strategy works towards resolving these factors by involving all instruments of national power, with military being only one of the options. Hence, only seeing the recent surgical strikes as being an avenging of Uri is not seeing the full picture. While, the surgical strikes are tangible actions seen by us and felt by Pakistan, they are in essence an integral part of the PAER strategy and thus work in tandem with the other instruments of State.

Evidently, from the fateful day that the Deep State Sponsored Actors undertook the Uri terror attack, India commenced its PAER strategy by taking diplomatic actions which worked towards the isolation of Pakistan, sensitising the global environment about India's right for equivalent reactions and rightfully calling for a labelling of Pakistan as a terrorist state. Hence, whilst Rawalpindi felt that it was business as usual, India was getting its time right by taking the above diplomatic actions. Once the time was right (remember the Indian Director General of Military Operations (DGMO) saying "We reserve the right to respond at the time and place of our choosing") the Indian Army undertook surgical strikes at a place which it deemed to be right. These places being terrorist launch pads which contained terrorists awaiting infiltration, after which, they would have committed further acts of terror. Thus, India's PAER strategy sends two signals: firstly, each Pak cut will be met with an equivalent response, and secondly, India can and will take pre-emptive actions. It will not wait for the next cut but will blunt the knife before it is wielded!

From what has happened over the fortnight following the strikes it would be fair to say that this strategy appears to be a well-thought-out one with the backing of a strong political will. Further, the fine-tuned orchestration between various organs of the State is also an extremely heartening thing to see. Besides India's PAER strategy, what has thrown Pakistan into a bigger logjam is that, after the surgical strikes, India has claimed responsibility for the same and kept the world informed about the strikes (so much so that, the Indian DGMO even informed his counterpart, the Pak DGMO, about them). Ideally, Pakistan would have liked India to execute the surgical strikes as covert operations so that it could have carried on its own covert activities of sponsoring terror without being burdened with the response of an overt response. That not being the case, Pakistan is now in a bind. For the moment though, it has carried on along expected lines by denying that the surgical strikes ever took place (akin to refusing to accept the bodies of its own soldiers post-Kargil operations). Further as per the same script, it has also engaged in a malicious false propaganda, claiming the death and capture of Indian soldiers during the aforesaid surgical strike.

However, Pakistan's past record shows that there would be a response sooner than later. Hence, what does India do in response? Before delving into the same, it is important to put to rest the belief that India's surgical strikes have put things into an escalatory mode. Such a thinking is absurd as it rests on the assumption that while Pakistan goes about its merry way of conducting acts of terror through its proxy actors, India has to behave in a supposed mature manner by limiting itself to diplomatic reactions and that too of the benign kind. Why? Because, if India undertakes a military response across the Line of Control (LoC), then the escalatory ladder would be activated and Pakistan would use its Tactical Nuclear Weapon that it has been brandishing all along. Deduction: While Pakistan keeps delivering its thousand cuts, India has to suffer silently as the onus of escalation rests on it. Guess what, India's Uri response has called this bluff too!!

Pakistan is most likely to respond by continuing its strategy of proxy war, albeit by attempting 'fidayeen' strikes which are more sensational. It could also attempt firing and shelling at the LoC or International Border (IB). In response to the same, India has to resolutely stick to its PAER strategy. Doing so involves employing all the instruments available to the State. On the diplomatic front, working towards labelling Pakistan as a terrorist state is of the foremost priority and has to be undertaken with the understanding that it is a long-drawn process which will yield results in the long run. Further, a global isolation of Pakistan in concert with the world, and more importantly, the countries suffering from Pakistan-sponsored terrorism, is to continue unabated. Both these actions are well underway and credit to the Government is in order for them. It is important to understand that both these diplomatic actions are a part of India's Preemptive Action strategy which is not restricted to the military domain only and hence have to be seen as such. Besides these, other diplomatic actions such as a rethinking of the Indus Water Treaty and working towards the denial of economic doles that Pakistan has been receiving for ages have to be consistently attempted as Pakistan cannot be comfortably allowed to pursue its India-centric policies without paying the price for them.

As concerns the military domain, India's military options should involve pre-determined responses. As is well known, no terrorist infiltration from Pakistan is undertaken without the complete support of the Pakistani posts on the Line of Control. There is also no doubt that the terrorists undertaking terror attacks in India are supported morally and physically by Pakistan. Hence, they should be made to pay a price for the support that they are extending. After any infiltration attempt, successful or not, the Pakistani post which has facilitated the same should be well taken care of by putting sufficient TNT on it to send home the requisite message. As regards fidayeen attacks, there is absolutely no doubt that the fidayeen attacks attempted against security installations would be repulsed professionally (as was proven by the recent failed fidayeen attack against the security camps at Baramulla). However, knowing the desperation of the Pakistan Army to preserve its primacy in Pakistan, such attacks would recur and the Indian security forces would do well not to lower their guard.

That said, following any infiltration attempt or fidayeen attack, India should continue to keep the option of surgical strikes at a time and place of its choosing open. Such surgical strikes cannot be seen as a one-off option only, sending a message that they were attempted for visual effect only, with no real intent in them. A continuation of such surgical strikes would certainly deter any infiltration and fidayeen attack as these would then come with an immediate tangible price. It is also important to note that, the military domain involves a wide spectrum of actions of which, the above-mentioned actions constitute effective responses taken at the lower end of the spectrum. Thus every time, they cannot and need not be approved at the highest level, but should rather be to left to the discretion of the defence forces' hierarchy.

Further, though certain quarters believe that such actions would lead to a limited war being initiated by Pakistan, the chances of the same are remote on account of the Pakistan Army having its hands full and thus being incapable of attempting any misadventure of this kind. Also, as in the recent past, Pakistan resorting to moving some of its forces from its western borders (which were deployed for counter-insurgency operations) to its eastern borders, worsens their situation even more as the Tehreek-e-Taliban Pakistan (TTP) now gets a better opportunity to take on the depleted Pakistan Army. As regards Pakistan choosing to violate the ceasefire outside J&K, it does so as its own risk for it would get an immediate befitting reply in the same kind.

India is a responsible power which is interested in economic development for the betterment of its people. To achieve this, it would ideally like a peaceful neighbourhood. However, this does not mean that India has to suffer Pakistan's strategy of a thousand cuts silently, mutely and reactively, any more.

While escalation is not in the benefit of both India and Pakistan, holding India responsible for maintaining the escalatory ladder at all costs to include an unending loss of lives of its citizens, is not justifiable by any count. While employing all the options available to it, India has to proactively and equivalently react to every cut that Pakistan tries to inflict on it. Pakistan has to be made to pay the price for every cut that it tries to inflict on India. While for the moment India's evolving PAER strategy is doing exactly this, it has to be ensured that the strategy stays in place as long as Pakistan persists with its policy of a thousand cuts.

Before concluding though, a word of caution would be in order. While India pursues such a strategy that would be in its best interests, we could well do without any chest-beating and warmongering about the same for, actions should always speak louder than words.

*

11

Breaking through a Strategic Logjam

General NC Vij

At the outset, the Modi Government needs to be complimented for administering a most befitting and unambiguous message to Pakistan that the continuing acts of terrorism perpetrated by its 'deep state', through its pet 'jihadists', would no more be tolerated in helplessness. That message was finally delivered after a decade of dithering during which political 'will' was held hostage to timid fears of 'escalation', and that in spite of being served by a highly professional military institution, when the present Government decided to call the bluff. Indeed, it was the most praiseworthy that the entire response was well-calibrated domestically, diplomatically and internationally.

On their part, by executing a clinically efficient operation along the Line of Control, India's defence forces have once again established their professionalism in the cause of national security. The bold action also shows that there could also be other ways to complement India's never-ending peace overtures against the innate animosity of a compulsively hostile neighbour that Pakistan is.

The Kashmir Valley has been on the boil for nearly three months. Though after stupendous efforts of the security forces the situation has been eased, peace and stability is yet to settle against continuous incitements—and incentives, as it is revealed—offered by the separatist elements to the gullible Kashmiri youngsters. Before that, a shorter but equally vicious version of the current turmoil in the Valley was enacted in 2010. In a parallel scheme, the separatists of the Kashmir Valley have been openly hobnobbing with the Pakistan embassy, begging the attention of certain Islamic countries and paying obeisance to the Pakistan-based and Wahhabi-funded fanatic groups. This crop of anti-nationals— Hurriyat, Wahhabi factions, rebellious 'intelligentsia' and 'mafia dons' who profit from anti-India activities—have undertaken to subvert the Indian nationhood from within. Simultaneously and in concert with the venomous propaganda spread by that class, there has been an unending succession of terror attacks emanating from Pakistan's soil to target the vulnerable stretches of the Indo-Pak Border, the Line of Control and even in the Indian hinterland. Combined with a diplomatic misinformation campaign, the entire sequence points to a concerted plan to create a situation when India comes really under unbearable pressure and is forced to make concessions.

India's response to the serious national danger has been restrained. It has so far been condemning the 'cowardly' acts of Pakistan-sponsored terror groups and holding out warnings of 'not tolerating' such attacks in the future, besides, of course, tightening the preventive measures. That restraint however, has failed to be taken seriously by the hardened terrorist groups and their benefactor—the Pakistani state. India's diplomatic efforts to curb Pakistan's policy of aiding, if not directly conducting terror attacks, too did not yield results barring hollow platitudes offered by global principals—till they themselves came under attack. Diplomacy in any case is feeble unless backed by military resolve—especially in those cases wherein only the language of force is understood.

On the other end too, there is compulsion. Having fed their people with lies and pumped them into an anti-India frenzy over the past decades in order to retain their stranglehold on power, Pakistan's elitist lords have no way to retract from sustaining their pathological 'K' dream, and turn it into the sole cause of Pakistan's nationhood. Having failed to get to their objective through wars in 1947 and 1965, they took to nurturing terrorist groups which then assumed the power of demanding, if not dictating, to the Pakistan state—the Army to be precise—the means and manners of launching terror attacks in India. The civilised world had in the meanwhile woken up to the dangers of the spreading mayhem, and has begun to expressing the fears of 'terror group', 'lone wolf' and 'nuclear jihad' descending upon them from Pakistan's soil. But then, it is very difficult to wean away a deranged 'deep state' from violating the norms of civilised behaviour just by sermons alone.

Thus far, any talk of India exercising the option of some form of military reaction against the elaborate terrorist infrastructure created by the Pakistani state has been sought to be countered by Pakistan's 'threat' of nuclear attack. Not wanting to feed brinkmanship, India has continued to exercise its 'strategic restraint' while trying many diplomatic and 'soft' methods to find an antidote to Pakistan's venomous ventures—but in vain. The narrative was therefore been clear: Pakistan's well-thought-out, carefully phased and steadily escalating scheme to externally and internally damage India's national integrity would remain in full operation, while India would have to remain deterred from retaliating through a legitimate application of military force.

India's strategic logjam was firm; in fact, it was so since the 2008 Mumbai carnage when India chose be passive in its response. It was becoming clear that only a political will to back up diplomatic efforts by a combination of bilateral sanctions and calibrated use of force could make sense to the habitual intransigent. The recent 'surgical strike' against terrorist launch pads was such a breakthrough out of this logjam and a message to Pakistan. However, a rap in the knuckle like the 'surgical strike' is not likely to make Pakistan see reason. If anything, its Army would already be in the lookout for 'revenge and glory', no matter how ridiculous it could turn out to be. Therefore, the Indian Government, having found the political 'will' and confidence, would do well to continue with all such measures that go to contain the unaccountable and conceited regime in Pakistan. No less important would be to remain in full alert against terror strikes which might affect citizens within and outside the state, all along the border and in hinterland India.

Seized by fanaticism and hatred, Pakistan is unlikely ever to let India progress in peace and stability—seven decades should be adequate to understand that. Time has also come to consider the issue of recovering the rest of the Jammu & Kashmir State—Baltistan, Gilgit—and work steadily towards its fruition. Further, concrete long-term measures need to be adopted to harness India's due share of water from the western rivers which have so far been allowed to flow into Pakistan.

India's minimalist and mature exercise of the military option has been globally appreciated in various manners. The virtual pull-out of all countries from the SAARC meeting in Pakistan is in itself a clear rejection of the policy of terrorism pursued by Pakistan. But as past experience reveals, global players would generally remain as fence-sitters while looking to squeeze individual advantages from either party. Therefore, while welcoming diplomatic support, India would do well to work towards the preservation of its national interests all by itself, and by all means at its disposal. In that context, Pakistan's flat denial of the said surgical strike points to its lies and bluffs. Pakistan would certainly react along the LoC, the IB and even in the hinterland.

We have to be vigilant and on the guard.

*

12

From Terrorism to Terror: Worrisome Developments for the International Community

Alvite Singh Ningthoujam

Ever since the territories under the capture of the terrorist organisation—the Islamic State of Iraq and Syria (ISIS)—began to be recaptured, several analyses have been made predicting the outfit's doomsday. The rapidly depleting financial sources and the reduction in the size of foreign fighters in the so-called Caliphate are other attributing factors for this prognosis. While the ongoing discussions about the trampling of the ISIS hold some substance, a complete defeat of its extremist ideology is nowhere in the vicinity. At the same time, it is doubtful whether the international community, mostly affected by this phenomenon, is doing enough to understand the theological and ideological underpinnings deployed by the outfit to attract fighters, supporters and sympathisers worldwide. An inability to counter the outfit's pernicious ideology is going to make its flame burn for a while.

The ongoing coalition military operations against the ISIS strongholds in Syria and Iraq are putting a tremendous amount of pressure on its fighters. But there are also a couple of parallel activities taking place beyond West Asia which require to be considered. The first is the exodus of well-trained foreign fighters to their native countries. The second comprises the rise of lone-actor/ wolf attacks, both in the United States and Europe. This is a particular phenomenon which is raising lots of security concerns as the ISIS is attracting a number of disaffected individuals and terror groups which continue to have illusions of establishing a global Caliphate.

Terrorism, earlier, comprised of coordinated attacks by existing organisations which had developed the wherewithal to inflict damages. But this is changing with the induction of unknown lone wolves whose actions are difficult to detect and deter. A vast majority of attacks in the Western world have either been carried by ISIS operatives or by the lone wolves who drew inspiration from the outfit. Activities by these individuals have gone in favour of this outfit which continuously attempts to spread its tentacles all over the world.

There is a growing concern about the security challenges the returning foreign fighters will pose to their countries. With the significant decline in the influx of fighters into Iraq and Syria, a pertinent question has arisen whether the "terrorism threat is actually easing or just morphing into a more dangerous new phase".[1] This is when the relevance of the returnees comes into the picture as a new phase may be in the offing. There is this possibility of the returnees teaming up with those radicalised who did not get an opportunity to travel abroad. In other words, the return journeys are likely to exacerbate the problem of violent extremism domestically.

The concerns emanating out of such reversal will be serious not only in countries such as Tunisia, Saudi Arabia, Russia, Turkey and Jordan (from where the highest numbers of foreign fighters have joined ISIS)[2] but also in Europe and as far as Australia. The problem is not solely anymore about people departing towards Syria/Iraq but the threats emerging from those who are fleeing the outfit's strongholds. Simultaneously, it has to be acknowledged that not all the returning foreign fighters will want to continue fighting or "form the next generation of global jihadists",[3] but the presence of even a small fraction with such an inclination should not be taken lightly. Some of them are still convinced "of the righteousness of their cause". This is mostly applicable in the European context where there has been an exponential rise in radicalisation. A study conducted by the Sydney-based Lowy Institute categorises "the future foreign fighter cohort in Syria and Iraq into four categories, and they are as follows: ...those who chose to remain in Syria and Iraq; those who leave in order to continue violent jihad in another theatre, either at home or elsewhere; those who seek to return to their country of origin; and those who go to a third country of refuge...".[4] Keeping a track of any of these groups is going to be a mammoth task for the law enforcement authorities.

Considering the recent surge in attacks, security officials from the European Union (EU) countries and the US have expressed their concerns about the likely fallout of the ISIS's military defeats. The risk is acute in France which has faced a few brazen attacks within a period of one year. French Prime Minister Manuel Valls mentioned that there are "nearly 700 jihadists who are either French or live in France are in Iraq and Syria at the moment", and "their return represents an additional threat to our national security… it's going to be a long fight".[5] As it is, the news of ISIS-connected lone-wolf activities and similarly terrifying incidents have been widely reported from Belgium, Germany and the US since the last few months. While some of them turned out to be ISIS-directed/inspired, there have been cases when the outfit's connections with the perpetrators were tenuous. Presently, there is a dreaded concoction of mental-health illness, violence streak and religion-based radicalisation which is on the upswing, resulting in acts of terror.

The lone-wolf attacks are gradually instilling fear amongst the civilians. This is more so because of the nature of their target audience and the locations such as theatres, pubs, malls, train stations, airports, etc. The recent bombings in New York and New Jersey, and the stabbing in Minnesota are cases which illustrate such trends. However, formal linkages of the attackers, namely Ahmad Khan Rahami and Dahir Adan, with faraway terror groups such as the ISIS, are yet to be ascertained. In-between inspired individuals who act alone and those terrorist operatives acting at the orders of leaders from Syria or Iraq, there are also individuals who "operate somewhere between the two extremes".[6] And as the ISIS has heralded many of these attackers as its "soldiers", a copious amount of investigation is required to get to the bottom of the matter and challenge this narrative. Their presence, however, is increasingly becoming a serious menace for the counter-terrorism agencies. As aptly expressed by Federal Bureau of Investigation (FBI) Director James Comey, "the so-called caliphate will be crushed. The challenge will be: through the fingers of that crush are going to come hundreds of very, very dangerous people. They will not all die on the battlefield in Syria and Iraq. There will be a terrorist diaspora sometime in the next two to five years like we've never seen before". [7]

The international community cannot afford to remain complacent by merely looking at the decline of ISIS in West Asia. As the outfit is losing ground, it is likely to turn to insurgency in its core areas while its fleeing fighters will likely conduct sporadic attacks in their native countries. The latter scenario is a matter of grave concern given the rising phenomenon of homegrown extremism in different countries. The undetectable nature of this radicalised lot will remain a major security challenge. In the wake of the threats coming from radicalised individuals, returnees and terrorist operatives, there is a need for a higher security vigilance and enhanced coordination between the agencies. One should be cognisant of the fact that the threats are fast changing from direct attacks to that of inspired attacks and they are rapidly spreading. Lastly, as the foreign fighters go home, they will carry the terror ideology along with them.

*

END NOTES

1. Griff Witte et.al, 'Flow of Foreign Fighters plummets as Islamic States loses its Edge", *The Washington Post*, 9 September 2016.
2. For further discussion, see 'Foreign Fighters: An Updated Assessment of the Flow of Foreign Fighters into Syria and Iraq', *The Soufan Group*, December 2015.
3. Liz Burke, 'Returned Jihadists: The Horror that comes after Islamic State', News.com.au, 28 September.
4. Lydia Khalil and Rodger Shanahan, 'Foreign Fighters in Syria and Iraq: The Day After', Lowy Institute, September 2016, p. 7.
5. "Ticking Time Bomb of Foreign ISIS Fighters returning Home", *NDTV*, 9 September 2016.
6. Mathew Levitt, 'The New York Bomber was not a Lone Wolf", *The Washington Institute for Near East Policy"*, 21 September 2016.
7. Allen Cone, 'FBI director warns of 'terrorist diaspora' after Islamic State crushed', *UPI.com*, 27 September 2016.

INDEX